"Bradley and Cole offer a thoughtful and timely look at the intersections between the abstraction of philosophical theory and the pragmatic reality of language learning. The result is an interesting set of approaches that pose important questions about the role of education within society."

—Barnaby Ralph, Professor of British Literature and Culture, Faculty of Humanities, Seikei University, Japan

"Bradley and Cole are two of the most active and proficient scholars to date working on Deleuze and Guattari. Their emphasis on language allows them to navigate through the emancipative project of a 'people to come,' a figurative species who speak the language of the most innocent of all destructions."

—Virgilio A. Rivas, Philosophy Department, Polytechnic University of the Philippines

Deleuze, Guattari, and Global Ecologies of Language Learning

Joff P. N. Bradley and David R. Cole

Deleuze, Guattari, and Global Ecologies of Language Learning

PETER LANG
Lausanne • Berlin • Bruxelles • Chennai • New York • Oxford

Library of Congress Cataloging-in-Publication Control Number: 2022061488

Bibliographic information published by the **Deutsche Nationalbibliothek.**
The German National Library lists this publication in the German
National Bibliography; detailed bibliographic data is available
on the Internet at http://dnb.d-nb.de.

Cover design by Peter Lang Group AG

ISBN 9781433191640 (hardback)
ISBN 9781433191657 (paperback)
ISBN 9781433191619 (ebook)
ISBN 9781433191626 (epub)
DOI 10.3726/b20421

© 2023 Peter Lang Group AG, Lausanne
Published by Peter Lang Publishing Inc., New York, USA
info@peterlang.com - www.peterlang.com

This publication has been peer reviewed.

Table of Contents

Acknowledgments

It was David R. Cole who got me (Joff P. N. Bradley) back into philosophy, who got me back into thinking as such. David remains the world's leading expert on Deleuze studies in the field of education. It was he who nearly 14 years ago told me that I should start writing. Before that I had been teaching a great deal but without a critical voice, all the while observing and cataloguing the everyday problems that I saw in myself, my students, my colleagues, and the commuters on the busy trains in Tokyo, but without a means to express my views and indeed any opposition to the way of the world. In frank discussions David said those societal problems were normalized under Japanese capitalism and I too was part of the problem. He suggested I give philosophical expression to my frustrations, resistance and skepticism towards the way that others organize education. It is for this personal reason, and while perhaps odd as one of the co-writers of this book, that I dedicate the book to him.

Permissions

We would like to thank the following journals, institutions and publishers for the permission to republish our sole and joint works.

Joff P. N. Bradley wishes to thank
Toyo University's *Dialogos* journal for permission to republish Bradley, J. P. N. (2012). On the materiality of thixotropic slogans. *Dialogos*, (12), 71–100;
Taylor & Francis for permission to republish Bradley, J. P. N. (2012). Materialism and the mediating third. *Educational Philosophy and Theory*, 44(8), 892–903;
The Liberlit Journal of Teaching Literature for permission to republish Bradley, J. P. N. (2015). Becoming-literature: Deleuze and the Craquelure. *Lit Matters–The Liberlit Journal of Teaching Literature*, 1(2), 79–11;
Micronesian Educator for permission to republish Bradley, J. P. N. (2021). Woe Betide You the Truth Be Told: Linguistic Corruption as Pedagogical Tool. *Micronesian Educator# 30*, 84;
Brill for permission to republish Bradley, J. P. N. (2019). Deleuze and Globish: Imperial Tongues, Faceless Coins, War Machines. In *Deterritorializing Language, Teaching, Learning, and Research* (pp. 87–109).

Bradley and Cole wish to thank the University of Singapore for permission to republish On Multiple Literacies and Language Learning: Video Production and Embodied Subjectivities which appeared in NUS CELC 5th Symposium Proceedings;

The Society for Teaching English through Media (STEM) in Korea for permission to republish Bradley, J. P. N., Cabell, C., Cole, D. R., Kennedy, D. H., & Poje, J. (2018). From which point do we begin?: on combining the multiliteral and multiperspectival. *Stem Journal*, 65–93;

Addleton and Linguistic and Philosophical Investigations for permission to republish Cole, D. R., & Bradley, J. P. N. (2014). Japanese English learners on the edge of 'chaosmos': Félix Guattari and "becoming-otaku". *Linguistic and Philosophical Investigations*, *13*, 83;

Journal of Engaged Pedagogy in Japan for permission to republish Cole, D. R., & Bradley, J. P. N. (2014). On conjuring the pea-and-thimble trick. *Journal of Engaged Pedagogy*, 1–9.

David R. Cole wishes to thank Edinburgh University Press for permission to republish Cole, D. R. (2013). Affective literacies: Deleuze, discipline and power. *Deleuze and education*, 94–112;

Discourse: Studies in the Cultural Politics of Education for permission to republish Cole, D. R. (2012). Latino families becoming-literate in Australia: Deleuze, literacy and the politics of immigration. *Discourse: Studies in the Cultural Politics of Education*, *33*(1), 33–46;

Power and Education for permission to republish Cole, D. R. (2009). The power of emotional factors in English teaching. *Power and Education*, *1*(1), 57–70;

Reconstruction for permission to republish Cole, D. R. (2005). Reading in the future: Literacy in the time of the internet. *Reconstruction*, *5*(2);

Wiley for permission to republish Cole, D. R. (2013). Deleuze and narrative investigation: The multiple literacies of Sudanese families in Australia. *Literacy*, *47*(1), 35–41.

Foreword

MARK FEATHERSTONE

In an age marked by the globalitarian power of digital code, the ways in which we communicate, speak, write, express our singular relations to the world, and bridge our social, political, and cultural differences, has become key political questions. In exploring the borderline space between a kind of absolute global indifference characterized by universal code and the hyper-local difference of a model of tribal communication that easily lapses into paranoid nationalism, Bradley and Cole's book interrogates the crux of the problem of troublesome self-other communication by reading the theory and practice of language learning through the work of the radical French thinkers, Gilles Deleuze and Félix Guattari. Writing from the 1960s through the 1980s, Deleuze and Guattari famously challenged authoritarian forms of repressive psycho-power and their oppressive material social, political, and economic expressions in the name of an alternative vision of subjectivity and collective formation characterized by desire, creativity, and freedom. Following the lead of Deleuze and Guattari, who essentially located the problem of domination in the ways in which we are coded by processes of Oedipal socialisation, Bradley and Cole explore the politics of language learning in terms of the contrast between major psycho-linguistic structures established in early childhood and beyond that screen culture in all its forms, and the possibility of minor or minority forms of communication capable of expressing desire, difference, creativity, freedom, and the imagination to think otherwise through their subversive and transformative interaction with the major form.

Readers of Deleuze and Guattari's work will remember that it is precisely this interaction that they explore in their book on Kafka, where the (con)fusion of Czech, Yiddish, and German produces ruptures in the majoritarian linguistic form. Before Deleuze and Guattari, the father of psychoanalysis, Sigmund Freud, similarly explored the possibility of escape from dominant socio-symbolic systems in his study of Daniel Paul Schreber. In the case of Schreber, the psychotic judge reacted to his over-determination by the law of the father and the law of the land by inventing his own way of talking, writing, and understanding the world. On the edge of the modern technological age, Schreber's new psychotic reality was characterized by a tangle of wires, rays of light, and strange writing machines that plugged him straight into the mind of God. Echoing Schreber, Kafka and Joyce, who we remember also invented his own minor cybernetic language for the coming electronic age in his famously unreadable *Finnegans Wake*, the key point of Bradley and Cole's work is that we must challenge the majoritarian, behaviourist model of language passed down by the tech giants and others who believe in the pure instrumentality of communication, command, and control. In the world of GAFA (Google, Amazon, Facebook, and Apple) corporations, which Bernard Stiegler writes about in terms of the four horsemen of the digital apocalypse, the internet is no longer a place of symbolic exploration, creativity, and invention, but rather a space of algorithmic governmentality where every form of communication is primarily understood in economic terms concerned with the need to produce some form of monetary gain.

Against this basic calculative utilitarianism, which threatens to translate our rich, symbolic worlds into a bland computational (un)world, Bradley and Cole turn to the theory of multiple literacies (MLT, multiple literacy theory), which they suggest has the potential to trouble, derange, estrange, or alienate our situation caught in a globalitarian, communicative system that in turn makes it seem impossible to escape our current thanatological trajectory that is playing out the dark destiny of the Anthropocene. In this regard, the stakes of Bradley and Cole's project are high. Indeed, they could not be higher. In their view learning and teaching language pitches students and tutors straight into what might turn out to be a life and death struggle between behaviour and creativity, intelligence and systemic stupidity, and thoughtless repetition and the possibility of new worlds conceived in the encounter with languages that are never finished, consistent, or self-identical, but rather endlessly dynamic, relational, and open to interpretation, reinterpretation, translation, mis-translation, and re-imagining. Akin to Schreber, Kafka, and Joyce, whose experiments with language led to new ways of thinking about self and world, Bradley and Cole remind us that learning language is a transformative experience. We cannot learn a new language, whether this is a new national tongue or a new regional dialectic, without encountering the other and the other in the self who poses the question—"who am I now?" In this context the Lacanian imaginary, the self-identical "I" which we develop when we look into the mirror and say "that's me", explodes and we lose our sense of certainty before a new understanding of the wide open spaces and possibilities of language that is no longer simply about the word / world of the father who came before, but also the strange, alien universe of the other who comes from somewhere else and opens up new horizons. Beyond the programmatic order words that translate language into a system that then defines reality in systemic terms that in turn transforms people into docile bodies set upon conformity, Bradley and Cole want us to creatively explore language. In their reading of Deleuze and Guattari's work, this creativity emerges from the productive unconscious that is no longer a store house for ghosts, ghouls, and other monstrous representatives of traumatic memories from the past, but rather a machine that floods language with creative potential and the ability to imagine new worlds and new futures.

In the contemporary world we might think about the opposition between this creative philosophy of language on the one hand and computer science, on the other, which exerts continuous control over communication for the sake of the eradication of the noise that breathes life into expression and the imagination. Thus, Bradley and Cole point out, in a manner which recalls Freud's joke book, that we should not seek to overcome noise. On the contrary, slips, stammers, stutters, mistakes, and mistranslations in the study of language must not be eliminated in the name of linguistic perfection, because they are the very life blood of communication itself. As Freud explained in his work on the joke, and then Deleuze and Guattari later outlined in their study of Kafka, it is precisely the gaps, breaks, and holes in expression that enable the new to emerge in between, and on the borderline, between this, that, and the other language. Building upon Deleuze and Guattari's reading of the schizophrenia of capitalism that is always undermining and working against the logic of territorialisation, Bradley and Cole take the view that noise is always productive, a sign of the rude health of language that is always running away with itself and that cannot be contained by computational code regardless of what the engineers and neoliberals want to believe. The truth is, then, that our hyper-mediated world saturated with language is defined by a state of unmooring, disembedding, and drift. There is no once and for all language, no pure symbolic system free of noise, that we can know in its entirety. Instead, we are always learning language, we are always translating, reaching towards the other, and having to come terms with uncertainty in meaning. Against this backdrop, we must conclude that the disciplinary vision of the school, where language is about instilling the kind of management of mind and body that Michel Foucault associated with all kinds of institutions, is fighting a losing battle. It is forever on the backfoot and will never be able to discipline language and eradicate the noise that characterizes communication in all its forms.

However, we know that such uncertainty about meaning can cause anxiety about otherness and our place in the world. For this reason, Bradley and Cole suggest the importance of scaffolding language learning in order to provide a level of security for students pitched into the chaotic sea of a new symbolic system. In this regard, the purpose of the psychoanalytic partial or transitional object is to simultaneously provide students with an object of desire and a sense of security to support their explorations. This *psychological* object, because it is important to recognize that this is not necessarily an object in the material sense of the term, might represent a vision of a future in another culture or another world, a fantasy of what life might be like, capable of transforming the classroom into a space of desire, hope, and the possibility of the new. Of course, the challenge of creating and defending this psychological object is that the contemporary education system resembles a knowledge factory, marked by neoliberal metrics, bureaucracy, and cybernetic channels of command and control that treat language in purely instrumental terms, more than an experimental space concerned with imagination, creativity, and becoming. The two models of learning and understanding language could not be further apart, but, for Bradley and Cole, they represent the key coordinates of the politics of contemporary language learning. Against the cybernetic view of language learning, where communication is about inputting information in the name of the output of monetary gain, Bradley and Cole challenge us to recognize the multiple perspectives disclosed by diverse languages, because it is only by understanding this multiplicity that we will be able to capture what it means to exist and be in the world and communicate this to others in ways that are never complete, but only ever partially coherent on the edge of chaos.

Given the state of our world, wracked by war, economic chaos, and potentially apocalyptic climate change, I think Bradley and Cole's key contribution is that we cannot see language as a computational system, because there is simply too much uncertainty in our world, but rather we must think about it in terms of an endless project concerned with making sense. In this context, lifelong learning is not the necessary disposition of the student who has to be prepared to constantly adapt to the vicissitudes of the market caught in ceaseless creative destruction, but rather about what it means to constantly strive to make sense with others in a community of significance essential to getting to grips with a hyper-complex world slipping into a state of chaos. The difference here is one of focus. Is language learning about ensuring seamless communication in the name of improving profit margins or is it about making sense in order to get a grip on the problems of the world? What we now know is that the imperial tongue of neo-liberal capitalism has no answers to the chaos currently enveloping our world. In respect of this ways in which the globalization of the Anglo-American system has led to the globalization of the English language, Bradley and Cole are clear that multiple language learning is essential today, if we are to escape the coming horror of the Anthropocene. We have to develop new ways of talking, new ways of writing, and new ways of thinking if we are to escape the fate set by the Anglo-American model. Ironically, Bradley and Cole suggest hope for the future in the very extremism of this mono-linguistic model that is in the process of exhausting itself in its over-reach. In referring to the globalitarianism of English, they consider the phenomenon of Globish, which is simultaneously universal in its expansion, but also strangely vernacular, empty, and beyond identity. In many respects, then, Globish is English in the process of emptying out a model of meaning that we also find in the writings of Schreber and Joyce, that is, the kind of becoming psychotic of language which is necessary to carve out a space for the new in the globalised techno *machina mundi*.

Introduction

This book is a selection of writings on Gilles Deleuze and Félix Guattari's philosophy on language learning. The authors are global experts in the field of language learning and schizoanalysis and have been collaborating on projects concerning Deleuze and Guattari for over two decades. And in addition to lecturing and co-writing together on this topic they have been working on projects concerning social ecology and the Anthropocene across the globe. This book is an attempt to put those writings focussing on language learning and teaching into a systematic order. As such, this book introduces the philosophy of Deleuze and Guattari and its use in the field of language learning in tertiary education sector and elsewhere. The authors will demonstrate how Deleuze and Guattari inform language learning and teaching in creative, unpredictable and sometimes rupturing ways.

The book introduces empirical research from Australia, Canada, US, and Japan that combines Deleuze's thought, literacies and multiliteracies theory to explain how students frequently have breakthroughs or breakdowns in language learning. In this book, an argument is made that the Deleuze and Guattari philosophical approach endeavors to understand the relationships between literacy, the literary, and literature use, and it extends multiliteracies into the multiple literacies theory of affect to push towards comprehending the many complexities of learning.

CHAPTER ONE

Ecological Crisis and Global Language Learning

Presciently, this book asserts that the state of global language learning is in a type of breakdown or crisis. This crisis has been created and prolonged by us. It is we, collectively, who are responsible. The crisis runs parallel to the advent of the Anthropocene, and it is largely due to globalization and its pernicious effects (also named late/high capitalism). The crisis involves the removal and integration of local teaching and language learning scenarios with and by global capitalism, a process that has become so seamless, absolute, and its effects so ubiquitous, that every theorisation of literacy and language learning seems to be redundant as soon as it is presented. This book does not proffer ready-made solutions to the takeover of local language learning scenarios and their dynamics with and by capitalist exploitation, nor does it offer a straightforward dialectic, rather, this book presents an evolution in thinking about the local teaching and learning of language, that extends globally to the ecology of the situation, and that owes much to the prophetic social ecology of Guattari (1996) in the 1970s and 1980s. Indeed, this book is intellectually based on the philosophy of Deleuze and Guattari (1983; 1980), with various necessary bi-ways and additions given the expansion and movement in the field of language learning since the 1970s. Firstly, this book may be comprehended through a cartography of language learning, and how it has evolved to respond to and been part of global ecologies.

The Social-Innate Rupture(s)

The traditional picture of Western language learning in education is a behaviourist one. Behaviourism is still the dominant paradigm in the practice of schooling (Manolescu, 2013), due to the ways in which operant conditioning works and conforms to the basic psychological modes in which children appear to learn;— i.e., through the reinforcement of receiving rewards (praise), or by having them taken away (Staddon & Cerutti, 2003). However, this analogue, psychological, and directly connective mode of educative practice started to rupture in the West along various lines that were inspired by thinkers coming from different paradigms to the still dominant and mainstream behaviourist one. Firstly, the translation and rein-terpretation of the work of Lev Vygotsky by Michael Cole and others (Vygotsky & Cole, 1978), led to the insertion of social-cultural learning into learning paradigms that responded to concepts such as the zone of proximal development (ZPD), scaf-folding and mediation, and concepts that lead language learning in certain com-prehensible directions (from expert to novice). The second significant challenge to the behaviourist paradigm in education came from Noam Chomsky (2011), and the theorisation of language learning as innate and generative, and its translation to, for example, the notion of "immersion" becoming an essential part of the lan-guage learning environment. Further, the rupture(s) to the behaviourist paradigm from social-cultural theorists were accelerated due to concentration on the social aspects of teaching and learning, and how entrenched disadvantage in education and the learning of linguistic complexity may be exacerbated by concepts from so-ciology such as class, power, wealth, and exclusion.

Since Marx (Harvey, 2017) and the development of the communist alternative to capitalism, a mode of dialectical questioning emerged to divert thought away from the capitalist real. In education, critical pedagogy has taken lessons from so-ciology and the analysis of capitalist influence and interference on education and has tried to counter the tendency (Riasati & Mollaei, 2012). In terms of language learning, critical pedagogy is not so much about turning all language into com-munist propaganda, but in giving students options and tools to critically analyze the rhetoric and deliberate language use that is, for example, solely designed to sell products. As such, the teacher may organize lessons around advertising, mar-keting strategies, and language use that are designed to critically analyze capitalist language and messaging with the intent of unpicking and unpacking it to the advantage of the student. However, the prescient counter argument to this so-cial rupturing of behaviourist language learning is that students need to learn the language of capitalism to survive and indeed thrive in the contemporary world, especially those emerging from disadvantaged positions (Suárez-Orozco, 2001). To this extent, a critical realist alternative to a strict Marxist critical praxis has emerged that gives an expanded option to the development of solely left-wing dialectical rupturing.

The French sociologist Pierre Bourdieu helped develop the critical realist approach, that has been extended and deepened, for example, by Roy Bhaskar and Margaret Archer (Vandenberghe, 2013). The critical realist approach emphasises the critical aspects of language learning, in the sense that the critical praxis of Marxism is broadened to include different types of capital such as social and cultural capital, and the notion of habitus, which describes the power relations whereby agency, values, and language emerge. It could be argued that critical realism is especially important in education, as schools, teachers, and indeed, society, produce, reproduce, and enable the thinking minds of students through their lessons, pedagogy, and assessment practices, and to an extent determine the language learning of the students through the matrix of relations that are created around and in them (Cole & Mirzaei Rafe, 2018). Critical realism gives the analyst the means to understand how to create a dialogue with capitalism whilst still holding a scientific position on the phenomena, i.e., not creating an ideal or imaginary social revolution or perfect social relations as an outcome, that might hide the actual power relations as they exist in a situation. In the specific frame of language learning of this book, critical realism helps to understand how language learning is created in context through the impingement of power relations, that carry with them specific codes, preferences, exclusions, and rituals that can be studied and understood in terms of how power works (Reay, 2004). However, both the social and innate rupturing of the educational context through the combined works as presented above, did not consider the shift from analogue relations, wherein relations are direct and accountable, to digital relations, whereby relations have become discreet, multiple, easily copied, and exteriorised through computer networks.

The Digital Rupture(s)

Something happened to the ecologies of language learning in the 1980s in the West that made much of the previous analogue theorisation of what was taking place in teaching and learning scenarios redundant and anachronistic. This acceleration in redundancy was harnessed and accompanied by two crucial movements that underpin the comprehension of ecologies of language learning, and hence the manifestation of this book: (1) The introduction of computers into education and work; (2) the neoliberal revolution that accompanied the introduction of computation into learning and which therefore made all relations accountable to the market (including education). Digitalisation and its accompanying marketisation have had profound effects on education, life, and work, and have severed and transformed the analogue modes of thinking that had previously introduced social and innate types of rupturing into the psychological, behaviourist means to comprehend how language learning works (Allsop, Briggs & Kisby, 2018). However, unlike the previous rupturing of social and innate "restructuring" of the normative and familiar modes of behaviourist teaching and learning, the digital rupture(s) happen due to exteriorised, discreet (1 0) and multiplied relations.

Firstly, the initial response to the multiplication, digitalisation, and market-bearing transformation of education was a pragmatic one. Pragmatically, the extension of codes from analogue to digital relations is a question of semiotics, and semiotically the field of operations is expanded from strictly linguistic matters to, for example, the important consideration of images, along with sound, and any other means to communicate that are present in the digital arena. Theorists such as Gunther Kress (2000) advocated concepts such as multimodality to explain the ways in which learning had multiplied under the influence of digitalisation. Further, the extension and coexistence of language learning with semiotics coincided with the use of genre theory to understand and organize language learning, especially in the primary context. Genre theory as applied to education and language learning took inspiration from theorists such as Jacques Derrida and deconstruction to examine and teach about text types, including digital texts (Duff, 2014). In sum, the combined influences of semiotics and genre theory encouraged educative practice and language learning away from traditional behaviourist modes of operant conditioning, and to take seriously the new conditions that were emerging in the West through the 1980s and 1990s.

In 1996, a group of educators called the New London Group published a landmark paper in the Harvard Education Review about multiliteracies (New London Group, 1996). Multiliteracies was a new theorisation of language learning that accepted and incorporated the moves into semiotics and pragmatics that had proceeded it. Further, the multiliteracies framework for language learning incorporated the gains that had been made through the critical ruptures to the stable and familiarized rendering of teaching and learning through behaviourism. Multiliteracies also incorporated the work of Foucault in education in terms of accounting for power relations through discourses that shaped and enabled the self (Hagood, 2000). The multiliteracies framework for teaching and learning, which accompanied the globalization of the 1990s, combined analysis of the new digital literacies with sociological considerations and an emphasis on designing social futures. Further to multiliteracies, multiple literacies and multiple literacies theory

(MLT) were developed after the 1990s and they have freed up the notion of language learning even further, which has led us closer to the ecologies of language learning of this book, and the contemporary educational situation (Masny & Cole, 2012). The initial conceptualisation of multiple literacies by Douglas Kellner (1998) and others was based on the social rupturing of behaviourism; MLT, and its accompanying theorisations took the ruptures further.

Rupturing from the Outside

MLT is based on the philosophy of Deleuze and Guattari (1980, 1988). Unlike the previous rupturing of the stable basis for understanding language learning through behaviourism as defined above by the social, innate, and digital aspects of language learning, the next rupturing of this understanding does not depend on an agentic or biological rendering of the self, or the interference of the digital. For example, multiliteracies are based on phenomenology which draws the learning that happens back to a human subject, and the fulfillment of educative mores by that subject (Clancy & Lowrie, 2005). Contrariwise, the multiple aspect of MLT as learning is based on the mathematical designation of multiplicities, which is beyond the human as a single entity (Meinrenken, 1996). There is some dispute about the differences between a strictly Deleuzian formation of the self, that he created from various philosophical investigations and other related areas such as theology and science, and the Guattarian notion of the self, which is a combination of a reversal of psychoanalysis and Sartrean existentialism. For the purposes of MLT and the development of ecologies of language learning found in this book, the important point is that language learning is ruptured from the outside, and in addition to the social, innate, and digital rupturing that had proceeded it, and the basic behaviourist model of a subject learning through conditioning, even though still present in the minds of educationalists and although it is practiced in schools, it becomes even more redundant (Masny & Cole, 2009). This new form of rupturing from the outside takes on two forms that will be explored in the book: (1) As modes of alienation, apartness, and segmentation, that have driven community and collective endeavor ever further to the periphery of the mainstream; (2) As a new requirement to explore environmental aspects of education, as demonstrated by the definition of the current epoch as the Anthropocene (Cole, 2021a), and the discussion over the probability of the sixth great extinction event.

Admittedly, the first form of rupturing from the outside as listed above has been recognised and theorized by Marxist critics for many years. Marx invented his theory of alienation in his *Economic and Philosophic Manuscripts* of 1844, that were published many years later in the Soviet Union in 1932. Latterly, the complex sets of relations that have formed around workers, labor, and production in time by capitalism were innovated upon through Deleuze and Guattari's (1983) *Anti Oedipus*, that should not be seen as in any way being a regressive or pro-capitalist/neoliberal step with respect to understanding and working with and through Marxist alienation. Rather, *Anti Oedipus* adds depth and insight into the hollowing out and taking over of the self by capital, in that the new and innovative reversal of psychoanalysis that is termed by them as schizoanalysis, sought escape routes from the iron cage of capital and its effects on subjectivity, the self, and learning. The difference that the Deleuze and Guattari (1983), and subsequent MLT approach to language learning (Masny & Cole, 2009, 2012) makes on the previous social, left-wing interventions in education as described above as critical pedagogy, is that the direct switch to anti-capitalist, pro-communist praxis is not primarily considered, rather, the flows and energy differentials of education (that may or may not lead to communism) are followed as material. These matter flows and their following present an innovation on the prevalent Marxist materialism of the time, of, for example, Louis Althusser (Lewis, 2017; Cole, 2012), and present a new mode of avoiding alienation through the ecologies of language learning that are the objects of this book.

Likewise, the second mode of rupturing from the outside, that seriously considers environmental education as a basis for all teaching and learning, and hence brings the external world into the arena of the Western educative subject learning and disrupts the picture of operant conditioning derived from behaviourism. The recognition that the world economy, driven using fossil fuels since the Industrial Revolution, is creating the conditions for the extinction of the human species, is perhaps reason enough to accelerate the rupturing of the self from the natural outside (Cole, 2021a). In a sense, the previous rupturing by the social-innate and digital modes of language learning with respect to behaviourism is negated and reversed when it comes to the extensive rupturing from the outside. Even though environmental education has been taken seriously as an academic discipline since the 1970s, it has largely not gained prominence in the curriculum or as pedagogy due to the overriding concerns of economic rationalism. In contrast, the Deleuze and Guattari inspired language learning practice of MLT (Masny & Cole, 2009, 2012) has the capacity to bring the outside of environmental education into the centre of education due to its refiguring of notions of human agency and the inclusion of non-human actors as being central to what education does. Furthermore, an enhanced social ecology derived from Guattari's (1996) solo work has the potential to drive the rupturing from the outside further to create the new worlds for thinking and learning that are necessary to escape the Anthropocene. As such, this book works through the combined rupturing as analyzed above, with the aim of encouraging new modes of education, targeted at the future and the enhancement of life.

Desire and Global Language Learning

Before the pandemic, Bradley gave a talk on Deleuze and Guattari and language learning at the Japan Association for Language Teaching conference (特定非営利活動法人全国語学教育学会). He was confident that this was the first time in JALT's history of 50 years that a presentation was given at length on Deleuze and Guattari. He thought that many would read the conference guidebook and ask what Deleuze and Guattari have to do with language learning. Further, they might ask: What has French philosophy got to do with language learning *in Japan*? Indeed, the Deleuze and Guattari approach has its detractors. For example, Professor Steve Kirk of Nippon Medical School, an expert on applied linguistics, asked: "Why do we need to talk about these guys (Deleuze, Spinoza, etc.) at all? Why can't we just talk about student motivation, 21st century technology, and means of expression, and using video in the classroom, without mentioning those guys?" I welcome his candour, but my reply was that motivation, the crisis of learning, the loss of attention, are issues precisely about breakdown and breakthroughs; it is about the ruptures in education. In effect, and confronted with endemic problems of language, literacy, and literature, Deleuze and Guattari analyze the relationships between literacy, the literary and literature, to extend multiliteracies into the multiple literacies theory of affect to grasp why there are breakdowns and breakthroughs in learning.

This book asks its readers to address the question of creativity in the classroom, and the school's interrelationships with the outside. The book is an institutional analysis of breakdowns and breakthroughs. In truth, language learning is much messier than the salespeople and designers of language courses let on. The use of Deleuze and Guattari is therefore intentionally anarchic, aiming to disturb and rupture the borders of established paradigms. The Deleuze and Guattari approach is promiscuous and allergic to the proclivity to narrow and fix disciplines to this or that taxonomy. What we do in the classroom and beyond is not and should not be confined solely to language education, as we do much more than that when we recognize how foreign languages and local knowledges produce moments of inspiration, rupture, experimentation, critique, and indeed art. The classroom has desire swimming throughout it, and it is important to appreciate that affect, otherness, strangeness, and alienation are intimately connected to transformation and learning. Indeed, learning literacies—whether through manga, video, and so on—is profoundly about desire, transformation, and becoming.

There are three quotations which demonstrate where the book's impetus springs from. (1) Silvia Grinberg (2013) from Argentina states: "A Deleuzian approach to the study of the pedagogical apparatus as it is experienced in schools on a daily basis means opening up a set of lines, of bifurcations and ruptures; it means approaching multiple situations of collapse and construction." And (2) Guattari who writes in *Molecular Revolution*: "At 20, attacks of anxiety. These could be schizophrenic syndromes that manifest themselves only at a certain point in one's life… The semiotic factors in puberty (new impressions, anxiety towards the unknown, social repression and so on) are enormously affected by such syndromes, and analysis should therefore be directed to considering the power formations that correspond to them: the high school, technical school, sports club, leisure arrangements, etc. At this point a whole new facet of society threatens to clamp down upon the desire of the adolescent, cutting her off from the world and leading her to turn in upon herself" (1984, p. 165).

And (3) Deleuze himself insists that language creation contains moments of rupture and dissonance: "One's always writing to bring something to life, to free life from where it's trapped… The language for doing that can't be a homogeneous system, it's something unstable, always heterogeneous, in which style carves differences of potential between which things can pass, come to pass, a spark can flash and break out of language itself, to make us see and think what was lying in the shadow around the words, things we were hardly aware existed." Writing is fundamentally about bringing something to life, he claims, "to free life from where it is trapped. To trace lines of flight." These quotations will help chart the direction of the book's overall project. What follows are concrete instances of the relay of breakdown and breakthrough which the authors of this book wish to convey through ecologies of language learning.

Eating the Dictionary

Interpreted through a Deleuzian lens, desire (joy/anxiety) for language operates on a pre-personal level, in terms of impersonal affect. There is no transparent desire to learn the language on the level of the first person singular. I do not just desire *in vacuo*. I am rather part of a network or *agencement* (assemblage) of desire. While we discern the desire for foreign language learning *as creative, energetic, replete and subtle* and through it a means to achieve certain ends such as learning in and for itself, or more instrumentally, for financial or professional gain, there is also present an existential desire: there is the desire to become-other through foreign language learning, a desire for a second self, which is to say, a desire to say something that can only be said in another language (Dörnyei & Gardner, 2012). We may find a desire for independence from families or to be a master of a minor language that few speak. We also find an investment in learning for amorous ends; a desire to be called "darling" in a foreign language; a desire to have "a" darling (Oguri, 2010); a desire to be told "I love you" in English. For example, in the 2003 South Korean comedy film 영어완전정복 [*Please Teach Me English*] we hear the following from Park Moon Su:

> When I find a woman to love, I'll confess to her in English. 'I love you' in Korean is so corny. I love you, darling. English feels different, doesn't it?

We also find a desire to be simply desired by the other (Takahashi, 2013). Furthermore, the desire to learn a foreign language can be linked to the desire to have Chinese, African, European, Russian, or North American friends: a desire to sing opera, hip-hop, or the blues in another tongue. There are also more complex desires which arguably are more manufactured or ideological fixed, desires to acquire a global identity (in Japan, this is called グローバル人材 or global human resource), a desire for global thinking or a global perspective, whatever that is, perhaps even a desire to be less culturally insular. My point is there is never simply a desire for someone or something (at its most manufactured and derivative for a white, blue-eyed, Western, English-speaking boyfriend for example) as one always desires an aggregate (living the American dream, a big house, baseball games, American fast food, working on an American navy base, the prom night, fast cars, owning a gun). Deleuze and Guattari say we never desire something to the exclusion of other elements. Moreover, one never simply desires an aggregate either, as one is always bound up from within an aggregate (compulsory English language learning from primary through to secondary, high school, university, graduate school, the workplace, endless evening classes and finally hearing and seeing English announcements every day during the train commute home). Through all of this, we are told again and again then we must learn this and that and for this and that exam, otherwise you will miss out on promotion and even *happiness in life*.

This point about desire and being told to do something is demonstrated well in the Korean film *Please Teach Me English*. Riding the bus on her way to register for English class and after seeing a schoolgirl rip and swallow indigestible pages from an English dictionary, Nah Young-ju bemoans the fact that English is desired: "Everybody's obsessed with English. What's wrong with being born in Korea and just knowing Korean?" (Sung-soo et al., 2006). Deleuze and Guattari will say that desire always flows within an assemblage. To affirm the joy of learning language desire must flow within an assemblage (less testing, less rote learning, more communication, escape from the teacher and classroom, the joy of contact with others from overseas—a joy in saying something in your name, or in a language of your choosing, free of the conventions, rules, formalities, strictures of Japanese honorifics, the selling of your own cultural belongings to cross distant seas for other exotic climes). Deleuze and Guattari add that to desire is to construct an assemblage. This means one imagines a self quite different from those ideologically manufactured by educational institutions. This is the becoming other of oneself. A becoming-speaker of other languages. There is an aggregate of a dictionary, a textbook, your first passport, of being totally lost in an exotic land, smells of foreign food, different climates, new alphabets, different writing styles, a different comportment of the body, an assemblage of foreign friends (parties, clubs, being given a foreign name or nickname), your first kiss, and then not knowing who you are any more. You are constructing an assemblage of language learning, enjoying a romantic sunset, and thinking about the future, with thoughts of international marriage or just being different, of getting away, breaking away from social mores and obligations, and finally saying "who the hell am I?" This is what desire is, Deleuze tells us. It is constructing an assemblage, constructing, assembling. Desire for foreign language learning is both creative and destructive; it is a "constructivism" (Deleuze & Parnet, 2012).

Perhaps all languages taste differently. I guess some people like this language for this or that reason, for its sound, or its romantic connotations, for the beauty of Japanese or Urdu, or German for its order, French for its romance, or English for its wondrous chaotic complexity. I guess there are some people who don't like one language for a particular reason, its harshness or loudness, its directness, its lack of nuance or subtleness. I suspect there are many people who indeed *hate* this or that language for this or that reason and that affects learning. But that does not tell the whole story. I am arguing that there's a kind of abstract impersonal force behind language, working upon it unconsciously, an army if you like, a drone machine. It is Deleuze and Guattari who help to explain this.

That which lies behind language inspires or deters people from learning a language; knowledge for example that the language you learn in school hails is from an imperial culture, which dropped nuclear bombs on your country. A language used by a military force in Okinawa which rapes young women. What does English taste like then? Here I think it is not a question of whether you simply like or dislike a language. Rather it is a question of affect. What affects are generated in and by language? What affects pierce the skin or assault the flesh? These words are those which Deleuze and Guattari call "order words". These are the words which carry illocutionary or even perlocutionary force. They have an effect. The affect has an effect. The judge adorning a black cap when passing a sentence of death is a form of illocutionary theatrics. Think about the effects generated in Harold Pinter's use of language, for example, in the menacing silences and the affects generated there; these are impersonal affects, not just emotions (Bradley & Kennedy, 2020).

Misono's Sweets

This is the story of Kazuo Misono. He tells me the story about his youth in Ochanomizu, the place where he grew up in central Tokyo. His childhood was formed in the immediate aftermath of the Pacific War, where American soldiers were conspicuous on the streets of Tokyo. As a primary school student, he is with his friends in the neighbourhood; a young American soldier comes up and talks to them. The Japanese kids don't understand a word. The American soldier is admiring one of the boys' bicycles; he's a friendly guy and gives the children some sweets for the exchange of pleasantries. The Japanese boys are grateful and try to find words to convey this; they look to Kazuo who knows a little bit of English. With much bravado, he replies with a hearty thanks to the American soldier which leaves his friends amazed. Kazuo is pleased by the reaction. It stays in the mind. And it just so happens that Kazuo grows up to become a famous professor of linguistics in Japan. This anecdote seems to me to show that affect and language are intrinsically connected. Language touches and inheres in the synapses. The affects of language concerned breakdown, leave positive memory traces in the brain; a connection between the sweetness of the candy, the positive effect of being praised, and the sweetness of language itself.

At this point, one could say that there is really no accounting for taste, but my pitch is that one has got to experiment with the affects of language. One example Guattari gives is of an autistic young man who prefers not to communicate with the doctors and the patients. He's suffering. But once he gets into a car, a serendipitous event takes place. His body almost explodes with excitement. He's found a way to connect. There is a breakthrough. Before this there is only breakdown, silence, frustration, and resentment. Things connect with other things, the question is how they work. In terms of my own teaching, it is a shame that in my large classes, I can't give more one-to-one treatment to individual students, to experiment with the kids, to find what makes them tick, what makes them work. For some, they've never had this kind of attention in their education. I think university teachers should be able to look at the student, to find out why things are working, or not. This is a breakdown of education, a breakdown of pedagogy. It is endemic in education in Japan and elsewhere. Breakdown is conspicuous. Deleuze and

Guattari's message is to dare to find the breakthroughs in teaching and learning, loving, and living. Their thought can create a new world through desire.

Breakthrough, Schizoanalysis, and Video Literacies

A student had a crush on a foreign lecturer, which had interrupted her learning and his teaching. The infatuation which lasted for a couple of years was never anything other than Platonic and was the kind of experience that we have all probably had in life or at school, at one time or another. What was really astounding was that the student in her own way worked through this experience, by making a video with her friend. The video represents this experience comically, for example, with both having a mock pistol shoot out, with special effects later dubbed in. I think that was an interesting way for them to work through a personal existential problem. The finished video was successful, very funny, and mature. Through making the video, the students were able to reflect on the emotional experience with humour and wit and draw something life affirming from it—such as the consolidation of their friendship.

In this case, there is confusion between the students as learners and the students as desiring the object of the learning, which isn't language, but the user of the language. In that confusion, that could lead to complications and difficulties in the learning context, such difficulties could seriously damage their relationship and the learning of the students. This is where a Deleuze and Guattari approach to understanding these processes differs from, for example, a straightforward psychoanalytical approach, which would look at repression, and the ways in which individual subjectivities of the Japanese girls respond to desire, to how they have been controlled and conformed from birth, for example, through the Oedipus complex. But the schizoanalytic approach broadens that psychoanalytic approach from merely registering the subjectivities as individualized and formed and reformed through the various ways in which their sexuality has developed into a bigger collective social platform and within that platform, desire can be seen to act in other synthetic, and more social ways. Desire is at the heart of the social.

For example, the desire for the lecturer might not just be one of individual desire, it might be expressing a relationship, for example, between Japanese and Western culture. It might be looking at the roles of women in Japanese society, or against the roles of men and women in Western societies. It might not just be a desire for one person or sexual contact or sexual liaison between the students and the teacher, but for a bigger gamut of desires, success, and power, which are part of contemporary global culture.

Making a video of this kind is a chance to express those entangled, bigger desires, which open the arena for expression beyond the singular sense of amour from the students to the teacher. It creates a broad arena, a wider focus for representation and expression. So the video works on one level as a representation of that, but other than a psychoanalytic understanding, or a simple exercise to express this desire, we can turn it into something that uses things like collages or images of video culture, from advertising, from all sorts of different sources, that could look to mediate and transform the particular desires of the girls or the girl for the lecturer into wider cultural, social questions; it is thought provoking to think about the question of these desires in a schizoanalytic way.

Literature Student

He was a first-year student. I taught him for the whole year. He struggled with virtually everything we did in class. At the end of the spring semester, I told the class to read all that they could get their hands on in the summer, because they would seldom get the chance after finding a job. I beseeched them to find something of interest. I told them don't just stare at their smartphones all summer. The young man came back in autumn and we talked about film. When I mentioned Leonardo DiCaprio's film *The Revenant* something clicks. He tells me about the film *Into the Wild* based on the true story of Christopher McCandless. His face breaks out with a smile. He tells me how he has fallen in love with this story and has started to read around it. He too wants to go into the wild. He pulls out a notebook full of quotations from Tolstoy and Nietzsche. Bits of French, bits of Sartre, big chunks of English and Japanese translations. A big thick notebook. He beams with joy, as he shows me it. I too smile, as I told him in spring to keep a notebook, to jot down notes for the whole year, as I had done as a student. He's enjoying the process. He's in love with life. When I see him on campus, he dashes over to me and tells me about his latest exploits. What he has read. The mad mixture of poetry and literature he has been reading—Baudelaire, Shakespeare, Henry Miller, Kafka. You could say from a Deleuzian point of view this is essentially what language learning is about. It's a connection with life. It's finding out how something works or doesn't, and you can understand that through a kind of schizoanalysis, which is what Guattari was doing at the La Borde clinic in France in the 1960s and 1970s, where he learned to think transversely about mental problems. I think this applies to language learning. But the examples above are concerned with a kind of breakthrough. Guattari's examples concern breakdown, kids suffering from mental illness, who struggle to talk and communicate, who struggle to follow the cognitive therapies which the doctors were prescribing. Guattari learned from this transversal aspect of language learning. And we should too.

In total, these examples serve as evidence for the type of transcendental empiricism that Deleuze espouses. *Difference and Repetition* (1994) shows how empirical evidence cannot be repeated, as it forms its own singularity of relations in whatever spacetime it is noted and observed. This is the fundamental problem for the science of educational research (Cole, 2021b), in that individual instances of learning are never repeated. Rather, only the differences between relations are repeated, but these are rarely noted or understood by educationalists. Hence, this book in essence is about difference, and the differences that are prised open and may be acted upon in education through ecologies of language learning. Deleuze and Guattari grasped that the fundamental object of analysis must be change, and it is the fulcrum of changing relations which is the central focus of this book.

References

Allsop, B., Briggs, J., & Kisby, B. (2018). Market values and youth political engagement in the UK: Towards an agenda for exploring the psychological impacts of neo-liberalism. *Societies, 8*(4), 95.

Bradley, J. P. N. & Kennedy, D. (2020). *Bringing forth a world: Engaged pedagogy in the Japanese university*. Brill.

Chomsky, N. (2011). Language and other cognitive systems. What is special about language? *Language Learning and Development, 7*(4), 263–278.

Clancy, S., & Lowrie, T. (2005). Multiliteracies: New pathways into digital worlds. *International Journal of Learning, 12*(7), 141–147.

Cole, D. R. (2012). Matter in motion: The educational materialism of Gilles Deleuze. *Educational Philosophy and Theory, 44*(sup1), 3–17.

Cole, D. R. (2021a). *Education, the Anthropocene, and Deleuze/Guattari*. Brill.

Cole, D. R. (2021b). A new science of contemporary educational theory, practice and research. In K. Murris (Ed.), *Navigating the post qualitative, new materialist and critical posthumanist terrain across disciplines: An introductory guide* (pp. 99–117). Routledge.

Cole, D. R., & Mirzaei Rafe, M. (2018). An analysis of the reality of authoritarianism in pedagogy: A critique based on the work of Deleuze, Guattari and Bhaskar. *Espacio, Tiempo y Educación, 5*(1), 41–56.

Deleuze, G. ([1968] 1994). *Difference & repetition* (P. Patton, Trans.). Columbia University Press.

Deleuze, G., & Guattari, F. ([1972] 1983). *Anti-oedipus: Capitalism & schizophrenia* (R. Hurley, M. Steen & H. R. Lane, Trans.). The Athlone Press.

Deleuze, G., & Guattari, F. ([1980] 1988). *A thousand plateaus: Capitalism and schizophrenia II* (B. Massumi, Trans.). The Athlone Press.

Deleuze, G., & Parnet, C. (2002). *Dialogues II* (B. Habberjam & H. Tomlinson, Trans.). Columbia University Press.

Dornyei, Z., & Gardner, R. C. (2012). *Motivation and second language acquisition*. Univ. of Hawaii Press.

Duff, D. (2014). *Modern genre theory*. Routledge.

Grinberg, S. M. (2013). Researching the pedagogical apparatus (Dispositif): An ethnography of the molar, molecular and desire in con-texts of extreme urban poverty. In R. Coleman & J. Ringrose (Eds.), *Deleuze and research methodologies* (pp. 201–218). Edinburgh University Press.

Guattari, F. ([1989] 1996). *The three ecologies* (I. Pindar & P. Sutton, Trans.). The Athlone Press.

Hagood, M. C. (2000). New times, new millennium, new literacies. *Literacy Research and Instruction, 39*(4), 311–328.

Harvey, D. (2017). *Marx, capital, and the madness of economic reason*. Oxford University Press.

Kellner, D. (1998). Multiple literacies and critical pedagogy in a multicultural society. *Educational theory, 48*(1), 103–122.

Kress, G. (2000). Multimodality: Challenges to thinking about language. *TESOL Quarterly, 34*(2), 337–340.

Lewis, T. E. (2017). A Marxist education of the encounter: Althusser, interpellation, and the seminar. *Rethinking Marxism, 29*(2), 303–317.

Manolescu, M. (2013). School competence between behaviourism and cognitivism or the cognitive approach to schooling. *Procedia-Social and Behavioral Sciences*, 76, 912–916.

Masny, D., & Cole, D. R. (Eds.). (2009). *Multiple literacies theory: A Deleuzian perspective*. Brill.

Masny, D., & Cole, D. R. (2012). *Mapping multiple literacies: An introduction to Deleuzian literacy studies*. Bloomsbury.

Meinrenken, E. (1996). On Riemann-Roch formulas for multiplicities. *Journal of the American Mathematical Society, 9*(2), 373–389.

New London Group (1996). A pedagogy of multiliteracies. *Harvard Educational Review*, 60, 66–92.

Oguri, S. (2010). Dārin wa gaikokujin. Media Fakutorī.

Reay, D. (2004). 'It's all becoming a habitus': Beyond the habitual use of habitus in educational research. *British Journal of Sociology of Education, 25*(4), 431–444.

Riasati, M. J., & Mollaei, F. (2012). Critical pedagogy and language learning. *International Journal of Humanities and Social Science, 2*(21), 223–229.

Semetsky, I. (2004). The role of intuition in thinking and learning: Deleuze and the pragmatic legacy. *Educational Philosophy and Theory*, 36(4), 433–454.

Staddon, J. E., & Cerutti, D. T. (2003). Operant conditioning. *Annual Review of Psychology, 54*(1), 115–144.

Suárez-Orozco, M. (2001). Education: The research agenda. *Harvard Educational Review, 71*(3), 345–366.

Sung-soo, K., Lee, N., Jang, H., & Kelly, A. (2006). *Please teach me English*. Tai Seng Entertainment.

Takahashi, K. (2013). *Language learning, gender and desire: Japanese women on the move*. Multilingual Matters.

Vandenberghe, F. (2013). *What's critical about critical realism? essays in reconstructive social theory*. Routledge

Vygotsky, L. S., & Cole, M. (1978). *Mind in society: Development of higher psychological processes*. Harvard University Press.

Materialisms

CHAPTER TWO

On the Materiality of Thixotropic Slogans

As a contribution to the critique of "pragmatic" communications theory, this chapter introduces Deleuze and Guattari's heterodox performative theory of the order word (*mot d'ordre*). It will be seen that the order word as a command or slogan implicit in speech acts plays a central role in the pragmatics of enunciation and charts a path between the Saussurean Scylla and Chomskyan Charybdis. The chapter will proceed to a conclusion which considers the limitative and expansive nature of the order word as an articulation and function of *strata*. I will consider the password as consistent with Blanchot's *mots de désordre (disorder words)* and argue that despite efforts to articulate a positive theory of the password by Lingis (2004), the thixotropic nature of the line of flight that the password embarks upon is soon recuperated by the ordering forces of the societies of control (Deleuze, 1995).

Genealogy of the Order Word

Although the idea of the order word is derived from Elias Canetti's *Crowds and Power* (1962), and denotes the function of language as the establishment of collective order, it is first mentioned by Deleuze in *Bergsonism* (1988). Considering the nature of *problems*, Deleuze remarks that order words "set up" ready-made opinions and perceptions (p. 15). He remarks that it is as if such shrink-wrapped problems were drawn from a bureaucrat's administrative filing cabinet so as to be quickly and easily resolved. Equally, social institutions such as education and language force the populace to "solve" them. They set the parameters of *the thinkable*. From this there is but a "thin margin of freedom" (p. 15). Obversely, true freedom Deleuze considers, is the power to decide and constitute problems *themselves*. Deleuze as such is interested in forms of invention and creativity which think the inaugural or that which is without pre-existing manifesto or programme. It is not a question of finding or discovering the solution but of inventing it. In *Difference and Repetition* (1994), Deleuze suggests we remain slaves to problems if we do not control or possess a right to them or participate in their management (p. 158).

There are clear parallels between Deleuze and Guattari's and Bakhtin's notion of slogans when the former discuss the term in relation to Lenin's pamphlet On Slogans in *A Thousand Plateaus* (1987). The slogan "All power to the Soviets" is read as effective within concrete circumstances during the critical time prior to the Russian Revolution. For Lecercle (2002), the illocutionary timeliness of this slogan produces a perlocutionary truth as its *effect* (p. 170). In a similar manner, Bakhtin makes references to the significance of indirect discourse for dialogism in his *Problems in Dostoyevsky's Poetics* (1981). Bakhtin also contends that a socially significant verbal performance possesses the capacity to "infect with its own intention certain aspects of language" (p. 290). If the comparison bears closer attention, what is novel in Deleuze and Guattari is a more comprehensive analysis of the working of power and control in relation to the infringement upon the body. After all, the slogan was originally a war cry. We can also detect a reworking and extension of Benveniste's model of the performative (1971) in Deleuze and Guattari's pragmatics. Deleuze and Guattari grant the performative a structural role in the collective assemblage of enunciation, which is an intrinsic component of the abstract machine of language. Language is formed through constraints on word formation made directly through the effect of group membership on individuals. The order word then expresses "the habits of speech of a social collective" rather than the gestures of a solitary, brooding, intentional and phenomenological subject (see Boundas in Protevi, 2005, p. 435).

Deriving much import from Foucault's analysis of *énoncé* (1972) or "serious speech acts" (Dreyfus & Rabinow, 1982), the order word, which is not defined as a function of a single kind of statement as it is with Austin (1962), is an integral part of the assemblage (*agencement*) of ideas such as indirect discourse, incorporeal transformation (a term borrowed from the Stoics) and collective assemblage of enunciation (*agencement collectif d'énonciation*). Foucauldian speech acts are interpreted as disclosing the history of truth judgments not in the ordinary sense of the cataloguing of the verisimilitude of truth claims but through a genesis or genealogy. Foucault thinks incorporeal transformations manifested through order words are discursively constitutive of what is meant by the "criminal" or the "mad" at a particular juncture in history.

The order word is defined as a series of regulated patterns formed through an ontological mixture of bodies, institutions and discourses (Lecercle, 2002), which combine to form the complex notion of a pragmatic re-interpretation of the illo-cutionary speech act and its perlocutionary effects, that is to say, effects which per-suade, cajole, frighten and inspire. According to Lecercle (2005, p. 74), the theory views interlocution as quintessentially *agonic* and expressive of *rapport de forces* (power struggle or differential relation between forces). And for Butler, the subject is the effect of power "in recoil" (1997, p. 6). Gender, she contends, is a construct, an effect of incorporeal transformation, a capture of the body from the insertion of order words into the subject's actions. Order words or slogans affect incorporeal transformations through bodies and only through bodies.

The Performative and the Imperative

The performative is prior to the constative or declarative, the assertion or the in-terpellation: the imperative insinuated in the performance is prior to the subject. At work in language is the performative or violent function of the order word. The key to understanding this is to see that meaning, intention and interpretation are replaced with the notion of capillary power and embedded relations of power. Insinuated among relations of power the linguistic cogito "I speak" is decentred. The "it speaks" dominates utterances. In a rather peculiar sense, the collective as-semblage of enunciation speaks the speaker (Lecercle, 2002, p. 88).

Indeed, for Deleuze and Guattari, pragmatics takes precedence over rival models of linguistics such as semantics. Indeed, writing separately, Guattari in making the case for incorporating signifying semiologies into a more expansive general pragmatics, says:

> [W]hile engaging with the Anglo-American tradition, pragmatics should stop being considered a great suburb of syntax and semantics; while engaging the Franco-European tradition, it should stop being considered a sub-discipline of linguistics. (Guattari, 2011, p. 335)

For pragmatics is the presupposition behind all of the other dimensions and "insinuates itself into everything" (Deleuze & Guattari, 1987, p. 7). Moreover, the order word—which according to Lydenberg (1987), bears close resemblance to William Burroughs' *word virus*—as it describes words as viral entities in a literal or metonymic, non-metaphorical sense. The order word forms part of an assemblage of ideas such as indirect discourse, incorporeal transformation and collective assemblage of enunciation which combine to form the complex notion of a pragmatics of the perlocutionary and illocutionary speech act defined as the set of "virtual-real" order words in a given society (Deleuze & Guattari, 1987, p. 110). The illocutionary—the enunciation of a statement or an act that modifies the relationship between two speakers—is therefore constitutive of the perlocutionary, which is conventionally deemed external. Austin's speech act theory (1962) is reworked to describe the order word in several ways as a kind of commandment, slogan or imperative for action. One might think of it as somehow operative on both symbolic and concrete power structure levels conferring orders to a body of individuals. It forms an integral part of the assault on the "molar" presuppositions of linguistics and lays the groundwork for Deleuze and Guattari's affirmation of a "molecular" linguistics of variation, which derives much of its geneologico-linguistic rigour and import from Labov (1973), who stresses variable rules and heterogeneity in language; C.S. Peirce (1931), who Deleuze and Guattari describe as "the true inventor of semiotics" (1987, p. 531); the critique of the Althusserian concept of ideology (Lecercle, 2006); as well as drawing on a host of influences from Benveniste (1971), Bakhtin (1973), Hjelmslev (1961) and Jakobson (1980).

Drawing on the pragmatism of C.S. Peirce, Deleuze and Guattari contend that linguistics needs pragmatics to isolate the condition of possibility and the usage of the linguistic elements (1987, p. 85). As Deleuze is interested in the conditions of possibility of language and linguistic signs, as well as the relations of forces enveloped in signs, there is no language intelligible outside of a generalised pragmatics, which is to say non-analogical expressions are inextricably entangled with the powers of the heterogeneous world or the collective arrangement of enunciation.

This pragmatism or transcendental empiricism—that is to say the disclosure of the empirical conditions of possibility of thought—is less concerned with the meaning of signs and their representations than with sign and its a-signification, its affect and functioning. The connected sign *qua* expression is dispersed amid a series of concrete arrangements. So the isolated "I" therefore asks of the forces which compel it to think *qua ipseity*.

Moreover, signs are re-read alongside Spinoza's notion of "expression" (Deleuze, 1990a, 1990b). The power of signs is interpreted as an illusion in collusion with the order of the signifier, the transcendental law and so on. In a gambit to transcend the horizon of images of death and negativity and to undermine Saussure-inflected semiotics and the Chomskyan linguistic paradigm, the problem of expression and expressivity is rethought in terms of an engineering issue, a linguistic theory of machinic pragmatism which cartographically sets out a semiotics of the clinical and critical. Emphasising the notion of variation and change, Deleuze and Guattari mischievously declare: "You will never find a homogeneous system that is not still or already affected by a regulated, continuous, immanent process of variation (why does Chomsky pretend not to understand this?)" (1987, p. 103). We can see here that Deleuze is aiming to oust a former representation and the problem of signs and their signification with a series of Spinozan-inflected problems pertaining to the expressed and the expression. So the question becomes one of invention and creation, a matter of machinic relay: what am I affected by and what do I affect? Through the prism of Spinozian ethics, Deleuze perceives signs as indicative of joyful or sad affects: an evaluation is taken in terms of whether signs increase or decrease the powers of living.

The order word receives its fullest explication in the chapter "Postulates of Linguistics" in *A Thousand Plateaus* (1987). At the heart of this argument are four issues which assess the following: (1) language as informational and communicational; (2) the abstract machine of language and its relation to extrinsic factors; (3) the universals of language and; (4) the scientific study of language under the conditions of a standard or major language (1987, p. 101). In this chapter I shall focus on the first and third notions. For Deleuze and Guattari, the "building brick" '(Lecercle, 2005, p. 71) of language is not the predicative sentence or assertion but the order word, the "elementary unit of language" (Deleuze & Guattari, 1987, p. 7). It is a function "coextensive with language", with a fallen state of language—and carries more fundamental import than subjects or signs, communication or information. The latter is but the "minimal condition" (Deleuze & Guattari, 1987, p. 79) for the transmission of order words.

The order word then is understood as the implicit speech act, a nondiscursive presupposition of a statement (*énoncé*) (Deleuze & Guattari, 1987, p. 77). Expressions are overcoded by impersonal collective assemblages, the manipulator of puppets in marionette theatre, while statements are individuated in the sense that the collective assemblage prepares them to be transmitted. They are anonymous for they are quickly relayed onwards—and no one takes responsibility for them. This idea reflects Beneviste's conception of subjectivity in language, which considers language as preparing empty forms which the speaker adopts in the constitution of the person (1971, p. 227). For Beneviste, language is primarily impersonal as it is the condition of the subject when personal pronouns are used. The subject only takes up the site of subjectivity by incorporating the impersonal and "empty forms" of language.

Language, which does not represent but rather circulates, is not the medium of communication of new information as such but more primordially pertains to the barking of lingering, dormant commands which convey not understanding as such but rather encapsulate miniature "death sentences" (Deleuze & Guattari, 1987, p. 88) or little "stings" or "stings of command" (Canetti, 1962, p. 351). Deleuze and Guattari give the example of the lion's roar in Canetti's analysis of commands in *Crowds and Power* as an order word and describe it in terms of affective intensity. Indeed, Brian Massumi, a translator of Deleuze and Guattari, argues that as the *mot d'ordre* means "slogan" or "(military) password" in modern French, Deleuze and Guattari use the idea to literally mean "word of order", that is to say, they contend that it commands a double sense of also creating a political order (Massumi in Deleuze & Guattari, 1987, p. 523). It can be said that the order word pertains to a command for action given by both a symbolic and concrete power structure (an army) to a large group of individuals. The word also designates the power wielded in a political party or union. In the essay "Deleuze and Signs", Colombat argues that the illocutionary, "subtends" the locutionary (see Marks & Buchanan, 2000, p. 16).

The order word is referred to as a command, judgment and death sentence and functions through the redundancy of its signification. Order words are spectral-like. They exist long after their initial utterance, long after they become redundant. For Cole (2010) they are governing, institutional structures which in some sense hover above the utterances of the everyday. They induce incorporeal transformations and adopt a death-in-life presence circulating "around institutions places of education like the routing of electricity in plasterboard walls" (p. 25). Order words soon pass over to the *"silent order" of things*, as Foucault would say (Deleuze & Guattari, 1987, p. 96).

Imperatives (commands, orders, injunctions), entreaties and requests, are performatives, that is to say, a form of speech act uttered by X person in Y circumstances, which compel a change in a state of affairs. Imperatives can also be found in declarative and descriptive sentences. If, for Deleuze and Guattari, the primary function of language is to affect others, then the "I" emits speech acts in self-expression for the "I" *is* an order word (1987, p. 84). Deleuze says that in the act of speaking, one does not simply indicate things and actions, but "commits acts that assure a relation with the interlocutor, in keeping with our respective situations. The verbs I command, I interrogate, I promise, I ask, *all* emit speech acts" (Deleuze, 1997, p. 73).

Assessed under the strictures of Jakobson's diagram of communication, the order word's exertive and conative (the vocative or imperative) element dominates the structure of the speech event. In Jakobson's formalist-functionalist model of communication, which is structured around six components—addresser, context, message, contact, code, and addressee—six functions correspond to the following: the emotive, the referential, the poetic, the phatic, the metalingual, and the conative. It is argued that in any communicative event, one of the functions takes precedence to a greater or lesser extent over the others—when one considers the point of view of the observer. The full meaning of the speech event is hence considered to be dependent on the context, code, or means of contact, and the combinations which ensue. The meaning of a message is grasped in the total act of communication, which entertains distinct extralinguistic factors and is comparable to the social relations organized by the collective assemblage of enunciation. While in Saussure's work there is a distinction between langue and parole, with langue taken as the systematic homogeneous aspect of language, and parole the individual use and variation, in Jakobson, we find the link between signifier and signified loosed to take better account of the role parole plays.

Fundamentally, primordial communication is considered to be the transmission, propagation and dissemination of order words. Language refers not simply to paralinguistic expression or extra-linguistic concerns, but to the always-already expressed which operates from "saying to saying" (Deleuze & Guattari, 1987, p. 7). The operation of the order word functions through memory and the memory of what has been said before. There is consistent correspondence between saying and saying. We can also find this idea in Nietzsche's *Genealogy of Morals* (1967), in which he argues that memory and pain are inextricably linked because it is through the internalisation of pain and the inscription of pain upon the body that one comes to know morality.

The transmission of the order word is a concrete event, and as such its effects are codified in the enunciation. Drawing on the speech-act theory of Austin, Deleuze and Guattari argue that the efficacy of a speech act is derived not in the meanings of words but in the specifics of the situation. The remit of speech act theory is therefore extended to analyze the implicit presupposition or "sense" of a statement. The order word takes notice not of signification or semantics *per se* but the vagaries of the concrete situation and the incorporeal transformations brought into existence and acted upon the body. The order word therefore reinforces the repetition or redundancy of production.

The problem of meaning is thus perceived as inextricably connected to the question of specific use. In terms of schooling and teaching of language, Deleuze and Guattari (1987, p. 75) claim that the compulsory education machine does not communicate education. Rather it imposes upon the student "semiotic coordinates" possessing all of the dual foundations of grammar. Put another way, the conversations at educational institutions—determine both the sayable, the iterable, as well as the unsayable and the outlawed. Moreover, vocabulary, grammar, rhetoric, and tone of voice are subject to the same determination.

To grasp the pragmatic interpretation of the order word, it is important to understand that it not simply a question of conscious decision, interpretation or understanding on the part of the isolated "I". With Deleuze and Guattari we find a relentless critique of the centrality of the subject and the system of representation. There is no axiological or existential decision to disclose. "We" obey blindly—unthinkingly. As Deleuze and Guattari insist, language is made not to be believed but to be obeyed, and to "complement obedience" (1987, p. 7). Obedience is thus perceived as the honouring of order words. Likewise, De Landa (1993, p. 14), argues that in small communities social rites and rules develop that register language as a "badge of identity" and ensure that dialect, patois or minor language are disseminated.

In speaking to others, we transmit to them what we have been told to say. Order words or slogans are the cues, prompts, watchwords and passwords—discontinuous utterances—which we attach and avail ourselves to as representatives of this or that discipline, body or group. Indirect discourse communicates what someone has heard and what someone has been told to say. The order words command the informative content of sentences. Learning a language would then seem to demand a blind affirmation of the "semiotisation" of reality derived from enforced participation in social practices. In other words, we carry out rules to avoid social exclusion and ostracism, to ward off the threat of social reprobation, to escape the label of mad, lying, stupid, or socially dysfunctional. We obey because others obey.

In the school, the grammar teacher imparts or *insigns* knowledge of a rule to be followed *compulsively* (Deleuze & Guattari, 1987, p. 75). The *docilised* body is unconscious of the "abominable faculty" instilled into it, which consists in "emitting, receiving and transmitting order words" (1987, p. 7). The language of order words is the language of the courtroom and of the law and is akin to Wittgenstein's form of life and language games. This processual semiotisation observes linguistic codes for social rites and pragmatic language use among peers as well as paralinguistic expression such as gesture, facial expression and posture.

In summa: the focus on exteriority shows language does not operate between something seen and something said, but relays from saying to saying. Language is connected to the outside because the dissemination of an order word is a concrete event, dependent upon the nature of the collective subject of enunciation. Deleuze and Guattari's theory of language and speech acts therefore pertains less to the conveyance of the meanings of words but more to the concrete context in question. Language appears to presuppose itself for order words are considered to be codified in every act linked to statements enforced by social obligation. It is this point which reveals Deleuze and Guattari's definition of language as such. They argue that language is the set of "all order words, implicit presuppositions, or speech acts current in a given language at a given moment" (1987, p. 79). Contra Austin, indirect discourse is primary because language *flows* through subjects, speaking through them, aiding the regulation and ordering of the life-world. Language is read as speaking in and through subjects, rather than being spoken by them. And as a consequence and in a similar fashion, politics affects language thoroughly from within (Grisham, 1991).

Interlude: The "I" Traversed

In eschewing the linguistics conception of subjectivity, Deleuze and Guattari's philosophy launches a full scale assault on the centrality of the thixotropic subject. Their philosophy singularly aims to "demote the subject from its central position" (Lecercle, 2002, p. 14). In other words, subjectivity is determined by effects. In the place of the subject, impersonal singularity is formed through connections with other singularities in a field distributed *about a potential*. For Deleuze, the world is "teeming" with anonymous, impersonal and pre-individual singularities (a term derived from the philosophy of Gilbert Simondon). Singularities are not individual or personal but oversee the genesis of individual and persons. A singularity is constitutive of a pre-individual transcendental field. The arrangement of singularities includes persons but also impersonal collections (Brott, 2011).

Thinking through the sense of the haecceity, that is to say, *thisness*, an occurrence or happening, an innocence of becoming or rhizomatic line of flight, Deleuze and Guattari consider the person as one among a series of possible individuations such as "a life, a season, a wind, a battle, five o'clock" (Deleuze, 2006, p. 355). The *haecceity* is a certain *gathering together* of the threads of life (Ingold, 2008). Moreover, subjectivity is an effect of impersonal processes of individuation. Impersonal effects—perceptions or emissions of singularities are irreducible to the individual or personal. The "it" is impersonal in every encounter. The poet Lawrence Ferlinghetti's "fourth person singular" (1960) or impersonal discourse is used to dethrone the centrality of the "I"—the subject that speaks in its own name. From this perspective, what is shown is the murmur of "*il y a du langage*" (there is language). There is no speaker or author but a system of utterances or enunciations—the anonymous murmur of the *on parle*. For example, we can think through the anonymity of the "it" in the following description of the battlefield: [the] "battle hovers over its own field, being neutral in relation to all of its temporal actualizations" (Deleuze, 1990a, 1990b, p. 116). It is impassive in relation to the victor and the vanquished or the coward and the brave. It is "never present but always yet to come and already passed" (Deleuze, 1990a, 1990b, p. 116). The event of the battle provides a prism through which to access the "fourth" person— "a genuinely impersonal dimension where everything is both collective and private" (Marks, 1998, p. 41).

For Deleuze, when we speak, a particular form of speech speaks through us. In our time, what speaks is not the individual, person or "sea without difference" but a world of pre-individual, impersonal singularities, which are mobile and nomadic. The fourth person is somehow entwined with a flowing, intensive, presubjective "I feel". While differentiated from the everydayness and idle speech of the Heideggerian *the they*, the fourth person partakes of its impersonality, "it is the 'they' of impersonal and pre-individual singularities, the 'they' of the pure event wherein it dies in the same way that it rains. The splendor of the 'they' is the splendor of the event itself or of the fourth person" (Deleuze, 1990a, 1990b, p. 152). The event *qua* language is devoid of subjectivity. Rather, it is embedded in the impersonal language of a kind of rustling *il y a* (there is) or the "fourth person singular". Singularity then is loaded with an impersonal power that forms local connections to produce transformation upon the body of the subject, that is to say, to produce a relay of subjectivation-desubjectivation. In questioning the concept of person (1990, p. 141), Deleuze cites a draft, a wind, a day, a time of day, a stream, a place, a battle, or an illness as haecceities which possess a nonpersonal individuality and a proper name. He goes so far as to say that individuality as such belongs more to the event as such (p. 141). The concept of haecceity avoids the habit of saying "I", or of speaking in one's own name. It ceases to be a subject but rather solicits events in assemblages (Deleuze & Guattari, 1987, p. 262). Put another way, in discussing the role of affect on subjectivity in the essay *Ritornellos and Existential Affects*, Guattari (1996) claims that affects engage the memory and cognition, with the result that the "I" is assaulted and deserted of interiority. It is but a tributary "to a multi-headed enunciative lay-out" (p. 160). He goes on to say that the "I" which speaks in the first person becomes a "fluctuating intersection", and a "terminal" for consciousness. Individuation is therefore an infinite process or constant movement. It is productive of untimely becomings. A haecceity is always intersticial, geometric and abstract (Deleuze & Guattari, 1987, p. 263).

Direct Discourse

Direct discourse is derived from the "anonymous murmur" (Deleuze, 1988, p. 18), and retrieved after the "dismemberment" of the collective assemblage (1987, p. 84). Reported speech is precisely the murmur from which the "I" assumes a proper name as it draws from the constellation of voices to compose its own. Deleuze and Guattari compare the collective assemblage to the murmur from which the "I" takes its proper name (1987, p. 84). Utterances in such an *arrangement* refer not to the subject of the statement because Deleuze discerns "subjectification processes" at work in the arrangements.

The pragmatics of the order word therefore considers the said as subordinate and dependent on what is being done in saying it. The focus is not on the construction of meaning in sentences possessed with declarative force but what is honed in upon is the force of language and the ensuing incorporeal transformations brought into being through speech-acts. For example, incorporeal transformations are engendered in the courtroom when the accused is convicted by the judge, who solemnly performs the utterance "I sentence you to life imprisonment". "I sentence you" carries illocutionary force as it instantaneously transforms the body of the accused into the body of the "convict". Moreover, saying 'I love you! expresses the condition of the sense of the statement and a real determination of the states of bodies and intervenes directly into the actions and passions that define them (Deleuze & Guattari, 1987, p. 82).

Order words—through the strange characteristics of the instantaneousness of their emission, perception and transmission (Deleuze & Guattari, 1987, p. 84)— also entreat the accused to speak in his own name without volition or will. This is the verdict or death-sentence. The accused must speak for silence implicates. Yet the accused who stands on his or her own and speaks in his or her own name succumbs to a process of subjectification which relays between both subjection and subjugation. Similarly, the accused can be convicted by public *doxa* whence sanctioned by the "mass-media act" (1987, p. 90).

Indirect discourse pertains not to communicating the visible but to transmitting the audible, what has been reported—in other words "hearsay" (1987, p. 76). We can take hearsay to mean cliché (Porter, 2003, 2010). Perhaps another way of thinking about this is to consider the "saying to saying" as the repetition of cliché, the banal everyday talk of Heidegger's *the anonymous they*. Heidegger interprets common knowledge as a multiplicity of statements that circulate, that is, picked up and passed on from one to another. The speakers appear as simple relay points, equivalent and interchangeable with one another. Yet, the talk does not circulate anonymously, but is always directed. Statements are taken up and repeated simply because they have been iterated before, because anyone, everyone, *the they*, says them. In this sense, no one speaks in his own name, no one takes responsibility for what is said. Here, we can invoke the Levinasian conception of speech as an address and command from the site of alterity. The murmuring indeterminacy of idle speech resembles background noise. There is but an anonymous murmur which all *re-iterate*. As a reading of the *material basis of language and* the impersonal form "one speaks", the pragmatics of the order word analyzes social relations as both prior to syntax and semantics and prior to information and communication. Impersonal or background words emerge prior to their enunciation in the first person.

Reflecting this focus in Deleuze and Guattari's *oeuvre*, Deleuze in *Negotiations* (1995), says he and Guattari were strict functionalists because they were essentially interested in how something works (p. 21). As "strict functionalists" Deleuze and Guattari reject the concept of "ideology" which for them does not exist (1987, p. 4). In its place, there is but the functioning of order words, which appear like lightning, full of promise and mischief, rich in perlocutionary effect. The events flash momentarily and explode before fading away, *before being forgotten*. Order words, for Deleuze and Guattari, by their very nature permit "one to feel absolved of the slogans one has followed and then abandoned to welcome others" (1987, p. 84).

Words are innumerable, but what do they mean? Words are many, but what do they do? The utterance of them is part of a constellation of always-already received *doxa*. The point is that order words are essentially evacuated of meaning and only ever receive a cursory analysis of their content. It is enough that they are obeyed. This contention connects with the idea of ideology and the repetition of the same. Order words form a pattern of clichés undergirded by innumerable others.

Communication

In Deleuze and Guattari's *What Is Philosophy?* (1994), we find a critique of the troubling desire for "universals of communication". They say one ought to "shudder" at this desire as it bespeaks of a will to excess—an excess of communication (1994, p. 7). Deleuze and Guattari return to the problem of communication and perceive it as the enemy of creativity. In a commentary on the perceived theft of creativity from academic discourse, Deleuze and Guattari say: "[T] he most shameful moment came when computer science, marketing, design, and advertising, all the disciplines of communication, seized hold of the word *concept* itself and said: "This is our concern, we are the creative ones, we are the *ideas men!* We are the friends of the concept, we put it in our computers" (1994, p. 10). Their objection is focussed on how the industries of communication and information erase self-reflection and critique of the very assumptions of their enterprise. Contra the process of communication as pure communication of itself, Deleuze and Guattari ask their readers to re-engineer and rescue life-affirming critique.

In a discussion with Toni Negri entitled "Control and Becoming" Deleuze (1995) sketches a prescient analysis of the change from disciplinary to control societies. Control societies, he says, no longer operate by confining people to set spaces and parameters but operate through continuous control and instant communication. Faced with this prospect, Deleuze calls for the hijacking of speech because creating is considered essentially different from communication (1995, p. 175). This epoché or critique of vacuous communication is similarly echoed by philosopher Peter Sloterdijk (2006, p. 84) who believes that more communication means above all else *more conflict* (see Žižek, 2010).

In Deleuze's societies of control, the code is the key. It is the password rather than the watchword that grants passage. Codes mark access to information. Deleuze (1992) says: "We no longer find ourselves dealing with the mass/individual pair. Individuals have become dividuals, and masses, samples, data, markets, or banks."

Deleuze's critical view of the widespread intoxication with *vacuous* communication in control societies discerns many dangers lurking in the universals of communication. Thinking in terms of the desire to desire repression he questions the thirst to be forever connected and "infernally" creative and productive. In a sense there is too much communication. We moderns do not lack communication, Deleuze and Guattari claim, for we have too much of it. Conversely, what is absent is futural orientation: "We lack creation. We lack resistance to the present" (1994, p. 108). What is missing is a people yet to come. This proclamation clearly contests the Habermasian communicational model of expression which assumes the centrality of the rational "I", the subject-object dualism, the free congregation of inter-subjectivity and the possibility of open and transparent information.

Deleuze (1995) throws down the gauntlet to his readers create "vacuoles of non-communication" or circuit breakers to elude capture (p. 175). What is valorised is the blocking of codes or anti-production as an anticipation of the production of the inaugural. In the next section we will turn to Lingis and his phenomenological theory of communication and language which puts Deleuze and Guattari to work.

Order word and Phenomenology

A more optimistic interpretation of the order word can be derived from Lingis's maverick phenomenological writing, who while critical of the model of communication as a relay of information, considers the order word a moment of fundamental understanding between selves. Phenomenologically, Lingis (2010) argues, communication is the exchange of information for it is through the order words (or the password as I understand it) that humans "utter words of welcome and ca-maraderie, give and receive clues and watchwords as how to behave among them and among others, gossip, talk to amuse one another" (2010, p. 15). He argues that the other is before the "I" not to issue meaningful propositions but as an agency that "orders us and appeals to us" (pp. 15–16). This fundamental communication exceeds the transmission and reception of signs sent from one ego to another. Communication is more than the translation of packets of data.

For Lingis, Serres' theory (Serres *et al.*,1982) is a model of a rational commu-nity and communication which operates as a phantasmagoria of harmonious dia-logic, through the purging and eradication of noise. Such a theory maps a milieu in which digitally encoded information and data is instantly graspable but only through the jamming of the equivocal voice of the outsider. In this ideal republic, Serres claims that communication is indeed possible as the "I" and its other are trained to code and decode meaning by using the same key. Communication is the said, the dematerialised. For Serres, the paragon is two modems, transmitting and receiving information-bits simultaneously. However, for Lingis, in the city of communication maximally purged of noise, universal, unequivocal communication would assume the horrific form of a transparent albeit machinic, inter-subjectivity, which he interprets as a plot to eliminate the other, a kind of homicidal xeno-phobia. As he says, the will to eliminate noise is an effort to silence the interlocutor *qua* outsider, (Lingis, 1994, p. 97).

If the pragmatism of Deleuze and Guattari can act as a prism to think the unconscious investment in the socius, Lingis contends that while there seems no question of escaping order words, one can flee the death-sentence and the verdict they inflict upon the body. Phenomenologically, the "I" who speaks in its own name, Lingis says, does not operate through the will to disclose or denude oneself in a manner of an epiphany or moment of Heideggerian authenticity. Rather, as words connect with other words, and statements support other statements, the "I" that speaks reaches back to the subject of the statements: The "I" says and what is said generates further statements. For Lingis, authentic speech is not simply a soliloquy before the night of death, so to speak, but in speaking in one's one name one disconnects from a vital environment and in doing so delimits one's possibilities as a process of subjectification, subjection and subjugation (2006).

Mots d'ordre or mots de désordre

Given the scope of its enterprise, linguistics, for Deleuze, has done a lot of harm (*la linguistique a fait beaucoup de mal*). Instead, it is the task of a more general linguistic exercise to interrogate the concrete exigencies through which the order word is uttered and to reveal the password as residing in every order word *qua* potential. The password carries the capacity to exceed the limits of the always-already circumscribed.

While the order word forms part of the apparatus of capture, the password is erected as a means to escape the strata and corresponds to the experimental use of language. In some not altogether straightforward way, it lies *behind*, perhaps above and beyond, perhaps lurking underneath order words. The *fabulative function* of the password (Deleuze, 1997) offers a trajectory of flight and proffers the hope of a *people yet to come*. It is therefore futural and expressive of a power that is capable of altering and immediately impacting the *socius* to engender change. The password throws content and expression into disarray, making it impossible to determine the limits of the possible. The password is difference in itself, formed in the immanence of production. Its function and matter circulate and interact on the plane of consistency. It breaks open both words and things. The password is multimodal: it can form in a variety of modes—in music, video and the textual. It is connective of difference, bringing different realms into contact, engendering new directions and possibilities. While the order word over-determines the relations of control within the strata, the password as its ever present other registers the excess of surplus value—it fractures. It is an experiment. If passwords do not re-present the world, they do in some sense reshape and reconstitute it in material ways. The question is how to elude the death-sentence of the order word so as to experiment with lines of flight that do not flair out or self-immolate. For Lingis, it is when we speak in our name (Lingis, 2007, when we take responsibility for what is said and connect with intensities and the otherness of the other, that we set in motion passwords which evade control. It is the password which disrupts the *mots d'ordre* and sets in train relays and transversal machines to impinge upon the smooth relays of barking orders.

For Blanchot (1993, p. xvi), there is a "background" behind words, whose murmuring interrupts the utterances of the everyday. The passwords which Deleuze and Guattari speak of bear close resemblance to Blanchot's "disorderly words", words which are "free of discourse" (Blanchot in Holland, 1995). Similar to the timeliness of the slogans articulated prior to the beginning of the Russian Revolution, the slogans or *mots de désordre* on the Parisian walls of 1968 *appear and disappear* in a circuit of immediacy and contemporaneity (Blanchot in Holland, 1995, p. 204). They have a transitory and ephemeral lifespan tied to the decision to act resolutely, the decision to say something in one's own name in the *hic et nunc*: with the act of saying deemed more important, for Blanchot, than the actual content of the said (Blanchot, 1988, p. 30). In the *evénements* of May 1968, there is a *détournement* of the meaning of the slogan "all power to the Soviets", which is transformed into, "all power to the imagination". There is a playfulness of language, a scrambling of the order words and mocking of the barking of commands. The writing on the walls, Blanchot says, is neither inscriptional nor elocutionary. The posters do not need to be read in the conventional sense but exist to challenge all law. The disorderly words accompany the rhythm of our steps. They are words which question, appeal and threaten but leave with haste without waiting for a reply (p. 204). There is a hyphenation of a disaster, of an astral change, according to Blanchot (Holland, p. 204). As Blanchot says:

> Tracts, posters, bulletins; street words, infinite words; it is not some concern for effectiveness that makes them necessary. Whether effective or not, they belong to the decision of the moment. They appear, they disappear. They do not say everything, on the contrary they ruin everything, they are outside everything. They act and reflect fragmentarily. They leave no trace: they are a trait without trace. Like the words on the walls, they are written in insecurity, received under threat, are themselves the bearers of danger, then pass with the passer-by who passes them on, loses them or forgets them (Holland, 1995, p. 205).

Taken another way then, the password is that which contests the cycle of machinic répétition *mortifère* or the deadly cycle of *repetition* and self-immolation (Guattari, 2000, p. 39). It questions and undermines the imperatives implicit in death sentences. It is through flight, becoming-nomadic and molecular, the innocence of becoming, that we find the expression of active and creative attributes, of active and reactive forces. The password is a word that forms a component of passage. If order words enforce stoppages, their underside may also conjure up creativity and becoming. It is therefore a question of isolating and fostering the password through modifying the formation of orders into components of passage (Deleuze & Guattari, 1987, p. 110).

But this is precisely the problem of how we come to speak in our name. It is unclear what the password unlocks or gives access to. How do we judge it is the right time to speak in our name if indeed to do so is to impinge upon ourselves a minor death sentence? Or taken another way, is in speaking in our own name an implicit concession to the outer command to denude ourselves to the otherness of the other? In terms of pedagogy, if the cues, watchwords, and passwords order and compel the student to speak and when to speak. How can the teacher jam the unthinking repetition of the "abominable faculty" which emits, receives and transmits order words? For Deleuze and Guattari, the teacher's role is to extract from the message an opening fissure or becoming. This ethology of the classroom would honour the injunction to remain vigilant to the serendipitous encounter that brings to life the thoughts and affects and considerations of the pupil. It brings out of torpor a positive affirmation of life. In Deleuze, there is a fundamental questioning of the critical and creative nature of thought, an exegesis of thought that is affirmative yet dissensual. This excess acts as a circuit breaker to distort the codes, to jam orthodoxy and *doxa;* to put into effect war-machines of a literary nature to entreat others to become-other, to contest the limits of received opinion.

In conclusion, we have seen that Deleuze and Guattari's account of language is an attempt to think otherwise than the Saussurean system of signifier and signified or Chomsky's universal grammar. Deleuze and Guattari's theory of linguistics tends to focus on the unconscious processes at work which reinforce norms and behaviour in society. In some way it helps us to understand the inscriptions upon and relations between bodies. The analysis of becoming-minor, of the stuttering and stammering of minor languages, offers a way to think otherwise than the major language of representation. For it is the minor language—or the foreign language within one's own mother tongue—which breaks open a passage in the order word to reform the redundancies of the major tongue.

References

Austin, J. L. (1962). *How to do things with words.* Oxford: Clarendon Press.

Bakhtin, M. M. (1973). *Problems of Dostoevsky's poetics.* Ann Arbor, Mich.: Ardis.

Bakhtin, M. M., & Holquist, M. (1981). *The dialogic imagination: Four essays.* Austin: University of Texas Press.

Benveniste, E. (1971). *Problems in general linguistics.* Coral Gables, Fla: University of Miami Press.

Blanchot, M. (1988). *The unavowable community.* Barrytown, NY: Station Hill Press.

Blanchot, M. (1993). *The infinite conversation.* Minneapolis: University of Minnesota Press.

Brott, S. (2011). *Architecture for a free subjectivity: Deleuze and Guattari at the horizon of the real.* Farnham, Surrey: Ashgate.

Butler, J. (1997). *The psychic life of power: Theories in subjection.* Stanford, CA: Stanford University Press.

Canetti, E. (1962). *Crowds and power.* New York: Viking Press.

Cole, D. R., & Hager, P. (2010). Learning-practice: The ghosts in the education machine. *Education Inquiry, 1,* 21–40.

De Landa, M. (1993). *Virtual environments and the emergence of synthetic reason.* Retrieved April 10, 2011 from: http://www.t10.or.at/delanda/delanda.htm

Deleuze, G. (1988). *Bergsonism.* New York: Zone Books.

Deleuze, G. (1990a). *The logic of sense.* New York: Columbia University Press.

Deleuze, G. (1990b). *Expressionism in philosophy: Spinoza.* New York: Zone Books.

Deleuze, G. (1992). *Postscript on the societies of control* October 59. Winter (pp. 3–7). Cambridge: MIT Press.

Deleuze, G. (1994). *Difference and repetition.* New York: Columbia University Press.

Deleuze, G. (1995). *Negotiations, 1972–1990.* New York: Columbia University Press.

Deleuze, G. (1997). *Essays critical and clinical.* Minneapolis: University of Minnesota Press.

Deleuze, G., & Guattari, F. (1987). *A thousand plateaus: Capitalism and schizophrenia.* Minneapolis: University of Minnesota Press.

Deleuze, G., Guattari, F., Tomlinson, H., & Burchell, G. (1994). *What is philosophy?.* New York: Columbia University Press.

Deleuze, G., & Lapoujade, D. (2006). *Two regimes of madness: Texts and interviews 1975–1995.* Los Angeles, CA: Semiotext(e).

Dreyfus, H. L., & Rabinow, P. (1982). *Michel Foucault: Beyond structuralism and hermeneutics.* Brighton: Harvester Press.

Ferlinghetti, L. (1960). *Her.* New York: New Directions.

Foucault, M. (1972). *The archaeology of knowledge.* New York: Pantheon Books.

Grisham, T. (1991). Linguistics as an indiscipline: Deleuze and Guattari's pragmatics. *Substance, 20,* 3, 36–54.

Guattari, F. (2000). *The three ecologies.* London: Athlone Press.

Guattari, F. (2011). *The machinic unconscious: Essays in schizoanalysis.* Los Angeles, CA: Semiotext(e).

Guattari, F., & Genosko, G. (1996). *The Guattari reader.* Oxford, OX, UK: Blackwell Publishers.

Hjelmslev, L. (1961). *Prolegomena to a theory of language.* Madison: University of Wisconsin Press.

Holland, M. (1995). *The Blanchot reader.* Oxford: Blackwell.

Ingold, T. (2008). *Bringing things to life: Creative entanglements in a world of materials.* Lecture at University of Aberdeen. Accessed 23 September 2011.

Jakobson, R., & Halle, M. (1980). *Fundamentals of language.* The Hague: Mouton.

Labov, W. (1973). *Sociolinguistic patterns / William Labov.* Philadelphia, PA: University of Pennsylvania Press.

Lecercle, J.-J. (2002). *Deleuze and language.* Houndmills, Basingstoke, Hampshire: Palgrave Macmillan.

Lecercle, J.-J. (2006). *A Marxist philosophy of language.* Leiden: Brill.

Lecercle, J.-J., & Riley, D. (2005). *The force of language.* Basingstoke, Hampshire: Palgrave Macmillan.

Lingis, A. (1994). *The community of those who have nothing in common.* Bloomington: Indiana University Press.

Lingis, A. (2004). Cues, watchwords, passwords. *International Studies in Philosophy, 36,* 4, 49–64.

Lingis, A. (2006). *Defenestration,* Presentation. Deleuze Conference.

Lingis, A. (2007). *The first person singular.* Evanston, Ill: Northwestern University. Press.

Lingis, A. (2010). Emanations. *Parallax, 16,* 2–19.

Lydenberg, R. (1987). *Word cultures: Radical theory and practice in William S. Burroughs' fiction.* Urbana: University of Illinois Press.

Marks, J. (1998). *Gilles Deleuze: Vitalism and multiplicity.* London: Pluto Press.

Marks, J., & Buchanan, I. (2000). *Deleuze and literature.* Edinburgh: Edinburgh University Press.

Nietzsche, F., Kaufmann, W. A., & Hollingdale, R. J. (1967). *On the genealogy of morals: Ecce homo; Friedrich Nietzsche.* New York: Vintage Books, div. of Random House.

Peirce, C. S. (1931). *Collected papers*, vol. 1. Cambridge, Mass. Harvard University Press.

Porter, R. (2003). *Habermas and the pragmatics of communication: Towards a Deleuze-Guattarian critique. Social Semiotics, 13*(2), 129–145.

Porter, R. (2010). From cliches to slogans: Towards a Deleuze-Guattarian critique of ideology. *Social Semiotics, 20*(3), 233–245.

Protevi, J. (2005). *The Edinburgh dictionary of continental philosophy.* Edinburgh: Edinburgh University Press

Serres, M., Harari, J. V., & Bell, D. F. (1982). *Hermes—literature, science, philosophy.* Baltimore: Johns Hopkins University Press.

Sloterdijk, P. (2006). Warten auf den Islam, *Focus, 10.*

Žižek, S. (2010). *Violence.* London: Profile Books.

CHAPTER THREE

Materialism and the Mediating Third

The hypertextual, multimodal and the virtual are transforming education at unprecedented speeds. Students think relationally, machinically, cognitively; they seldom sit to write with ink and parchment. As a consequence, schools are reorganizing the way they teach literacy to adjust to the intensification and widespread fever for technological *fixes,* as in the case of constant monitoring, feedback and assessment. As students engage enthusiastically in complicated semiotic registers, forging multimodal, multimedia practices, the implementation of machinic complexes informs and remoulds the concept of literacy. Despite operating out of a different intellectual milieu, multiple and multimodal literacies are, in a sense, a response to what has been designated the "techno-materialist semiotics of info-capital" (Genosko, 2008, p. 11). In this light, the often bewildering impersonal flows of people and images, not to mention the sonority of accents, languages and noise across the planet, and indeed across our spectacular fields, can be seen as demanding a rethinking and repositioning of the concept of multiple and multimodal literacies.

A critical multiliteracy theory shares a striking similarity with the thought of French psychoanalyst and activist Félix Guattari with respect to tracing the effects generated from the decentring of subjectivity when coupled to machines and impersonal relations (Guattari, 1995).

Guattari examined the role of machinic assemblages and collective regimes of enunciation (systems of statements such as marks and sounds), which engender subjectivities on both a-signifying and affective registers. As communication is mediated and manufactured by plastic universes of reference, which is to say that the subject is not the sole engineer of meaning but a node in a wider circuit of sounds, signs and images, what is under investigation is how meaning is generated in multimodal environments. Moreover, the array of learning practices is diffused with cultural difference as a consequence of increasingly unfettered globalizing and runaway processes. The student—uprooted, transhuman, always on the go—is hooked up with people and cultures and traditions from remote, distant places.

Multiple literacies theory (MLT) is one resource to think the concept of educational materialism. MLT examines the unconscious workings of creative crackups, breakthroughs, breakdowns, blockages, neuroses and misunderstandings that are produced in the classroom and online (Masny, 2006). It notes the ethological tempo, the dissonance, relations of control, and transversal creative processes at work in the school, between both the teacher and student and among and in between peer relationships.

Ronald Day (2001) claims that Guattari warned against the reduction of "learning" to institutions such as schools, churches, the family and so on, and was critical of prioritizing particular object-tools for "affective engagement and production" (Day, 2001, p. 77). Day claims that Guattari found it unnecessary to prioritize the written word over music, chairs over moving objects, or writing over speech. Day argues that Guattari saw the adoption of certain contexts, modes, and products of learning as serving the interests of power and capitalism. For Day (2001, p. 77), Guattari's contention that a child's semiotic inculcation comes about through habits, class inscriptions, moral rules, and the ability to recognize certain forms of sense as information or knowledge, mirrors Foucault's theory of capillary power and his description of carceral, panoptic, or disciplinary societies. The child learns through the internalization of the rules and rites of passage almost on an unconscious level.

Day (2001) also notes how the subject incorporates and carries out the rules, rites and regulations of continuous education. Established structures of learning and recognizing informational value-content are internalized beyond the context of the original institutions. Continuous assessment then is not simply about formal knowledge but *training* according to already sanctioned and established modes and codes. He goes on to say that the reshaping of the traditional classroom through more use of technology must take into account other deep-seated problems which "can be masked even more subtly in digital formations and standards" (Day, 2001, p. 78). He warns that the "revolutionary" promise of information and communication technologies should be measured against what he sees as "formal controls upon language".

Through the Image Darkly: Critique of Technology Fetishism

John Marks has defined materialism in terms of computers expanding the potentialities for thought in new and perhaps unpredictable ways (1998). The brain and the computer take part in the construction of an "abstract machine" (Marks, 1998). What is of key relevance here is the brain's transmitting of information as discrete differences. In a similar vein, Verena Conley argues that it is through the transmission of differences that people connect and reconnect with other humans, animals and the world (Conley, 2005, p. 259 ff.). It is argued that it is through computer-aided subjectivity that humans increase virtual potentialities—be they good or bad outcomes. A "becoming-radio" or "becoming-television" can yield "good or bad connections; productive or nefarious becomings" (Parr, 2005, p. 235). While computers and the Internet have "great potential" as rhizomatic war machines, they can be recaptured by the capitalist machine that deploys the order word (*mot d'ordre*), consumer codes, and multifarious redundancies. The result is that computers can become ends in and for themselves in a sphere of "techno-narcissism" (Parr, 2005, p. 235). However, a positive Deleuze & Guattarian reading of this process would suggest that co-optation is never final and complete. The capitalist war machine in its schizophrenic operations is always under threat by nomadic, surreptitious war machines that wield technologies to form new rhizomes and becomings.

For Maurizio Lazzarato (2006), techniques of control operate through the modulation of brains, by tinkering with the psychic life of memory and attention, general intellect and mental disposition—to engineer a new kind of knowledge/power microtechnology. What are the new modalities of power in the school and outside? For Lazzarato, in societies of control and when mediated by technology, power relations gain operational effectiveness through action undertaken at a distance "of one mind on another", through the neurological power to affect and be affected. In his essay *Life and Living in the Societies of Control*, Lazzarato claims that collective assemblages of enunciation—a neologism used heavily by Guattari—such as law, knowledges, languages, public opinion—function as affective machines, reinforcing the dominant coda disseminated in factories, prisons and schools (Lazzarato, 2006, p. 172). Yet even here, the question for Lazzarato is how long capitalism can keep pace with the increasingly intense creativity of its interconnected, disenfranchised populace or what he terms "progressive no-longer-individuals".

The question arises: does MLT pay sufficient attention to the apparent unconscious, neurological role of affect? Proponents of MLT proffer an account of the lived experiences of the subjects, such as home life, the influences of the media and the impact of technologies upon the self. Diana Masny (2006) claims that literacies are not exclusive to a second language coda *per se* but inhere in desire, transformation and the becoming-Other of the student. The process of becoming-Other occurs through a reading of the world, the word and self as texts in multiple environments. For MLT, literacy is linked to power and as such the theory looks to connect power, literacy and minority language education. Moreover, it deploys a poststructural and micrological analysis of power through the examination of the interplay of the rhizome and regimes of affect in the classroom and beyond.

For Cole (2007), MLT is a mode of poststructuralism that can be applied to education as a kind of minor thesis, to probe questions of identity and representation. This affective reading takes the view that there is much to learn from "alternate routes for learning" (Cole, 2007, p. 125), and from observing how populations intimately entwine to learn and work. Cole asks how reading, reading the world and reading the self transform the processes of learning. For Cole, reading comprehension is overcoded through excessive testing by overseeing powers. Accordingly, theorists of MLT contend that other literacies embrace different immaterial universes pertaining to music, plastic forms, animal and vegetable becomings—a view with clear similarities to that of Guattari's political brand of psychoanalysis—schizoanalysis. MLT perceives the transformative potentialities inherent in social institutions and their practices and places emphasis on micrological group dynamics and discerns change through cartographically tracing this movement.

Differentiating itself from phenomenological models of the experiential and the emotional dimension of learning (Masny & Cole, 2009, p. vii), MLT, in Spinozian mode, is concerned less with the centering of the subject and more with the power to affect and be affected. The theory views affects as relational forces, derived not from anecdotal impressions of class dynamics but from a relational analysis of joyful or sad affects or being the products of those affects—the "I" traversed, the "I" dividuated. MLT foregrounds affects, viewing them as operating beyond meaning and signification and reading them as intensive aspects of language. Coupled with the issue of creativity and becoming, MLT derives the improvisational nature of learning from the transcendental materialism or schizoanalysis of Deleuze and Guattari (Semetsky, 2009, p. 449). In this respect, Deleuze and Guattari's philosophical ideas serve as a new vocabulary and set of conceptual tools through which to analyze literate behaviour afresh (Masny & Cole, 2009, p. 10). Deleuze, in particular, is read as expanding quantitative multiplicities to include a qualitative aspect (Deleuze & Guattari, 1987, p. 30) with the latter producing differences in nature. For pedagogical purposes this is a question of creativity and transversality among, between and in-between assemblages. As qualitative multiplicities make apparent the working of the creative unconscious, the issue goes beyond dualism or binary machines to imagine the effects and distribution of multiplicities. At work in the classroom is the qualitative unconscious, a machine to escape boredom and rigidity, the machinic *répétition mortifère* or the deadly cycle of repetition and self-immolation (Guattari, 2000, p. 39). MLT assesses the processes of literacy within diverse literacy practices, noting the complex demographics at work. Multiplicity is posited in the very idea of literacy and, as such, communication is perceived as detailing the workings of multiplicity, with singularity rendered equivalent to a self-organising assemblage of components, working in tandem with each other. The stress is on the non-linear nature of development in literacy skills and in the classroom. To understand the different speeds, feedback loops and aggregates in literacy learning, MLT traces the contours of difference and designates the multi-lateral nature of literacy. The dynamics of communication are construed in terms of positive and negative feedback, active and reactive desires.

Students learn at different speeds primarily because affect, the body, and multiplicities are intrinsic to communication. Change is accounted for in terms of qualitative and chaotic factors as well as spatial referents and can be understood through the notion of "style", those "small but effective ways of skewing the potential movements composing the field" (Massumi, 2002, p. 77). Qualitative multiplicity is important for thinking communication as nonlinear as it notes the processes and reversals, flips and knots, jokes and false pathways (Masny & Cole, 2009, p. 3). While media and technology are important issues for literacy, MLT disagrees with the emphasis on metanarratives—such as the overarching modernist story of technological progress—as they erase the role of qualitative multiplicities. In terms of MLT's transcendental materialism, the social agenda of literacy from life passes through the subject and helps constitute memories and desire. In exploring the role of desire and collective enunciation, MLT is a pedagogy which recognizes agency and views the construction of meaning as transforming agents and identities through the very constitutive act of meaning. There is an emphasis on underscoring the significance of local knowledges, which are deemed productive of inspiration and experimentation. Literacies are viewed as texts expressive of multiple meanings in local contexts with resistance to one dominant signifier or arbitrator of truth. MLT contests the modern notion of the rational, universal, autonomous agent, free of local, historical, and cultural contingencies, a stance which links up with Deleuze's transcendental empiricism and its own emphasis on contingency.

Literacies—personal, critical, community, school-based or otherwise—are directed to reading, reading the world and reading the self as texts. Students, in the language of Deleuze and Guattari, are perceived as desiring machines. As such, written literacy and acquisition are perceived through the prism of becoming, becoming creative and becoming-Other. MLT addresses the key issue of bodily literacy and *habitus*, noting the dimension of corporeality in the process. Reading is intensive and immanent. Intensive reading reads disruptively: it is not a question of meaning but of what works, how things are produced. In *Dialogues* Deleuze maintains that concepts are equivalent to sounds, colours or images, or intensities which one extracts pragmatically in *bricolage* fashion (Deleuze & Parnet, 2006, p. 4). Paraphrasing Deleuze, at work are nonsignifying machines, "for there is nothing to explain, nothing to understand, nothing to interpret" (Deleuze, 1995, p. 8). This sense of machinic interlock is captured well by Henry Miller in *Tropic of Cancer* (Miller, 1961, p. 28): "It is as if we are merely plugging into an electric circuit. I am a writing machine. The last screw has been added. The thing flows. Between me and the machine there is no estrangement. I am the machine."

Reading is also about sense, where sense is construed as a value of interpretation. As such, sense is a virtual event, activated when words are actualized in interesting ways (Colebrook, 2002). Although MLT acknowledges the objectivity of books, Internet, equations, and buildings, it foregrounds sense as emergent when relating experiences of life to reading the world, word and the self as texts. One concept of key importance here is the refrain. Think of daydreaming in the classroom, an emotional flashback from a pristine reverie, of being with friends, of past and future loves, non-productive thoughts—all of these are understood in the Spinozist sense as affective literacies. Or in terms of machinic coupling, if viewers watch TV and become "hooked" to the PC screen, the refrains produced are of a narrative and affective nature (Guattari, 1996, p. 200).

In Spinozian terms, learning is a creative, affective encounter, joyful or sad, capable of accessing inaugural materials of expression, which can engender fresh universes of reference. Smooth and striated spaces intersect and overlap in complex ways and there is always movement between the actual and virtual, territorialization and the accompanying reterritorialization. The issue is how literacies intersect in becoming. A person is a text "in continuous becoming" (Masny & Cole, 2009, p. 15). Creativity is an event that produces novel connections, different assemblages and becoming. Deleuze called for the liberation of the concept from dogmatic paradigms and perspectives (Deleuze, 1988, p. 4), arguing that: "As long as thought is free, hence vital, nothing is compromised. When it ceases being so, all other oppressions are also possible". In pedagogical terms, the success or failure of learners is measured in the ability to use multiple literacies in multimodal ways to engineer meaning. Gestures and things, voices and sounds are at play in the same operatic drama, "swept away by the same shifting effects of stammering, vibrato, tremolo, and overspilling" (Deleuze & Guattari, 1987, p. 109). The methodology of MLT explores nonlinear narrative forms of openness and hones in on the escape routes or lines of flight that lurk deep in the structures of language.

A Peep at *L'Anti-Œdipe*

To understand the unconscious thirst for machinic couplings, a critique is necessary of the enthralldom with *techné* and the belief that *techné* is a panacea for classroom ills. An analysis of the febrile intoxication with *techné* exposes the blackhole of nothingness, in which one finds the fetishism for technological funk. We can imagine an abstract machine or a *deleuzo-guattarian* diagram which traces the black-holes of machinic *répétition mortifère* (sadness, spinning in the void) and moments of n-1 "plus three" creativity (joy, intensity). Slicing the two deadly spirals of ipseity would be the Freinet-Guattari mediating third object, which breaks and interrupts the immolating cycle of autopoietic repetition and the eternal return of the same.

The Guattarian-inflected impersonal critique of matter raises several methodological and interpretative challenges regarding the construction of a radical, multimodal environment for teaching and learning. The production of new modalities of subjectivity, existential territories (modes of becomings) and incorporeal universes of reference (found in music and the plastic arts in *institutional* and *ethological*-level contexts which affect the subject in varying ways) takes place at accelerating speeds and on different ecological plateaus. It is therefore apposite to examine the cognitive and semiotic ecologies governing social, cultural, environmental or technological assemblages.

Why does it seem impermissible to allow children to play with their own miniature machines *in vacuo*? To understand this, it is time to appreciate the affective and machinic relations which ensue as a consequence. Semiotically, it is important to grasp the way miniaturization becomes a tool of capitalism, equipping users with devices that surreptitiously and neurologically remould perceptual fields. It is through the plugging of consumer electronics into the machinic phylum, defined as a continuum, a mathematical physical complex, a technical innovation and the military machine, which engenders a certain craziness or thirst for self-medicated consumer highs.

One literary example of this is Kenzaburō Ōe's (大江 健三郎) haunting and hideous figure of a paternal *certain party*, which captures much of the suicidal tendency and surplus value investment of machinic junkies. In his novel *Teach Them to*

Outgrow Their Madness (1994), the headphone-clad, underwater-goggle-wearing, taciturn father, whose name the narrator dare not utter, goes mad and locks himself away to play ecstatically with the machines of communication. Is this "becoming-radio" evidence of an ever-present psychotic threat? To account for this process, it is important to account for the unconscious workings of affect that sweep through and across the subject, to make sense of the dialectic involved in the power to affect and be affected. Guattari's notion of subjectivity examines the process of becoming-Other in relation to itself. The lust for technology transforms users and reorders mental ecologies. For Deleuze and Guattari, there is no distinct biosphere or noosphere as such but one identical and infernal mechanosphere (Deleuze & Guattari, 1987, p. 69). The subject is at sea, without land to fall back upon; it is ruptured. Hardt and Negri (2000) write of the development of cellular telephony and portable computers as "unmooring" the communicating points in the network, intensifying the process of deterritorialization. A splintered subject enters into relations with the machines of the universe in a fluid, multiple, and fragmented fashion. A pedagogy which accounts for this would assess the interplay of desire and the virtual in the formation of identity.

Returning to the question of educational pedagogy, Guattari's model of group creativity, derived in part from the radical pedagogy of French educationalist Celestin Freinet (1896–1966), founder of the Modern School Movement, at first glance invokes a responsive, creative and engaged mode of learning. Like Freinet, Guattari was interested in creating a de-Oedipalizing institutional context for education, to escape the stifling cocoon of classrooms and textbooks, to forge connections with the outside. Writing before the invention of the Internet and on-line technologies, Freinet encouraged students to trace their material connections to the world, through objects, machines, people and places. Through reading, discussion, performance and reflexive journal writing, Freinet envisaged the classroom as a space for collective imagination and engagement. The core concepts of Freinet's philosophy of education are as follows: (1) student work must be productive and useful; (2) co-operative learning is necessary in the productive process; (3) group enquiry-based learning is based on trial and error; (4) the natural method is based on an inductive, global approach and (5) centres of interest are grounded in children's learning interests and curiosity. For the purposes of this chapter, I shall focus on the second issue.

The printing press is seen as the organizing principle for intellectual, individual and group work. Classwork is focussed on making a collectively created journal, which is used as a basis for lessons and correspondence between classes and schools. Guattari was attracted to Freinet's ideas because of their shared stress on heterogeneity, the singular and collective assemblages. Guattari interpreted creativity as a way to transcend dogmatic institutional practices which might preclude the emergence of heterogeneity. Through triangular experiments, which used a mediating object or a collectively produced monograph the purpose of learning was to create progressive scenes of subjectification, which is to say, the construction of new forms of subjectivity, to overcome what Guattari's mentor Fernand Oury (1920–1998) designated the *encaserné scolaire* (school-as-barracks). Both Oury and Freinet were concerned with the interrelationship between the group-subject and creativity. Oury emphasized the act of writing as an individual and collective project that not only allowed for expression of meaningful interests by individuals, but also realized a sense of success in communication—in being read or heard by one or many others. Teachers set up a pedagogical scene of subjectification that guaranteed the certainty of being read through the circulation of published, reproduced texts. This entailed reading before the class, but only from those sections of one's personal "free text" that would interest the group. The group would then pass a certain kind of judgment, making corrections and suggestions and carrying out editing towards its inclusion in a collective publication. Work would also be addressed and readdressed in correspondence between individuals, in groups, and group-to-group exchange of collectively written manuscripts, between geographically diverse schools. In this sense, the school journal works as a third object that opens the students *to the world*. Two becomes three, but three is not just three, more precisely it is 3 plus n. It is with the triangle and threes that micropolitical pedagogies manifest. In the meeting, the teacher is one among many participants and, although they may veto any motions, the class remains active as a self-directed group. Similar to Guattari's schizoanalytic reading of a subject group that formulates its own projects, speaks and is heard, the creative classroom puts itself at risk in pursuing its own ends and taking responsibility for them. The school journal, in a sense, brings the group to language. It is created, reinvented and maintained by the group over time. And furthermore, this mediating third object operates outside of face-to-face relations. The subject group is formed in its own making, speaks and is heard and is tested against these goals and ends. A creative pedagogy has the capacity to call subject groups into being, to bring a group to language, through which situated knowledges of the students literally call the subject group into being to form a group identity that is delinked from a common spatio-temporal subjugation to institutional power. There is a shift of power relations away from the teacher towards the more diffuse, situated knowledges of the students.

Guattari in his critique of the "ritualized griddings of the socius" (Guattari, 2000, p. 64) saw in the dynamics of group therapy a method to engender social transformation, a means to produce, collect, enrich, and reinvent. His inquiry asked how to foster mutant universes of value where reinvention is presupposed as a guiding principle. It is here that Guattari and MLT advocates such as Inna Semetsky (2004; 2013) again share common ground. The breakdowns, crack ups and frustrations in the classroom are not always pessimistic omens of failure and lines of flight that turn inward, implode or immolate but can remould subjectivity as affective events. For Semetsky (2004), the teacher's remit is "to get things moving" by outlaying appropriate conditions through which the new can be produced. The inaugural is engineered in an experimental setting where "desire, curiosity, trust, and interest" manifest. Semetsky invokes Deleuze's exhortation to teachers to explore and play with questions, to make them machinic.

Bottle Rack

In artistic terms, when an everyday object is read in isolation from its typical regime of circulation, a trigger point is reached, producing virtual regimes of reference. The detachment of the object opens up unknown virtual universes. In a pedagogical sense, MLT registers the affective bottlenecks that block the free and open the act of writing, connecting it to forces other than the order of representation. From Guattari's ethico-aesthetic perspective the question is of being open to the affective event, engendered by partial objects. Partial objects act as a point around which mutant subjectivity might crystallize, like a school journal, a webpage, a shared presence in virtual reality. In a collaborative manner, they act as points of entry into different incorporeal universes, different regimes of thinking and doing. Guattari (1995) argues for an ecology of the virtual to address the performative modalities of poetry and music. For Guattari, poetry introduces both corporeal and incorporeal universes of signification and generates new existential terrains or subjectivities.

Duchamp's *Bottle Rack*, one of the early readymades from 1914, is a good example of how affective literacy might work. Guattari interprets Duchamp's *Bottle Rack* as setting out the potentialities of inaugural virtual universes of reference, new mutant nuclei of subjectification. He writes that the work functions as "the trigger for a constellation of referential universes engaging both intimate reminiscences (the cellar of the house, a certain winter, the rays of light upon spider webs, adolescent solitude) and connotations of a cultural and economic order" (Guattari, 1996, p. 164). Into the *Bottle Rack* enters life. Affective heterogeneity splits and shatters the object and subject, and releases mutual and mutant becomings. The readymade engenders a multiplicity of prepersonal affects, a haecceity or unique entity unto itself. The *Bottle Rack*'s change of direction is suggestive of the aesthetic practice of creative subjectivation. In detaching an object, putting it somewhere else, the field is opened to different virtual universes of reference. There is an opening of the possibility of something different. The stammering and stuttering of minor languages, disordered and fragmentary genealogies, the a-signification of language effects, are plugged in to question extant affective regimes. A-signifying language is productive of involuntary memories and images, productive of generating micro perceptions, generative of affects and becoming. Guattari saw in subject groups a way to formulate a creative pedagogy through transversal elements, by which relations to the institution are subverted through play—the subject group becomes active in questioning existing academic divisions of labor. A critical pedagogy of multiliteracies and the machinic therefore examines the microphysics and ethology of affect in the classroom. Guattari viewed Freinet practices, such as the learning walk, the printing press, the free text school journal and so on as machines to foster new mutant subjectivities. It is students who call the group into being, who engender new modes of living and thinking, who produce transversal relations. Group pedagogy becomes creative, collaborative research. The subject group shifts the question from the potentially disempowering, to what can and must be done. The question for teachers and learners is to examine to what extent can new subject groups come into being through collaborative research. For Guattari, extra- or non-human, a-signifying, intensive regimes and the prepersonal elements of subjectivity are crucial for generating heterogenic becomings.

Writing in the 1980s and early 1990s, Guattari was prescient in noting the effects of the acceleration of the technological and data-processing revolutions. In his *Three Ecologies* (2000), he noted how computer-aided subjectivity offered the promise to open up or unfold animal, vegetable, Cosmic, and machinic becomings. But he also forewarned of the risks along the way. As he says: "We should not forget that the formation and 'remote-controlling' of human individuals and groups will be governed by institutional and social class dimensions" (Guattari, 2000, p. 39). Obviously, this again has clear import for MLT. What is of clear importance is Guattari's notion of machinic subjectivity which explains why people go "crazy" for machines, for a "machinic kind of buzz". In *Anti-Oedipus* (Deleuze & Guattari, 1983), commenting on the ideas of André Gorz, Deleuze and Guattari inquire into why people who return home exhausted from a hard day's work, "automatically" turn on the television to experience artificial and personal reterritorializations. Gorz in his brilliant *Strategy for Labour* (1967) speaks of the plight of the immaterial "creative" laborer (in this case the nuclear industry technician) who after gaining the order word to access elite institutions, "spins in a vacuum" from a dearth of opportunity to operate such skills. Gorz argues that the desire for "autonomous activity, creation and communication" is transmigrated and reengineered, psychosomatically and existentially, into "the acuteness of sharp pain" (Gorz, 1967, p. 106). The worker at his workstation is bored to the nth degree as the machine hums and murmurs along autopoietically. Such boredom turns into despair and neurosis. The skilled worker is superfluous, a powerless witness in a universe engineered by others. He takes refuge at home taking apart radio and TV equipment to prove he is useful, to make his work valuable and something more than what Marx called *pure abstraction*, an empty activity. Although molecular, machinic subjectivity fosters creativity, and there are indeed dangers and traps along the way, the question is how to proliferate an inventive machinic collective passion "without crushing people under an infernal discipline" (Genosko, 2002, p. 126).

Conclusion

Axiomatised stupidity: it is important to question therefore whether machines are a means to control rather than "enhance" or "support" learning. If students are tracked in the system through notes, contact, messages papers, projects and so on, to what degree do institutions *motivate* through top-down control and constant supervision? How can teachers qua state functionaries become cognizant of their "abominable faculty" (Deleuze & Guattari, 1987, p. 84) of emitting, receiving and transmitting order words, words that are not to be believed but obeyed? Ultimately, for Deleuze and Guattari the capitalist machine through order words and codes formats computers as ends in and for themselves in a sphere of techno-narcissism. Deleuze and Guattari in *A Thousand Plateaus* (1987) contend that the compulsory education machine no longer communicates education as there is a radical difference between learning and actually being at school. Moreover, if real, transformatory education were to take place, collapse would ensue. Deleuze writes: "If the protests of children were heard in kindergarten, if their questions were attended to, it would be enough to explode the entire educational system" (Foucault, 1980, p. 209).

Guattari's perspective is futural because it begs the question of the ethics of media and the prospective orientation of new communications technologies, artificial intelligence and control alongside ecological problems. This kind of educational materialism provides a critical tool because the triangulation of transversal singularity, mutating machines and bodies melded to the technologies of virtual reality do not simply represent the cataclysmic end point of modern technology's nightmare. For Guattari (1995), virtual reality is but an actualization of machines of virtuality. For example, "computer-aided design" expands the production of images to "unprecedented" plastic universes. To understand the attitude Guattari might have towards literacy it is crucial to examine his stance vis-à-vis the impersonal machinic production of subjectivity, which can work for "the better or for the worse" (Guattari, 1996, p. 193). At one extreme there is the potentiality for creation, invention, and new universes of reference. At the other extreme there is the "deadening influence of the mass media to which millions of individuals are currently condemned" (Guattari, 1995, p. 5).

In *Chaosmosis* (1995), Guattari asks how one can make a class operate like a work of art. His answer is to seek out aesthetic techniques of rupture, paths to singularization and the source of a "purchase on existence" (Guattari, 1995, p. 133). How then shall the infernal machinic *répétition mortifère* be transformed? How can students stop "spinning in the void"? For Deleuze, motivation is a part of the society of control, a condition of permanent supervision, continual training, ticking boxes or passing gates. Deleuze is sickened by the fact that young people desire being "motivated", desire apprenticeships and permanent training. Why does the self place itself under constant supervision? If the "coils of a serpent are even more complex than the burrows of a molehill" (Deleuze 1992, p. 7) has this much to do with the micro-management of the machinic self qua learner? In conclusion, if the precautionary principle holds true, it is advisable to hold fast to the Deleuzian view that the coils of the serpent are indeed complex, rhizomatic and, if left unattended, fraught with all manner of dangers and strange becomings.

References

Cole, D. R. (2007). Virtual terrorism and the internet e-learning options. *E–Learning and Digital Media, 4*(2), 116–117.

Colebrook, C. (2002). *Understanding Deleuze.* Allen & Unwin.

Conley, V. (2005). Rhizome & technology. In A. Parr (Ed.), *The Deleuze dictionary* (pp. 234–235). Edinburgh University Press.

Day, R. E. (2001). *The modern invention of information: Discourse, history, and power.* Southern Illinois University Press.

Deleuze, G. (1988). *Spinoza: Practical philosophy.* City Lights Books.

Deleuze, G. (1992). Postscript on the societies of control. *Cultural Theory: An Anthology,* 139–142.

Deleuze G. (1995). *Negotiations 1972–1990* (M. Joughin, Trans.). Columbia University Press.

Deleuze, G., & Guattari, F. (1983). *Anti-Oedipus: Capitalism and schizophrenia* (H. R. Lane, M. Seem, & R. Hurley, Trans.). Athlone Press.

Deleuze, G., & Guattari, F. (1987) *A thousand plateaus: Capitalism and schizophrenia* (B. Massumi, Trans.). University of Minnesota Press.

Deleuze, G., & Parnet, C. (2006). *Dialogues.* Continuum.

Foucault, M. (1980). *Language counter-memory practice: Selected essays and interviews.* Cornell University Press.

Genosko, G. (2002). *Félix Guattari: An aberrant introduction.* Continuum.

Genosko, G. (2008). A-signifying semiotics. *The Public Journal of Semiotics, II*(1), 11–21.

Gorz, A. (1967). *Strategy for labour: A radical proposal.* Beacon Press.

Guattari, F. (1995). *Chaosmosis: An ethico-aesthetic paradigm.* Indiana University Press.

Guattari, F. (Ed.). (1996). *The Guattari reader.* Basil Blackwell.

Guattari, F. (2000). *The three ecologies.* Athlone Press.

Hardt, M., & Negri, A. (2000). *Empire.* Harvard University Press.

Lazzarato, M. (2006). The concepts of life and the living in the societies of control. In M. Fuglsang & B. M. Sorensen (Eds.), *Deleuze and the social* (pp. 171–190). Edinburgh University Press.

Marks, J. (1998). *Gilles Deleuze: Vitalism and multiplicity.* Pluto Press.

Masny, D. (2006). Learning and creative processes: A poststructural perspective on language and multiple literacies. *The International Journal of Learning, 12*(5), 149–156.

Masny, D., & Cole, D. R. (2009). *Multiple literacies theory.* Sense Publishers.

Massumi, B. (2002). *Parables for the virtual: Movement, affect, sensation.* Duke University Press.

Miller, H. (1961). *Tropic of cancer.* Flamingo.

Ōe, K. (1994). *Teach them to outgrow their madness.* Grove Press.

Parr, A. (Ed.). (2005). *The Deleuze dictionary.* Edinburgh University Press.

Semetsky, I. (2004). The role of intuition in thinking and learning: Deleuze and the pragmatic legacy. *Educational Philosophy and Theory, 36*, 433–454.

Semetsky, I. (2009). Deleuze as a philosopher of education: Affective knowledge/effective learning. *The European Legacy, 14*(4), 443–456.

CHAPTER FOUR

Affective Literacies: Deleuze, Discipline, and Power

This chapter explores the philosophy of Gilles Deleuze in order to understand classroom management in terms of the shifting power-structure(s) in the teaching and learning context. The classroom dynamic presents a form of affective literacy or literacies in the framework of multiple literacies theory (Masny, 2006). This is because the flows of communication in the classroom demonstrate an affective map of the power flows in that context; and in this chapter this power differential is dealt with through "affectus". The affective interactivity of literacies in classroom management is complementary to and congruent with the conceptual framework of this writing. This chapter will focus on the Deleuze-Guattarian concepts of "anti-production" (as presented in *Anti-Oedipus*) and the order words (in *A Thousand Plateaus*), which will be unpacked and analyzed in the specific educational context of classroom management and as pertaining to teacher education. The two conceptions of desire from *Anti-Oedipus* and *A Thousand Plateaus* will be reconciled in this chapter through the communication of affective literacies and in the power relationships of affect as affectus.

Anti-production locates the immovable and yet invisible points in the socius that Deleuze and Guattari (1984) subject to analysis and synthesis in *Anti-Oedipus*. The primarily Marxian-Freudian concept of anti-production explains how traces remain of classroom management strategies being deployed, in institutions of teaching and learning, which pertain to desire. Anti-production shows how this "holding" of disciplinary events takes place, and provides a bridge between being in a school, and the collective memories of the resident population, spreading contagiously among them. The second concept that acts as a platform for affective literacies, discipline and power in this chapter is that of the order words. Deleuze and Guattari (1987) offered the idea of the order words to connect the "collective assemblage" and enunciation, or how we use language socially. The order words "flow" around places of learning like the routing of electricity in plasterboard walls, and present a means to explain how disciplinary triggers are shared communally and linguistically. This chapter includes scenarios to illustrate classroom management as affective literacies and how to deploy Deleuze and Guattari's (1984, 1987) concepts in teacher education. It also shows how teacher education and classroom management could be modified through the Deleuze-Guattarian philosophical perspective, by emphasising that students and teachers competently analyze the affective literacies that are at work in schools and how they impact on teaching and learning. This chapter contends that classroom management is made easier through understanding and applying affective literacies to questions of power (affectus), and by combining an analysis of anti-production with order words.

Classroom Management and Deleuze

Deleuze did not present a theory or model of classroom management during his career. Whilst this should not surprise one, it doesn't mean that his philosophical toolbox of ideas cannot be crafted into a workable notion of classroom management. In contrast, Guattari was directly influenced by the radical pedagogy of Freinet and Oury, which implies a notion of classroom management through the augmentation of the group to act as subject (see Guattari, 1995). It is in *Anti-Oedipus* and *A Thousand Plateaus* that the philosophical toolbox of Deleuze meshes most closely with the practical materiality of Guattari. However, pre-service students and teachers often have little use for such ideas, as they look for directly applicable models of classroom management that will help them in their chosen profession. It is therefore worth considering the conjunctive aspects between the affective literacies of this chapter, that are built on the Deleuze-Guattarian concepts of anti-production and the order words, and classroom management theory at its most open and liberal. The ideas that most readily join with the focus of this chapter are those of William Glasser (1998a, 1998b). This chapter is not a comparative study between Glasser and Deleuze, but it does show how Deleuze's philosophy is compatible with classroom management theory. Glasser was influenced by the constructivism of Dewey, and worked against the dominant paradigm of behaviourism in classroom management. In summary, he proposed that classroom management required educators to satisfy the needs of the students, and these needs are driven by (Glasser, 1998a, p. 5):

1. Survival, safety, security
2. Love, belonging and acceptance
3. Personal power, competency and achievement
4. Freedom, independence and autonomy
5. Fun and learning

Glasser (1998b) proposed that teachers conduct analyzes of needs to make sure that their pedagogy takes into account the drives as listed above. The problem that most teachers find with this process is that there is not enough time in "normal" teaching and learning contexts to inquire into students' needs in such depth. The classroom management model from Glasser is radically student-centred, and this fact could potentially jeopardise the position of the teacher, and the teaching and learning structures that could help with classroom management. However, Glasser's ideas are meant to give the teacher the greatest possible chance of allowing the students to make the right choices in education, and to make classroom management a matter of being a lead teacher, and not a boss teacher (Glasser, 1998a). These tactics from Glasser do resonate with the affective literacies, anti-production and the order words of this chapter, yet if one takes the ideas of Deleuze-Guattari seriously, one cannot straightforwardly fall back into choice theory in terms of classroom management. This is because understanding and working with drives in the classroom does not necessarily imply choice according to Deleuze and Guattari (1984, 1987).

One could say that the classroom management model of this chapter is more akin to conducting an orchestra, or like being a DJ at a dance. The teacher must acclimatize and become one with the atmosphere of the class, and through this acclimatization process work out how to make learning happen. The classroom management plan of this chapter is a highly disciplined and rigorous practice, which replaces traditional power hierarchies with subtle pulsations in energy and drive. Such a discipline could include some of Glasser's ideas, yet one shouldn't presuppose any needs before one has experienced a particular context. Rather, one should firstly understand how every context is permeated by affective literacies and power through affect.

Affective Literacies and Power (Affectus)

When one goes to a school, college or university for the first time, one may discern affect. This is the atmosphere of the place, which has been produced by the historical and material presence that the institution emits. For example, a school may have been run on military lines, and the experience of teaching and learning at the institute would seem as if one has entered the army. In an opposing example, a college might specialize in the creative arts; the pedagogic affect that one experiences in the space would in this case be more liberal, open and spontaneous. Affective literacies involve the reciprocal articulation of such affects, and can be bodily, visual, audio or linguistic (see Masny & Cole, 2009). Affect in these affective literacies is the act of changing in encounter with another. In places of teaching and learning this is entwined with power relationships that permeate such institutions due to classroom management, discipline and control.

For the purposes of this chapter I am interested in the notion and Latin term "affectus", or subjective modulation. In his book *Spinoza, Practical Philosophy* Deleuze (1988) says that affectus is "an increase or decrease of the power of acting, for the body and the mind alike" (p. 47). In relation to this chapter, this increase or decrease in power is when the teacher and students experience changes in atmosphere through classroom interaction and any lines of conflict that are present. According to the philosophy of this chapter, the teacher cannot straightforwardly control the class, but has to assimilate with the prevailing atmospheres in the context and work through the affective literacies that are present. He or she must not attempt to quash or nullify "affectus", but should rather try to understand, articulate and work with the presence of affects in the classroom—like moving with an energy field or dancing. I have elsewhere named this movement with affect in education as the two-role model of affect (Cole, 2011). Deleuze expands his definition of affectus by arguing that it is crucially separate from emotion; affectus is simultaneously the physical and non-physical increase or decrease in a body's power of acting. Deleuze (1988) states:

> The *affectio* refers to a state of the affected body and implies the presence of the affecting body, whereas the *affectus* refers to the passage from one state to another, taking into account the correlative variation of the affecting bodies. Hence there is a difference in nature between the *image affections* or *ideas* and the *feeling affect.* (p. 49)

Put differently, affectus is the sum total of material and immaterial elements of change and importantly for educational use may be understood as:—*the act of learning.* Affectus is the passage from one state to another, which occurs in relation to affecting bodies, and in the case of classroom management, due to conflict, power and discipline. Affectus is also what theorists such as Hickey-Moody and Haworth (2009), and McWilliam (1996) have called pedagogy; in other words, affectus is a relational practice through which knowledge is made and transmitted. This relational practice is here transcribed into affective literacies, which are multiple opportunities to work with affectus in an educational context and via the energy penetration of classroom management strategies. The image affections or ideas, to which Deleuze (1988) refers above, are generated by a specific kind of movement in affect. This change involves increasing or decreasing one's *capacity* to act, or the modulation of affectus; and such a plane of action prompts affection or the feeling of affect in the consciousness of the body (See Hickey-Moody, 2009), read as a plane of materiality. Affectus therefore differs from notions of subjective change as a contained pedagogy, as affectus is a type of "non-human" pedagogy, and as shall be illustrated in the examples of classroom management below (1–10) as a machine.

The affective literacies that correspond to affectus and that we are using in this chapter for classroom management are grounded in terms of interrelated, non-personal connections; and they are necessarily a response to, and part of, becoming in the world (c.f. Semetsky, 2006). This "becoming in the world" will be explained below (1–10) in terms of practical examples in classroom management. One could say that the affectus of affective literacies is a rhythm, and that affectus may be incorporated into transversality (see Guattari, 1984). Affective literacies are an articulation of an encounter between form and forces that are non-human and chaotic. In terms of classroom management, affectus necessitates institutional administrators, teachers, computer programmers and students to understand and work with the lines of force and power as they are represented through and in context.

A vital aspect of using affectus and affective literacies for classroom management is to understand that they do not signify closed systems, i.e., functioning only inside the physical classroom. Teachers and students should be able to explore the affective economies of learning in community spaces, in and out of schools. For example, the multiple and complex processes of political activism on the Net makes for excellent affective literacy activities and engagement in today's wired and globalized classrooms (see Pullen & Cole, 2009). Understandings of power are often reversed and subtly questioned and renegotiated on the internet, and teachers need to engage with these movements of power that regularly take place in mediated environments. Such understanding and articulations can take one into a new vision of society that permeates educational institutions and the requisite classroom management of these spaces. Affective literacies connect with power and classroom management in that the new worlds that are emerging due to digital connectivity are relayed into action. Teachers need to stay up to date with these cultural shifts, and engage contemporary group dynamics through affectus, digital hierarchies and protocols that are currently emerging in post-industrial societies. This is also the nexus of what Masny (2006) calls "creative process", or research, that is about:

> ...[c]onfronting teaching as unknowability and learning as literacies or [the] different ways of becoming [that are] involved in uncontrollable and uncontrolled ways of "reading-learning". (p. 148)

Anti-Production

Affective literacies, that foreground power as *affectus*, are importantly involved with and about desire. The idea at this point is that the teachers and students, working through affectus, and effectively moving within the classroom management situation by pertinently attending to the contextual and situational power relationships affectively, necessarily tap into the desires of the host population and any group dynamics. There may be censors and problems with this scheme in education, if, for example, the children and teachers are not allowed to talk overtly about sexuality or violence. The other major drawback of this idea might be the complexity of the desires involved; if, for example, the local situation is mired in poverty or suffering due to alienation, because the specific understandings accessed in this situation and the desires that living a life of poverty or as an outsider create may be insurmountable for the educator to address (see Anyon, 2005) in full. However, these examples of desire in education draw us closer to understanding the Deleuze-Guattarian concept of "anti-production". Desire is not enjoined with lack according to Deleuze and Guattari (1984) although one could say that educational desiring production is imbricated with circuits of anti-production, as the desire for continual learning production leads to the habitual repetition in concepts such as: "lifelong learning". This is because it could be argued that lifelong learning is a containment strategy of post-modern capitalism and does not lead to revolutionary change (c.f. Wallin in Cole, 2012).

Furthermore, the operations of anti-production in education can be seen in the political economies of schools, colleges or universities. Capitalist surplus value incorporates students and teachers into enveloping circuits of educational production to make money from learning ("edu-debt"). To exemplify the conjunction between surplus value, capitalism and anti-production (edu-debt), one could say that in a culture driven by semiotics, there is always more to learn. In an age of rapidly developing computerized information technologies, there are always new computer skills to be mastered and new software programs and gadgets to be bought and managed. In a system of global educational rankings, there is always progress to be made; there is always another scale upon which one can compare performance. This exteriorising surplus capitalist economy drives education into processes of interminable production and debt (see Lazzarato, 2006). Anti-production can be detected in the many ways that the labor of teachers and students never catches up with the motility of surplus value. The educational containment by surplus value is commensurate with the functioning of capitalism, which ensures the interconnected nature of production through anti-production at all levels of the social assemblage (Deleuze & Guattari, 1984).

Therefore, one must include anti-production in the affective literacies, affectus and classroom management as discussed in this chapter. One could say that anti-production produces an atmosphere of "unrealisation" in the classroom, as the potential of teenagers and teachers is often thwarted by the societal processes of capitalism and desiring-production that swirl through teaching and learning contexts. There is an important political message attached to "anti-production"; and this states that the ways in which the youth are socialized in contemporary society often gives them unrealistic expectations as to what they can achieve. The lure of fast cars, glamorous models and luxurious lifestyles is communicated through advertising and film, and a gap between material needs and desire is created as a function of living and being schooled under the sign of capitalist endeavor (see Darder, Baltodano, & Torres, 2009).

There are serious consequences of anti-production in terms of classroom behaviour and the management skills necessary to deal with such a situation. Deleuze and Guattari (1984) do not give a straightforward solution to the behavioural and adaptive problems produced by anti-production, yet by theorising anti-production as being liminal with desire, one may begin to recognise the complexities of the situation. If one goes too far in the direction of capitalist endeavor in one's pedagogy, and tries to utilise the desires that capital produces, the resulting knowledge work can be contrived and artificial—except perhaps if one makes money through teaching and learning! Contrariwise, if one ignores contemporary capitalist society altogether, one may come across as being a dinosaur only interested in knowledge for scholastic or purely scientific purposes. This chapter suggests that there is a middle way that may be gleaned from a detailed understanding of Deleuze and Guattari's (1984) anti-production. This middle way takes capitalist production and explores and explicates the desires that flow through its processes—good and bad.

Such a strategy should demonstrate the value of knowledge in contemporary society, whilst providing engaging and dynamic lesson plans.

For example, in terms of anti-production in education, one may analyze the reasons for the 2008 Global Financial Crisis (GFC) with the students, but not in a purely analytical or statistical fashion. The educator and group can draw social and cultural consequences from the facts of the GFC, as well as understanding how this event has ramifications for the global financial system in the future. Anti-production is being used here purposefully and with the intention of dealing with potential behavioural problems associated with the striations of desire caused due to economic collapse. The last element of this chapter's concept-construction to understand affective literacies, power and discipline in the classroom involves language and Deleuze and Guattari's (1987) order words.

Order Words

> [I]t is in this sense that language is the transmission of the word as 'order words', not the communication of a sign as information. Language is a map, not a tracing. (Deleuze & Guattari 1987, p. 77)

When teachers implement classroom management techniques, they invariably use language. Therefore, one must take into account language use on power and discipline in the classroom. In *A Thousand Plateaus*, Deleuze and Guattari (1987) deploy the notion of the order words, which is taken from a non-normative approach to linguistics. This means that the order words are immediately drawn away from mainstream linguistics, and this is because linguistics is interested in fixing language by according primacy to constants and a secondary role to variation. In contrast, Deleuze and Guattari (1987) had a reversed take on constants and variations within the systems of language. Variations are in their terms primary, and exist on a virtual plane, as one can never fully predict how a word is actualized in advance. Such actualisation of words depends entirely on the context, and in the instance of this chapter, on behaviour management situations involving affect, anti-production, discipline, power and conflict.

Deleuze and Guattari (1987) were interested in the multiple and crisscrossing relations that are possible between the statement and the act. These relationships, though complex, are importantly political for Deleuze and Guattari, and the political nature of language becomes integral to language. For example, when a teacher asks/directs/tells a student to do something, this is a statement that is politically empowered by and through the context of teaching and learning, and is potentially empowering in terms of the learning that could take place and any ensuing group dynamics—as well being disempowering if the statement fails in its intent (see Cole, 2009). All behaviour management statements have a political and relational dimension according to this schema, which can be analyzed by understanding the order words.

The language that we are primarily concerned with in classroom management is about command, instruction and its reception. With the desired action of learning stemming from speech, transformations in the agent must occur accordingly. Deleuze and Guattari (1987, p. 92) refer to this context of change as "incorporeal transformation". An example of such a change that is specific to this chapter could be when a teacher reprimands a student for disobeying the class rules. The physical bodies of the teacher and child have not altered in the exchange, hence the notion of incorporeality in this context. Yet by making such a statement about power in the classroom, i.e., reasserting the class rules, this has altered the relationships of bodies that are encountered in the particular context and the overall form of the classroom "assemblage". The statement of "rule adherence" turns into an act, that of compliance or defiance on the part of the student(s). This particular type of transformation has social implications that alter the bodies that it affects, i.e., those of the teacher, the student, the cohort and anyone who is listening or who hears about the speech act. One could say that the statement and reinstatement of class rules is an immanent act, actualized once the teacher is in a particular time and space that is related to the context of being a teacher and that implies a previously defined role of what it means to be a "good teacher" (see Rogers, 1998) who can manage the class. Yet the realization of the political and pragmatic level of the order words also allows the teacher to question the presuppositions inherent within the order words, i.e., the statement and reinstatement of the school rules.

Classroom management through language and class rules is a social activity. The social character of language is according to Deleuze and Guattari (1987) the "transmission of order words, from one statement to another or within each statement in so far as each statement accomplishes an act and an act is accomplished in the statement" (p. 72). Order words therefore importantly demonstrate a social order through language. Order words may concern directions, commands, instructions, questions, requests or promises that are linked to statements by a "social obligation". Order words are part of a matrix that codes, possesses and potentially enhances or restricts action. For example, the order words can be the instruments of the state that defines education in a particular territory and in a certain manner (see Masny, 2005). In the context of this chapter, the order words of the state will refer to previously defined, normatively correct and acceptable behaviours in the context of teaching and learning.

The recognition and analysis of the order words used in classroom management by the state is therefore a potentially subversive activity, and one that can undermine governmentally dominant forms of control through social acquiescence and quietism. Deleuze and Guattari (1987) affirm that in addition to the order words, language consists of indirect discourse, which refers to speaking in a received, "passed on" or clichéd style. In the case of indirect discourse, it may not be clear who is speaking or where the words have come from. Indirect discourse has a collective style because of its generalized form (see Grisham, 1991). The order words of classroom management situations relate to and bleed into indirect discourse as the teacher typically lives in society, interacts with the media and deals with groups of students who also live in society. Therefore, dominant forms of socialization and normalization can be transmitted through indirect discourse as much as through the order words, and teachers should be aware that clichéd and colloquial forms of language can be detrimental to working with knowledge because of the conditioning and coding that lies in indirect discourse.

In corollary, language is a set of statements and propositions, order words, implicit and explicit presuppositions, indirect discourse and incorporeal transformations that make social processes. For Deleuze and Guattari (1987), the primary role of language, contra traditional linguistics, is neither to inform nor to communicate, but to produce order words according to an overriding and dominant social reality. Therefore, language has a negative status in the analysis of Deleuze and Guattari (1987), as their philosophical approach to understanding language continually undermines the potential homogenization inherent within communication (see Roy, 2008). Their approach is one that invites experimentation and the creation of new language. If one uses cliché or mindlessly restates the rules without sensitivity or empathy to a particular context, one is immediately caught out by the ideas of Deleuze & Guattari.

To take their notion of the order words seriously for classroom management purposes, one must be able to take apart socially dominant forms of using language, and be able to ask searching questions about the purposes and grounds whereby these statements have been made. The consequence of applying the order words in this chapter opens up the use of language in education as a means to comprehend contextual and practical adaptations in teaching and learning—and as they happen, affectively. This chapter does not tell teachers how to speak, or what to say in order to control their unruly class. Rather, the challenge here is to continually analyze the typical order words of control, e.g., "be quiet" "sit down", etc., in order to get to a level of language production and reception that achieves affective auto-reflexivity in moments of classroom management and disciplinary crisis.

The Classroom Management Machine

This chapter proposes a means to understanding classroom management in terms of affective literacies, which focus affectus as power, anti-production and the order words. The responses to classroom management situations below demonstrate how the non-human pedagogy described above in terms of affectus may be figured. This is because the classroom management ideas in this chapter are a machine, and not a matter of experience, judgment or subjectivity. The proposal of the chapter is to show that this amalgam of elements from the work of Deleuze and Guattari helps to deal with classroom management situations. This link to the practical and im-manent life of education may be illustrated by thinking through the responses that an "affective literacies (affectus)-anti-production-order words" machine produce:

Examples of classroom management

1. A student approaches you and tells you that he has ADHD (Attention Deficit Hyperactive Disorder). He can't take the test within the time allotted, can't turn in assignments on time, or can't take notes, etc. He is requesting special consideration. Other students in the class overhear your conversation and start to whisper among themselves.

This example very well illustrates how affectus, anti-production and order words are connected to classroom management. The teacher should choose their response to this situation carefully, as the wrong tone, and the reproduction of order words related to learning conformity, could augment a potentially disastrous situation. The teacher needs to grant special consideration to this student, whilst not being seen to give spe-cial privilege to one student's needs. The best way to handle this case would be in a neutral context, without the other class members being present, where the problems that this student is experiencing may be discussed in full, and affective literacies may be achieved between student and teacher. These literacies would articulate the stu-dent and teacher's perspectives on ADHD and the consequences in the teaching and learning context. These affective literacies would help to establish a sound working relationship between the student and teacher for the future, and also deal with the anti-production of submitting this student to uniform assessment processes.

2. You've assigned online discussion groups. You are reviewing their postings and dis-cover inappropriate language and sexual references to you and/or other students.

These postings are clearly not acceptable; yet show how educational practice relates to societal tendencies, which has been dealt with in this chapter, through anti-production. These postings should not be addressed in an overly judicious or moralistic manner, or by assigning the order words of reprimand to the (unknown) subjects. Rather, the postings should be discussed with the class members, not in terms of reprimand or punishment, but to articulate the affects that have been conscribed as forms of affective literacies. Offensive and obscene material should not be simply castigated or nullified in education; but worked through to show how it communicates hurt (affectus). This example of turning a classroom management and potential conflict-situation into a pedagogic process demonstrates how to conjoin affectus, anti-production and the order words. The authors of this material should understand that online environments are not neutral, and that they are engaging with affective literacies that are connected to the anti-production of contemporary society and the order words of control.

3. John recently began teaching at college. In the fourth week of the term, he administered the first exam. Mary, a bright student, was a 'no-show' and had also missed the previous week. After the exam, John telephoned her at the number she had provided on her student profile. A middle-aged man answered the phone. John identified himself as Mary's teacher and asked for her. The man identified himself as Mary's father, told John that Mary was not home, then asked the nature of the call. John replied that Mary had missed the test and went on to speculate about its impact on her grade.

John should not discuss Mary's grade with her father, and this is because of the affectus that would be produced by such an exchange. John needs to arrange a time and date to speak to Mary in person and to ask her what has happened. Speaking to her father in the first place could potentially damage the relationship that John has established with Mary and therefore make communication harder in the future. This example shows how discussing matters with parents can influence the affective literacies necessary to make classroom management work. Furthermore, Mary's father could pass on order words connected to grading (simply put: A = good, E = bad), and this might also impact on the anti-production of grading, in terms of Mary's likelihood not to benefit from future assessment results.

4. You are presenting a new concept to your class. You've worked very hard to organize your presentation and find the material very interesting. However, the energy level in the class is very low. The students appear to be falling asleep and are not interested in the lesson.

One might refrain from overtly demonstrating disappointment in the students' reaction to one's material—however interesting one might think it to be, and this is an example of affectus in the classroom. Such disappointment could lead to further and increased disruption and a potential split between your ideas about the material and that of the cohort, or eschewed affective literacies. Rather, one needs to take the time out from the prescribed curriculum and examine the reasons for the lull in energy. Maybe the students just need a break or a change in the presentation of the material.

Furthermore, they could be experiencing 'information overload' and might need a more interactive teaching and learning environment. This example shows how order words can be multimodal and not only instructive or explicitly directing knowledge work, and that anti-production has to be engaged with affectively.

5. A student comes to class who is obviously on drugs or drunk.

This is a delicate situation that should be treated carefully. According to the affective literacies of this chapter, one should not immediately reprimand the student, or make an example of them, as this could provide a basis for an irrational outburst or enflamed situation (affectus). Rather, one could start the lesson off as had been planned, and when the rest of the class has become engrossed in the focus of the learning, one should address the student personally and ascertain the details of the intoxication (affective literacies). Once this interaction has been achieved, the student should either be asked to leave the class, or reminded of the class procedures that will happen during and after the lesson; and they will have to remain within these parameters to successfully negotiate the teaching and learning context. One could say that the teacher is working with affective literacies in terms of building relationships, anti-production in terms of the impact of intoxication, and order words in terms of not using language to express reactive indignation to drug/alcohol use.

6. Many of your students come from different cultures with different ethnic and linguistic backgrounds. You have been lecturing and students are complaining that they cannot understand you or follow your logic.

The linguistic diversity of student backgrounds will add to the richness of the educational experience, and is an important part of the affective literacies of this chapter. However, this situation could lead to the increased possibility of misunderstandings and subsequent conflict and disruption (affectus). Therefore, the teacher must take time to create specific sessions that aid inter-cultural literacy (by using affective literacies) by avoiding the order words and clichés connected to cultural differences. These pedagogic actions may include looking at the different languages represented in the cohort and showing what different cultures bring to the particular knowledge field that is being studied. No group should be highlighted as being in particular need of help, as this can lead to the anti-production of that group; cultural diversity will be complemented and included in knowledge work on an everyday basis by deploying affective literacies.

7. Marina finds spelling and grammar errors in your sentences on the board with embarrassing consistency, and she comes around after class to give you her critical opinion of the course. When she's in class, you feel like you're being constantly monitored.

Making spelling and grammar mistakes will attract criticism. However, the relationship between yourself and Marina needs to be addressed. This situation would be best handled outside of the class when she has come to complain, and affective literacies may be constructed mutually. One needs to be able to handle personal criticism as a teacher, yet if it is ill-directed or a cover for a different problem, this also needs to be looked at. In this case, Marina has suggestions that will help with the running of the class and these suggestions should be used. If Marina has a social difficulty, this should be addressed and suggestions made to help, e.g. changing of seating plan, less or more group work, a different means to discursive pedagogy in the lessons (e.g. using an IWB). The aspect of changing teaching and learning patterns involves affective literacies by thoroughly discussing the pedagogy, anti-production in terms of the culture of the classroom, and the order words in terms of the terminology used when changing practice.

8. Patrick is critical and outright insubordinate in class, always challenging your information and interpretations on the basis of readings from the textbook. Though he often remembers the text incorrectly, you sometimes start to wonder if it was in fact you who failed to master the material.

Patrick's behaviour needs to be addressed as soon as possible in this situation as it is an on-going problem. This means that the ways in which he is reacting to your pedagogy need to be examined in terms of the affective, relational and anti-production consequences. One could counter Patrick's claims by stating that it is healthy to consider if one has mastered the material of the lesson, as this should lead to increased knowledge and engagement with the topic. However, it is unhealthy to feel belittled by a student. The power relationship (affectus) between you and the student should be addressed, whereby; the teacher may be put back in tune with the knowledge field that they are exploring, and one can deal with any critical remarks that arise during the lesson and Patrick is less inclined to make outbursts. Patrick's manner should be explored through class-wide engagement with knowledge and the objects of inquiry, and not through a 'power war' with Patrick or by using order words; as this could lead to a narrowing of affective literacies and intensification in the impact of the conflict.

9. Teri had a class in the past similar to yours, and constantly compares your instruction to her other experience. Inevitably, your class always comes up short in her eyes.

Comparative pedagogy could be a positive aspect of the lesson. Yet if this process is initiated with a negative intent, using order words and anti-production, the outcome will be negative. This is why the teacher should lead an affective literacies session to show how knowledge can be shared and transmitted via different means. For example, the teacher could introduce the use of ICTs, or change the affectus and power relationships by asking students to lead sessions. The point here is to not get caught in one circuit of pedagogy that can lead to anti-production. This example shows how affective literacies, anti-production and the order words are a form of non-human pedagogy, as the reciprocal relationships that develop with knowledge are not personal, but straddle non-human divides between participants in the teaching and learning context.

10. Clearly disappointed in her test grades, Kathryn always challenges your grading of the tests. In an effort to seem accommodative, you once relented on strict scoring for one minor point, but this has only emboldened her, and she now calls openly for you to 'be more fair' with the grading.

The point here is not to completely hand over one's pedagogy and educational experience to the anti-production and order words of examinations. Exams are important and highly valued by society and schools; however, they can also lead to anti-production as they delimit educational possibilities. The teacher needs to make this point for Kathryn through affective literacies and affectus. Kathryn has become embroiled in the minutiae of the exam result rather than seeing the overall and broader picture of the lessons as an experience. While one has to engage with the marking of exams, the affective literacies here should direct the conversation outwards and to the bigger picture, for example, to the content, knowledge and purpose of the lessons, rather than always going inwards and to the exact reasons for a grade.

Conclusion

Deleuze did not theorise society in disciplinary terms in the same way as did, for example, Foucault (1995). Yet, one may see from the examples above how the classroom management machine in this chapter has potentially strong consequences for power and discipline in the classroom. The affective literacies operate constantly in the teaching and learning context, especially because society has given education a high priority, and therefore the affect of teaching and learning lives on beyond the time accorded to the actions of teaching and learning—and this enhances both anti-production and the order words. Deleuze (1995) speaks of the "control society" in his later statements about social processes and the ways in which the technologies of the self have evolved recently to monitor and define how one should behave and think in any context. This chapter should not add to the impression of a control society by enhancing classroom management to increase more normatively determined modes of behaviour. Rather, the affective literacies, anti-production and order words of this chapter work together to unleash behavioural constraints from the ways in which teaching and learning are currently orchestrated in education.

Certainly, there are resonances in this philosophy with alternative modes of education that prioritise the acts of learning, and look to diminish the traditional effects of schooling such as conformism, powerlessness, subjugation under the sign of capital, etc. (e.g. Reimer, 1971). Yet, this chapter also points to a new way of performing the work of classroom management, one that is stimulated and stimulating due to the action of affectus (power), understands anti-production and works with order words to creative effect. The mode of classroom management proposed by this chapter sits within the currently defined ways of doing education, yet ceaselessly looks to overturn and remodel these processes. This work is immanent now, and should be acted upon by teachers, pre-service students and teacher-trainers alike in their practice of teaching and learning.

I would like to acknowledge the Central Florida University (CFU) teacher-training unit for supplying these examples of classroom management.

References

Anyon, J. (2005). *Radical possibilities: Public policy, urban education, and a new social movement.* Routledge.

Cole, D. R. (2009). The power of emotional factors in English teaching. *Power and Education, 1*(1), 57–70.

Cole, D. R. (2011). The actions of affect in Deleuze—Others using language and the language that we make…. *Educational Philosophy and Theory, 43*(6), 549–561.

Cole, D. R. (2012). *Surviving economic crises through education global studies in education.* Peter Lang.

Darder, A., Baltodano, M., & Torres, R. (Eds.). (2009). *The critical pedagogy reader* (2nd ed.). Routledge.

Deleuze, G. (1988). *Spinoza: Practical philosophy.* City Lights.

Deleuze, G. (1995). *Negotiations, 1972–1990* (M. Joughin, Trans.). Columbia University Press.

Deleuze, G., & Guattari, F. (1984). *Anti-Oedipus: Capitalism and schizophrenia* (R. Hurley, M. Steem, & H. R. Lane, Trans.). The Athlone Press.

Deleuze, G., & Guattari, F. (1987). *A thousand plateaus: Capitalism & schizophrenia II* (B. Massumi, Trans.). The Athlone Press.

Foucault, M. (1995). *Discipline & punishment: The birth of the prison* (A. Sheridan, Trans.). Random House.

Glasser, W. (1998a). *Choice theory: A new psychology of personal freedom*. Harper Perennial.

Glasser, W. (1998b). *Choice theory in the classroom* (Rev. ed.). Harper & Row.

Grisham, T. (1991). Linguistics as an indiscipline: Deleuze and Guattari's pragmatics. *SubStance*, *20*, 3(66), 36–54.

Guattari, F. (1984). *Molecular revolution: Psychiatry and politics*. Penguin Books.

Guattari, F. (1995). La Borde: A clinic unlike any other. In S. Lotringer (Ed.), *Chaosophy* (pp. 28–46). Semiotext(e).

Hickey-Moody, A. (2009). Little war machines: Posthuman pedagogy and its media. *Journal of Literary & Cultural Disability Studies*, *3*(3), 273–280.

Hickey-Moody, A., & Haworth, R. (2009). Affective literacies. In D. Masny & D. R. Cole (Eds.), *Multiple literacies theory: A Deleuzian perspective* (pp. 79–93). Sense Publishers.

Lazzarato, M. (2006). The concepts of life and the living in the societies of control. In M. Fuglsang & B. M. Sorensen (Eds.), *Deleuze and the social* (pp. 171–190). Edinburgh University Press.

Masny, D. (2005). Multiple literacies: An alternative or beyond Friere. In J. Anderson, T. Rogers, M. Kendrick & S. Smythe (Eds.), *Portraits of literacy across families, communities, and schools: Intersections and tensions* (pp. 71–84). L. Erlbaum Associates.

Masny, D. (2006). Learning and creative processes: A poststructural perspective on language and multiple literacies. *International Journal of Learning*, *12*(5), 147–155.

Masny, D., & Cole, D. R. (Eds.). (2009). *Multiple literacies theory: A Deleuzian perspective*. Sense Publishers.

McWilliam, E. (1996). Pedagogies, technologies, bodies. In E. McWilliam & P. G. Taylor (Eds.), *Pedagogy, technology and the body* (pp. 79–87). Peter Lang.

Pullen, D., & Cole, D. R. (Eds.). (2009). *Multiliteracies and technology enhanced education: Social practice and the global classroom*. IGI Global Publications.

Reimer, E. (1971). *School is dead*. Penguin Books.

Rogers, B. (1998). *You know the fair rule and much more*. ACER.

Roy, K. (2008). Deleuzian murmurs: Education and communication. In I. Semetsky (Ed.), *Nomadic education: Variations on a theme by Deleuze & Guattari* (pp. 159–171). Sense Publishers.

Semetsky, I. (2006). *Deleuze, education and becoming*. Sense Publishers.

Wallin, J. J. (2012). Remachining educational desire: Bankrupting Freire's banking model of education in an age of schizo-capitalism. In D. R. Cole (Ed.), *Surviving economic crises through education* (pp. 229–246). Peter Lang.

Multiplicities

On Multiple Literacies and Language Learning: Video Production and Embodied Subjectivities

The dialogue below is a reflection on the cutting-edge research around video literacies being undertaken in several universities in the Tokyo metropolitan area in Japan and looks to link this up with equally progressive work being done in the Australian context (Cole, 2011, 2012a, 2012b, 2013, 2014; Cole & Bradley, 2014, 2015; Cole & Moyle, 2010; Masny & Cole, 2012; Pullen & Cole, 2010). It is the theoretical counterpart to findings in the recent colloquium held by Bradley *et al* at the National University of Singapore. Philosophically and in terms of educational pedagogy, the dialogue and discussion extend, undergird and contextualize the development of affective, multimodal and engaged literacies and pedagogies through student-created and student-led video production (Pullen & Cole, 2010; Cole & Bradley, 2014). Bradley and Cole's recent joint and singular work considers what it means to present an embodied subjectivity (Bangou & Fleming, 2014) through multimodal, multiple literacies in the foreign language classroom (Masny, 2013; Cole, 2013). The dialogue discusses one of the core focuses of the colloquium and considers the view that experimental and creative methodologies—that is to say, processes which encourage points of breakdown and breakthrough in education— are vital in sustaining critical and transformative pedagogies in the Japanese university setting. Without them, it is argued, students are left to spin endlessly on their own axes. So the University's traditional remit remains true—to nurture *Bildung* or self-cultivation, which is to say creation, image or shape, the overall purpose of which is to engender personal and cultural maturation—but it has to grasp also how students are utilizing and manipulating different technologies and media. Embracing and combining some of the tenets of the multiliteracies and multiple literacies theory, student-led video projects, it is argued, is a way to short-circuit the obsession with the world of work, in order to return students to themselves as a site of self-cultivation—to "record and represent oneself", as Cole says in the interview below.

What Is Multiple Literacy Theory?

Bradley: The purpose of this interview is to consider some of the emergent, on-going concepts in higher education and to situate these in view of what can be broadly conceived as a philosophy of education, which is your specialty Professor Cole. A key approach which I'd like us to focus on as we proceed in this interview is the blending or merging of content, language and new technologies. I'd like to examine this not only in terms of the core issue of literacy, but also the series of new literacies which have developed in recent years—for example, multiliteracies, digital literacies, multiple literacies theory and more recently pluriliteracies (Meyer et al., 2015). I would like to try and see how your theorization of new technologies, for example, can be differentiated from the New London Group (Cope et al., 2000), or from the multiliteracies approach more broadly. The first question would then be, "what is multiple literacy theory?"

Cole: Multiple literacies theory (MLT) (Masny & Cole, 2009) is a theoretical approach that I have developed, or helped to develop with Professor Diana Masny from Ottawa University. Diana and myself had two different ideas about MLT, but we came to the agreement that multiple literacies theory crystallized some ideas on literacies and literacy theory and especially regarding where we'd like to take it. Obviously this is within the context of an evolving environment that includes video, the internet, and mobile phones that can seemingly do everything under the sun now. A good theory has to be able to explain these new ways to record and represent oneself and one's ideas.

Just to differentiate very quickly between the multiliteracies from the New London Group, and multiple literacies theory. In the 1990s multiliteracies came about as a collaboration between linguists and theorists such as Allan Luke, who was influenced by Foucault and discourse theory. This was still quite linguistically based, but took into account things like Gunther Kress's semiotics (1995). This pertained to the notion of meaning-making, but they called it design—which is a very important concept with respect to multiliteracies. So it was quite a phenomenological approach—connecting this big world of representation that we have through the internet, through different means of presenting ourselves, our ideas and meaning-making, and then to a theory of the mind, and how that works.

It is a semiotic, phenomenological approach, and so is quite a mainstream take on connecting education with business needs, or with different technologies, and using them to positively make meaning and connect together things like image, language, gesture, and space in a reasonable fashion. So that was a big focus on critical literacies and critical literacy through Foucauldian discourse—analysis of power, social justice, and things like that. Multiple literacies theory picks up on that, but tries to cut this connection between subjectivity and the mind, or this exterior world of representation, for example in video and in thought. It tries to contest the mainstream notion of what literacies are in terms of work, thoughts, and play in the world, and tries to interpret this through what Guattari calls a-signifying semiotics.

A-Signifying Semiotics

Bradley: Could you possibly explain a little bit about a-signifying semiotics?

Cole: Again in contrast to Gunther Kress's approach to semiotics, which is indeed about making meaning, what it does say is a lot of literacy studies are not literacy studies as such, they are rather illiteracy studies. What people are doing is looking at all the things that go wrong in literacy, all the mess and mistakes. It's not helping often with articulation, for example, in new mediums like video. A lot of research has found that a lot of new technologies do not help students and their articulation of themselves—who they are, what they believe in, what they find truly interesting. Why? Because it takes an excessively mainstream approach. So students tend to reproduce what they see in the media, what they see on the internet *as themselves* when in fact it isn't. It's a false identity they're producing. Félix Guattari especially, who I've been highly influenced by, thought that you have to look at what escapes these mainstream modes of representation.

We do find moments of this in cinema. This is why we wrote *A Pedagogy of Cinema* (2016), where we take stills from cinema or from things like documentaries, which seem to encapsulate a different way of thinking around image, around thought. We then use those for pedagogy, using them for what Guattari calls a-signifying semiotics, which escapes mainstream representation. What multiple literacies theory says is that within any context there are all these embedded literacies going on. For example, in Australia, you've got more than 60 languages being spoken on the streets by an immigrant population and then you've got the indigenous languages as well.

Critique of Representation

Bradley: So the critique of representation is a key concept for MLT?

Cole: Such languages with their culture, thoughts, and values are not usually represented in the mainstream English-speaking classroom. Multiple literacies theory (MLT) goes the opposite way, and says, no, this is a resource for meaning-making; but it's an a-signifiying semiotics, it's not a mainstream approach, it's not about the majority. Students make meaning outside of the classroom. MLT says we can take any of these minor literacies—which are all interconnected through the unconscious—through the fact that we're here in this environment, and we're living, and we're breathing, and we're chaotically doing things. All these actions create meaning, but we're not trying to dominate one or the other. It's not about trying to overlay other meanings with our meanings. It's not about the ego, it's not about who's the brightest, most powerful or most beautiful. It's about trying to …. use is a bad word …. work with all these minor literacies and the meaning making resources we have in the classroom. Students are definitely part of that.

Bradley: Is meaning-making empowering for the students? Is it demanding of the students to be more autonomous in their learning? Or does it invariably remain teacher-centered?

Cole: The a-signifying semiotics goes hand in hand with the Guattari-inflected notion of what pedagogy entails. Guattari was a practitioner and worked at La Borde, a psychiatric institute in France, and he experimented with power, in the sense of rethinking the roles of doctors and staff in such institutions. Who are we in this classroom? What's your role? What's his or her role? This can be very scary for some teachers, because they're the ones who are being paid to get the kids through the class. Bringing in video or whatever medium as a *mediating third* (Bradley, 2012) is a powerful technology. It's not about me, or you. It's not about power, it's not about who's in charge, it's about the product, what we produce: *what is the video?* And how do we understand it? Is it in any way useful or meaningful, and how does it *do* something for us to articulate something in the world? And therefore not just to reproduce banal, commercial, capitalist rubbish. You have to get beyond the mainstream. You have to think about other artists, poetry, that which can help you to think differently about the media, about representation.

Bradley: Can something like the meaning-making generated from video, let's say how the meaning generated from the use of play in the video contributes to that sense of escape? Does it do something which textual approaches cannot and if so how does it do it and what are some of the effects of that approach?

Cole: Video has a different quality to it, which is more immediate. It's all about the viewer and the viewed, isn't it? It's all about this relationship between spectatorship, and then actively participating in it. We can become, as Deleuze and Guattari say, machinically enslaved within these relationships, these image-based relationships just by watching TV, just by turning a TV on, or turning a computer on. If I look on the internet now, within seconds I'm bombarded by these very highly specific advertising regimes. These are semiotic. They seem to know what I desire somehow. They're targeting me. The question for our students using video is how can we think beyond that type of bombardment and immersion?

Video Practice in Australia

Bradley: May I ask how you've applied video in your own practice?

Cole: I've done it mainly for research purposes. I've done projects on using camcorders (Pullen & Cole, 2010) with middle school students who used them to record their reflections on their literacy learning, and then I've done research with African immigrants in Australia. I've given them small flip cameras (Masny & Cole, 2014), just to record their daily lives, and then discuss what it means, what these videos are about that they're recording. Research and video go well together I think.

Bradley: What was the purpose of that, if I might ask, about the use of flip cameras?

Cole: It was actually a multiple literacies theory (MLT) project looking at immigration in Australia and Canada (Masny & Cole, 2007), and trying to understand the connection between very specific problems and challenges that the new immigrants face in the two countries, and then what possible ways in which these problems or challenges were overcome, either by external agencies or through their own ingenuity or their own ability to deal with immigration issues.

Bradley: So video became essential as a specific way to explore their material lives as textually based literacies proved impossible?

Cole: We interviewed them and transcribed interviews. I went to their houses, sat and interviewed them. But this is not the same as videoing what happens in their everyday lives. For example, they videoed a wake. In the Dinka culture, during a wake, everybody they know comes to the house, and they sit in the house for a certain number of days. It was very interesting, almost being present as a researcher myself, looking at this experience of being in an African wake in Australia in a suburban house. You go past the house, but there's no way that you could ever visualize or understand what was happening inside. So the video gives you that sort of texture. It's the *real*, isn't it, a type of ethnography?

But I don't like the term ethnography, because it sort of assumes that we are looking at ethnic minorities and kind of trying to make them more mainstream. I think the Deleuze and Guattari approach or the multiple literacies theory (MLT) approach is that these videos, that these people are making, are kind of singularities. They're sharing very specific instances of time and space, and how they're coming together, and we can think about them in that way.

Deleuze and Guattari and the Real

Bradley: As you mentioned the real, how do you connect the idea of the real with desire—a very important concept for Deleuze and Guattari, and how does that work in practice?

Cole: That's a huge question in Deleuze and Guattari as I've been reading quite a lot about the new materialism stuff. There's a connection clearly in Deleuze and Guattari between Spinoza (Deleuze, 1988), where a lot of this desire stuff comes from, and then Bergson, vitalism, different kinds of theory of the real. The problem with philosophy, according to Deleuze, according to Nietzsche, is the real. The real is out there: life, chaos, blood, sweat, it's all happening, and what are the philosophers doing? They're sitting around pontificating this, that and the other, turning it all into language, logic, into a very boring philosophical, technical explanation of how the world works. Whereas the world always will trump it and do something else. To get closer to how the world works, Deleuze takes bits of Spinoza, which doesn't relegate desire to a sort of underling of reason or to something that's just to be thought out. Actually we're really taking desire seriously as we do the will, and as we do all motive forces that drive our thinking.

Nietzsche (1967) is the other figure, especially with respect to his theory of the drives, and how that connects with reality, and then nature or some sort of understanding of the physical world that doesn't negate the powers, the natural ... again you struggle against language here because often the concept of nature is riddled with romantic, scientific, all sorts of paradigms which pervade that concept and detract from the real, from desire.

Bradley: Speaking of desire, one of the inspirations for the colloquium in May 2016 at the National University of Singapore with four other colleagues from Hitotsubashi, Kanto Gakuin, Tokyo and Toyo universities in Japan is drawn from a video that was created some years ago by a female student at a university in

Yokohama, Japan. Just to give you a quick synopsis of the content of the video, a student had a considerable crush on a foreign lecturer which interrupted her learning and his teaching to some extent. The year-long infatuation was never anything other than Platonic, and was the kind of experience that we have all had in life or at school, at one time or another. What was really astounding, was that the student in her own way worked through this experience by making a video with her friends. The video represents this experience comically, for example, with both of them having a mock pistol shoot out, with special effects later dubbed in. I think that was a really interesting way for them to work through a personal existential problem. The finished video was successful in that way and very funny, and mature in the end. Through making the video, the students were able to reflect on the emotional experience with humour and wit and draw something life affirming from it—such as the consolidation of their friendship.

In terms of language education, the students needed hands-on, by-the-book instruction, with somebody to work with them and teach them the grammar of the target language, the phonology, pronunciation and spelling and that kind of thing. The argument of Joe McKim, the professor in charge, is that after a certain point the explicit studying of the rules of the language becomes almost counterproductive and therefore at that point the students and teacher need to progress into a situation where students use the language but in some way forget that they're doing it. In a way, video production distracts them from the whole arduous task of learning the language in the sense that they are motivated to do the task at hand, they pick up the language naturally, especially by using drama and incorporating actions. Language is embodied—with the body active and in an affective relation to language acquisition when and where communication is made. This positive motivational aspect to video production engenders neural connections that assist the student to remember the vocabulary and the lines, intonation and so on. So when you get into similar communication situations, you can actually call up the same bits of language, the same chunks of language that you used in making the movie. That remains the view of the professor in charge. From your research paradigm, how you would respond or interpret such a video?

Cole: Having seen the excellent video, and commenting on the video of the Japanese girls who express their feelings for their lecturer, I suppose I would agree with the idea that the linear progression of language-learning through understanding phonics, grammar, vocabulary building—all of these technical aspects of learning a target language are extremely important and need to be addressed—but outputs or use of that language, those things that are very connected to the feelings, the emotions, affectivity, the senses, what the student really is interested in, that is highly connected to progression in that language. If the student just knows a lot of technical aspects of the language, that will be removed from their more fundamental desire, their stronger more instinctual, intuitive behaviours. If those stronger forces can connect with language learning, then that clearly has a more powerful effect for the learner.

Student-Teacher Dyad

Bradley: Could you say something more about the student-teacher dyad?

Cole: In the particular case you mentioned, there is confusion to a certain extent between the students as learners and then the students as desiring the object of the learning, which isn't language but the user of the language. So in that confusion, clearly that could lead to complications and difficulties in the learning context. And these difficulties could seriously damage their relationship and the learning of the students. So this is where I would say a Deleuze-Guattari approach to understanding these processes differs from, for example, a straightforward psychoanalytical approach, which would look at repression and the particular ways in which individual subjectivities of the Japanese girls respond to sexuality or desire, to how they have been controlled and conformed from birth, for example, with the Oedipus Complex. But the Deleuze-Guattari schizoanalytic approach broadens that psychoanalytic approach out from merely registering the subjectivities as individualized and formed and reformed through the various ways in which their sexuality has developed into a bigger collective social platform and within that platform, desire can be seen to act in other synthetic, more social ways.

Bradley: To contextualize this argument, could you explain a little bit more about the dialectic between Japanese and Western culture?

Cole: The desire for the lecturer might not just be one of individual desire, it might be expressing a relationship, for example between Japanese and Western culture. It might be looking at the roles of women in Japanese society, or (comparing) against the roles of men and women in Western societies. So it might not just be a desire for one person or sexual contact or sexual liaison between the students and the teacher, but for a bigger gamut of desires which are part of contemporary global culture. Making a video of this kind is a chance to express all of those entangled, bigger desires which open up the arena for expression beyond the usual clichés or singular sense of sexuality from the students to the teacher. It creates a bigger arena, a bigger focus for representation and expression. So the video works on one level as a representation of that, but if it challenges a simple psychoanalytic understanding or a simple exercise to express this desire we can turn it into something that uses things like collages or images of video culture, from advertising, from all sorts of different sources that could look to mediate and transform partic-ular singular desires into bigger, cultural, social questions; it could be very helpful to think about these desires in a schizoanalytic way (Carlin & Wallin, 2014; Cole & Bradley, 2016; Cole and Woodrow, 2016; Graham & Cole, 2012; Ringrose, 2012; Thompson & Savat, 2015; Sellar, 2015).

Bradley: In terms of literacy, what are the ramifications of this approach?

Cole: In terms of literacy, in terms of building language, I've worked on two aspects of this: The multiple literacies theory, which is taken from Deleuze and Guattari, which simply put states that, within any of these learning episodes and scenarios—like making a video of these desires—there are always multiple forms of expression. You can keep on dividing this learning environment into smaller modes of analysis, until you get down to very molecular modes of desires, motivations, feelings and senses—all of which can make a difference. So it doesn't just become a question of embracing this molar desire, desire for the lecturer, de-sire for Western culture, it can become a question of who the student is, what they think, what type of submerged feelings enter into this scenario as well as the bigger cultural and social senses of what the desire means. Multiple literacies theory ap-plied to this particular scenario would look at different modes of representation, the ways in which desire can be cut up, used and thought of in different ways, es-pecially in the Japanese context. Multiple literacies theory gives you that sense that literacies aren't just about English progressing in a certain way through writing more, but rather about the regressions and ups and downs of what it means to read, write, speak and listen in different ways, in multiple ways, in English and Japanese, in hybrid Japanese-English, and according to different literacies and vocabularies that you can take or inject into this environment or that, in this expressive medium for example, from global media or from film, documentaries, videos, YouTube. It's an endless series or set of different semiotic registers and signs that can be brought in to cut up and play with the way in which desire works in the language-learning context.

Furthermore, I have worked with the idea of affective literacy which tries to locate and work with the notion of affect. In this context between the lecturer and the student, with feelings of being in love and having this sense of contact and wanting to feel close to the lecturer …… That situation is full of affect, a kind of potential, tension or energy. And that is a mode of expression as well. It's often not represented in language, it's not rational or sensible. It's hard to put down into words. But you can play with it, you can do things with it. Affects lead to other things, other interconnected emotions and senses. Not just feeling alone within that context but rather, how does the student relate to other students, how do they see themselves before or after? How do they resolve their sense of anticipation, expectation, wants, desires in the world for other people, other objects, other feelings, other emotions? Affect is about movement. It's about change, it's about thinking through the ways in which emotion and feelings and subjectivity aren't repressed or turned into diminutive senses but can really change the dynamic of the language learning situation.

Multiple literacies theory and affective literacy both work in this kind of Deleuzian sense to open up and play with and change desire, as much as (would) a work of art. If you can get to that level, you can look at the positive transformatory effects of this methodology. I suppose what you've got to do then is to take this further, to think about cinema, art, philosophy. How does that dialectic get resolved, and how can we add other complex elements to it to make it more interesting? Otherwise it can be a very clichéd type of video production. So it is a question of trying to allow the students to express themselves, to create desire, but also to relate this to the larger world in which they live, and where desire is packaged, used, and is part of the sales promotion type of culture, which again takes us away from the a-signifying semiotics.

Bradley: One of the problems with multiliteracies in my view is the under theorization of the body. Yet in your work with Diana Masny the body is a central thematic. It seems to have a very important place within your framework, and from the practice of video-making with the students over the years, what I've noticed is the way the body is used in video production, the comportment of the body, the acting, the gestures. Video is a very empowering way for them to learn language in a very real sense, which multiliteracies doesn't pick up on. I was wondering if you have any thoughts about how your theory maps that out.

Cole: Multiliteracies is based on semiotics, and phenomenology. The proponents of multiliteracies explicitly say in one of their books that they're trying to connect phenomenologically with the experience of these types of literacies. Both semiotics and phenomenology tend to diminish the power of the body. The exception to that would be someone like Merleau-Ponty. His theorization of the body is a very conscious attempt to bring the body into phenomenology. But in terms of what we get out of the students, Spinoza seems to be a better way to understand what they really do, and how important the body really is to all thought, all articulation, enunciation—their affect. It becomes an affect theory approach to understanding what is their video production, why is it important, what it means. That can be more productive than the phenomenological analysis of it.

Video Modalities

Bradley: One of the main components of video production has been the use of different literacies and modalities in the generation of video—using subtitles, images, different speeds of frames and things like that—and of course multiliteracies does pick up on this celebration of different literacies and media—but what differentiates that approach from your perspective in particular?

Cole: Yes, the multimodal. I'm not necessarily criticizing multiliteracies as being a bad approach; it is not as simple as that. I think it can be good as an introductory way into understanding how to use these different modes of representation. But it doesn't go far enough. I suppose multiple literacies theory takes you further as you can apply a more rounded material analysis. I have been theorizing this under the banner of immanent materialism recently, and really trying to get into a deep material analysis of any situation, and you can do that through video.

You have to be able to push it, you have to know where to go, and how to use it, how to analyze it. I think you need to study examples—writers, philosophers, filmmakers—who have pushed the material analysis, material forces of nature as far as they can. This gives the students the intellectual and aesthetic tools, but it gives them a conceptual ability to go further than just a banal, obvious representation. Mixing up the different genres within a film production, using collage, using different time speeds as you say, mixing up the different ways in which video can be documentary, it can be time-lapsed, it can be a memory, time can go in different directions within the same film. From all of these concepts taken from different films, different artists, different thoughts, the students can put that into their production. That for me takes it further than multiliteracies into multiple literacies theory (MLT).

Conclusion

A critique of the insufficiencies of the student-teacher dyad (the linear passage from the teacher as imparter of knowledge to the student as empty vessel) has been undertaken in this dialogue to show how at once technology and multiliteracies may contest this dynamic and at the same time engineer new forms of exploration of student identity, sexuality, race, class, and lifestyle choices. While video production may be disruptive to the aforementioned dyad it is also productive of new literacies and knowledges which the students bring into the classroom (their Outside) and which may, if wielded aptly, inspire and motivate students to reexamine assumptions about themselves, their families and communities and the wider society as a whole.

A-signifying semiotics as described in this paper is a means to redraw the flows of *capillary power* and relays of power/knowledge, which are active both inside and outside the classroom. MLT is well aware of critical feminist approaches which are concerned with relations of power and dominance in patriarchal Japan for example, but is not delimited to these parameters of analysis. In its place, MLT pinpoints languages, sub-culture, thoughts, and values underrepresented in the mainstream English-speaking classroom and reads them in terms of meaning-making. It is here that a-signifying semiotics returns to the meaning-making generated outside of the classroom which prevents breakthroughs inside. It is concerned with those minor literacies—interconnected through the unconscious—which do not assume a dominant mode. It is therefore not prescriptive and does not look to reintroduce out-of-date clichéd plans and worldviews.

References

Bangou, F., & Fleming, D. (2014). Deleuze and becoming-citizen: Exploring newcomer films in a Franco—Canadian secondary school. *Citizenship Teaching & Learning, 10*(1), 63–77.

Bradley, J. P. N. (2012). Materialism and the mediating third. *Educational Philosophy and Theory, 44(*8), 892–903.

Carlin, M., & Wallin, J. (Eds.). (2014). *Deleuze & Guattari, politics and education: For a people yet-to-come.* Bloomsbury.

Cole, D. R. (2011). *Educational life-forms: Deleuzian teaching and learning practice.* Sense Publishers.

Cole, D. R. (2012a). Latino families becoming-literate in Australia: Deleuze, literacy and the politics of immigration. *Discourse: Studies in the Cultural Politics of Education, 33*(1), 33–46.

Cole, D. R. (2012b). Matter in motion: The educational materialism of Gilles Deleuze. *Educational Philosophy & Theory, 44*(1), 3–17.

Cole, D. R. (2013). Affective literacies: Deleuze, discipline and power. In I. Semetsky & D. Masny (Eds.), *Deleuze and education* (pp. 94–112). Edinburgh University Press.

Cole, D. R. (2014). Latino families becoming-literate in Australia: Deleuze, literacy and the politics of immigration. In D. Masny & D. R. Cole (Eds.), *Education and the politics of becoming* (pp. 33–47). Routledge.

Cole, D. R., & Bradley, J. P. N. (2014). Japanese English learners on the edge of "chaosmos": Félix Guattari and "becoming-otaku". *Linguistic and Philosophical Investigations, 13*(1), 83–95.

Cole, D. R., & Bradley, J. P. N. (2015). Educational philosophy and "New French Thought". *Educational Philosophy and Theory, 47*(10), 1006–1008.

Cole, D. R., & Bradley, J. P. N. (2016). *Pedagogy of cinema.* Sense Publishers.

Cole, D. R., & Moyle, V. (2010). Cam-capture literacy and its incorporation into multiliteracies. In D. L. Pullen & D. R. Cole (Eds.), *Multiliteracies and technology enhanced education: Social practice and the global classroom* (pp. 116–133). IGI Global Publications.

Cole, D. R., & Woodrow, C. (Eds.). (2016). *Super dimensions in globalisation and education.* Singapore Springer Publishers.

Cope, B., Kalantzis, M., & New London Group. (Eds.) (2000). *Multiliteracies: Literacy learning and the design of social futures.* Routledge.

Deleuze, G. (1988). *Spinoza: Practical philosophy* (R. Hurley, Trans.). City Lights Books.

Graham, L. J., & Cole, D. R. (2012). *The power in/of language.* Wiley-Blackwell.

Kress, G. R. (1995). *Making signs and making subjects: The English curriculum and social futures* [Personal lecture]. London, UK: Institute of Education, University of London.

Masny, D. (2013). *Cartographies of becoming in education: A Deleuze-Guattari perspective.* Sense Publishers.

Masny, D., & Cole, D. R. (2014). *Education and the politics of becoming.* Routledge.

Masny, D., & Cole, D. R. (2007). *Applying multiple literacies in Australian and Canadian contexts.* Sydney University Press.

Masny, D., & Cole, D. R. (2009). *Multiple literacies theory: A Deleuzian perspective.* Sense Publishers.

Masny, D., & Cole, D. R. (2012). *Mapping multiple literacies: An Introduction to Deleuzian literacy studies.* Continuum.

Meyer, O., Coyle, D., Halbach, A., Schuck, K., & Ting, T. (2015). A pluriliteracies approach to content and language integrated learning—mapping learner progressions in knowledge construction and meaning-making. *Language, Culture and Curriculum, 28*(1), 41–57.

Nietzsche, F. W. (1967). *The will to power* (W. A. Kauffman, Ed., and R. J. Hollingdale, W. A. Kaufmann, Trans.). Random House.

Pullen, D. L., & Cole, D. R. (Eds.). (2010). *Multiliteracies and technology enhanced education: Social practice and the global classroom.* IGI Global Publications.

Ringrose, J. (2012). *Postfeminist education? Girls and the sexual politics of schooling.* Hoboken: Routledge.

Sellar, S. (2015). A strange craving to be motivated: Schizoanalysis, human capital and education. *Deleuze Studies, 9*(3), 424–436.

Thompson, G., & Savat, D. (2015). *Deleuze. Guattari. Schizoanalysis. Education.* Edinburgh University Press.

CHAPTER SIX

From Which Point Do We Begin?: On Combining the Multiliteral and Multiperspectival

Having students of beginner or intermediate proficiency think philosophically in the English language classroom in Japanese tertiary education, on postmodern or poststructural topics, might appear an impossibility for some and flatly a waste of time for others. However, this chapter contests this self-defeating assumption by proffering a content and language integrated learning (CLIL) multiliteracies approach to the problem of considering different points of view. Although having students adopt different perspectives seems fraught with difficulties, in this chapter the authors suggest ways in which various media and forms of multiliteracies may inspire students to adopt alternative perspectives and to think critically about the world at large and about their place within it. For example, how might a particular set of problems be approached in new ways by considering different genders, social classes, ages, colonial subjects and races, identities or viewpoints? How might a particular debate be informed by the perspectives of feminism, queerness, and of various subcultures and legal statuses? What are the differences between the Western, Eurocentric view of knowledge and Asian-centred or multicultural stances (cultures of the North and South)? To answer such questions, we look at how the CLIL-multiliteracies approach has been applied in a new content course entitled Japanese Society 日本の社会 at a large private university in Tokyo.

The use of a 'pataphysical dialogue in the chapter creates a space that unexpectedly, and perhaps discomfortingly, resists the tyranny of academic assumptions that dismiss any possibility of insight into ways of being and living to be gained from approaches that depart from entrenched methodologies—wherein truth is defined a priori as systemic, static, verifiable, quantifiable, and able to be abstracted in ways that allow translation into Big Data—And this in turn can be added incrementally to a teleological pyramid of progress upon which rests the academy's claim to authority over universal human knowledge. Through such a claim, the Eurocentric locus of globalization is constantly reproduced in universities throughout the world in ways that facilitate the dismissal and destruction of alternate knowledges, languages, cultures and ecologies. In contrast, the dialogic, peripatetic model applied here focuses attention on the spontaneous, the experiential, the affective, the interdisciplinary, the irreducible, the local and the dynamically communal. If we acknowledge teaching as a series of impossibly complex discrete events that can never be fully directed, designed, controlled or repeated, a state of affairs that might be acknowledged in equally creative ways to expand the range of permitted interactions in scholarly conferences and academic journals; then the turn to the dialogic model allows us to reconsider how spontaneity, creativity and emotion—as well as social position, fragmented, indeterminate experience and scale of perspective—create meaning, shaping our understanding, knowledge and behaviour. The use here of the 'pataphysical dialogic model thus puts into practice, or "performs", the multiliteracies approach that is being thematically explored. As should become evident, the ideological space created to take into account varying perspectives and structures of knowledge creates at the same time new possibilities for interactions with students of varying English levels and subjectivities. We hope to show that adult university students, even with relatively limited English ability and expression, are capable of grappling with issues that might otherwise be assumed as questions better reserved for higher levels of education.

Despite the theoretical nature of the chapter, its significance in English-mediated classrooms in the Japanese university should not be overlooked. As a market-driven model of globalized neoliberal education has risen to a position of dominance around the world, including in Japan, an instrumentalist evaluation of learning has led to the shrinking or elimination of any subject matter not easily packaged as a marketable asset of the "global human resources" considered the desired end products. In Japan, shifting a greater portion of university courses into English threatens to radically reduce the intellectual and ethical demands as well as the cultural content of higher learning. In more concrete terms, this shift results in increasing numbers of students who seldom, if ever, study history, feminism, psychology, sociology, literature, non-western cultures or non-nationalistic ethics, to say nothing of philosophy. Failure to find ways to scaffold abstract thinking into English language education may thus condemn such students to a system of learning that can be expected to produce largely ethnocentric, patriarchal, un-critical and disempowered students passively obedient to institutional and social hierarchies of power, who perceive of themselves and others primarily in terms of their latent economic value. Readers are encouraged to find throughout the dialogue alternative practical solutions to such a bleak proposition and prospect.

'Pataphysical Dialogue

The following conversation took place at a scholarly 'pataphysical meeting in Akasaka, Tokyo on July 10, 2017. It was later transcribed by B as the basis for a potential screenplay on the state of foreign language learning at the tertiary education level in Japan. The main characters in the dialogue are as follows:

A: The likeable, open hearted, "good cop" teacher.

B: The pseudonym for Joff P. N. Bradley of Teikyo University, Tokyo, Japan.

C: The irascible "bad cop" critic of experimental, critical pedagogy.

D: The pseudonym of Deleuze pedagogy expert David R. Cole of Western Sydney University, Australia.

E: The pseudonym of social semiotics scholar David Kennedy of Nihon University, Tokyo, Japan.

F: The pseudonym of Japanese literature expert Charles Cabell of Toyo University, Tokyo, Japan.

G: The pseudonym of graphic artist and assistant professor Joseph Poje of Teikyo University (Poje, 2018), Tokyo, Japan.

A: By Jove, you have changed your tune? You have been looking so glum recently, B? What has happened to you?

B: I have been trying to teach critical media studies and to ask philosophical questions in CLIL classes without much success, banging my head on the proverbial wall as it were, but I had a Eureka moment recently, so I am returning to an idea that I became very much interested in a few years ago, namely the idea of multiperspectivism and scaffolded thinking skills in the language classroom. I suppose I am reacting to what I recently found to be a deficit of explanation as to what scaffolded thinking might entail, especially as presented in Rear's chapter "Scaffolding Thinking Skills through Debate" (Breeze & Sancho, 2017), where scaffolding appears in the title but is not explored in any concrete detail whatsoever. There is material out there, such as Laura MacGregor's (2015) work at Gakushuin University in Tokyo but alas it is fragmentary. Sadly, in the Japanese context, a conspicuous lacuna haunts the practical aspect of scaffolded thinking in the CLIL classroom.

A: A Eureka moment? How intriguing! Care to explain?

B: Indulge me. I shall first introduce a CLIL module for a new, administration-led university elective on global Japanese studies held in the 2017 academic year at a private university in Tokyo, Japan. The student demographic had 30 registered students, two-thirds Japanese and the rest from other Asian countries. Employing a hybrid methodology of CLIL-multiliteracies designed to develop students' higher-order thinking skills (techniques and strategies) through the use of scaffolding techniques, lessons aimed to increase students' critical media literacy in ways that would enable them to better comprehend multiperspectivism and cultural difference. The course asked students to confront two philosophical and epistemological questions regarding (1) access to the whole "truth" and (2) the significance of the position of the subject (whether the Japanese subject, the foreign subject, the female subject, the illegal subject, invalidated subject or other formations). I wanted the students to appreciate different and changing subject positions and points of view (socially, culturally and personally). The problem was that teaching this skill in the traditional argumentative fashion (a single discursive essay) proved nigh impossible. I was forced to rip up previous methodologies on problem-solving strategies and "go multilateral and multilateral" as it were. I collated "non-argumentational discursive forms" and materials to present a philosophical idea linked to critical media literacy. This is what I call the scaffolding of thinking skills.

C: "Go multilateral and multilateral"? I have no idea what that means, and it sounds profoundly difficult. Moreover, I am unaware of the difference between the scaffolding of critical thinking skills and the scaffolding of argumentation.

A: May I interject something at this juncture? You are an exponent of the CLIL approach (Coyle, 2008; Koike, 2016) to language learning, B? This I take to mean the interweaving of content and language, or the passage from studying English to studying in English. Would I be right in thinking that? Could you enlighten us all on this and how it works with multiliteracies?

B: That is indeed true. I am interested in how to best use multiliteracies (Cole & Pullen 2010; Elsner, Helff, & Viebrock, 2013; (Herzogenrath, 2013); Pullen & Cole, 2010) in the CLIL-led language classroom in Japan (Bradley & Cole, 2016; Bradley, Hunt, & Cole, 2017). I wonder if you scholars might offer some critical advice and response regarding this model.

A: We shall do our best.

C: What is this task upon us? Critical media studies? What's that? Why teach such a subject in an English class in a Japanese university? I already see manifold problems with this approach. From which perspective linguistic or literary are you responding from?

B: Having students think philosophically in the foreign language class in Japan with respect to postmodern or poststructural issues might appear nigh impossible for some or a waste of time for others. However, I want to contest this view by proffering what I call a CLIL-multiliteracies and multiperspectivism approach to the problem of considering different points of view. I wanted the students to clarify the nature of a central problem (can we know the whole?) and to evaluate the reliability of information (what is fake news or constructed documentary views?)

C: May I ask why?

B: Why? You might well think that we all have the innate skill to be able to reason and think about the lives of those who are not of our own group, class, gender, nationality, age, and so on. You might think it is common sense and unnecessary to teach. Yet, I have found it to be otherwise, as undergraduates increasingly appear to lack the conceptual knowledge to understand different points of view, to empathize as such, or to think beyond the linguistically ingrained binaries of self and absolute other, that is to say, the Japanese and the forever foreign. Innovative lesson plans consequently are necessary to challenge such parochial forms of thinking, which often migrate unconsciously to the target language. Although at first glance and for the most part, having students adopt different perspectives (feminism, post-colonialism, classism and all the other isms) seems fraught with numerous difficulties, I have tried to set out a critical media and multiliteracies approach to the problem at hand, suggesting some ways in which various media and different multiliteracies (*mise en abyme* in art, TV commercials, film, political cartoons, film, documentaries) may inspire students to adopt alternative perspectives, and to thus think critically and laterally about the world at large. The playfulness of adopting subject positions of course is a form of lateral thinking and has some basis in Edward de Bono's work on the six thinking hats (1985). In terms of adopting different subject positions, how might different genders, social classes, ages, colonial subjects and races, changing identities and viewpoints approach a particular set of problems? How might the perspective of feminism, queerness, different subcultures or legal statuses inform a particular debate in Japan regarding marriage, racism, or exploitation? What are the differences between a Western, Eurocentric view of knowledge and Asian-centred or multicultural stances? Is this division no longer valid? How stable are these received identities and distinctions? How might a fluid or fragmented sense of identity better explain the current realities of Japan and the world we are living in at present? I must admit I have come up against numerous theoretical cul-de-sacs in this pedagogical task but I continue to challenge colleagues and students alike with the question: Is it possible to understand the whole?

C: By Jove, that is a lot to take in all at once; it needs unpacking, but I admit it's thought-provoking. How do you start to teach such a thing?

B: I have been inspired by Nick Sousanis, the graphic artist whose dissertation was set out entirely as a graphic narrative. Are you aware of it? It is now published as *Unflattening* (2015) by Harvard University Press. In it, Sousanis says the following remarkable thing: "Nothing changed, except the point of view—which changed everything" (Sousanis, 2015, p. 33). I was most intrigued by this idea.

Sousanis has explained to me his rationale for engaging with Deleuze and Guattari. He writes: "I can say I found Deleuze and Guattari's ideas resonated well with how I was thinking about comics and the way they could hold separate fragments together in something cohesive (something comics theorist Thierry Groensteen discusses in his work), and at the same time, I found the difficult nature of their writing as potentially ideally, suited for comics. That is, they are talking about rhizomatic structures and doing so in an inherently non-rhizomatic form, whereas comics could let them make the connections in a more natural way (comics support fragments and connections). I tackled very little of their work, but I like the idea of addressing it deeply through the form and seeing where that goes" (private communication).

F: The Copernican Revolution is a great example of how the warp and woof of our lives are shaped by the point of view we adopt. To take a case from Japan in the 1940s, novelist Sakaguchi Ango (1947/1990) referred to how fixed perspectives can control us through "the march of history" (p. 93). Academics nowadays might favor an expression such as "dominant discourse", but it is basically the same thing. Ango felt that he and other Japanese regained their humanity when defeat at the end of WWII shattered their adherence to a belief in self-abnegation under the Emperor system. He was skeptical that the Japanese, or any humans for that matter, could live for long without constructing some dominant perspective that would control the thoughts and behavior of members of society. Yet he also appeared to hold out hope that we could resist social control by fully embracing our humanity.

C: You lost me there!

F: OK let me help. Please imagine. If you travel through time or space or history, or just look around you, you'll encounter countless people dressing, speaking, behaving and thinking in ways that you would never emulate. Why? Because you're (fill in identity position here such as a "proper lady", "professor" or "German"). Without realizing it, you've allowed codes of belief and conduct that adhere to your identity position to curb your ideas and behavior in ways that rule your life.

C: Well, what if I'm happy with my identity and don't want to dress like some 19th century cowboy?

F: That is actually not a bad state to be in because, as you're undoubtedly aware, philosophers and theologians alike often remind us that we cannot love others unless we first love ourselves. Media scholars, on the other hand, warn us that much advertising is designed to make us feel anxious and insecure; so if you're happy, you're ahead of the game! Even those of us who find a way to be happy with who we are, however, must heed the ethical demand to listen to others.

C: Can you walk that back a little and explain what you mean by an ethical demand?

F: Just what I was getting to. As we come to a greater understanding of how we are shaped by our personal history, our family, our class, our gender, our culture, our community, our ethnicity and our sexual orientation, we realize that we see the world differently from others. The closer our identities approximate to what I have called the dominant discourse of our society, the more power accrues to us and the more difficult it becomes for us to listen to and acknowledge the voices of minorities. Maintaining a sense of difference from them may be a key psychological mechanism by which we justify to ourselves our relative privilege. When we fail to heed their challenges to our dominant perspectives of the world, however, we unknowingly add to their oppression by sustaining hierarchal systems that ignore their suffering or contribute to it. Let's take a look at a couple of examples to help clear things up. Consider the case of an educated, wealthy white American man who lives comfortably in New York City. Can he hope to understand without tremendous effort the perspectives of an American Indian family in North Dakota protesting an oil pipeline being built across their traditional homeland? The man may invest in the corporation that's destroying their community. Unless he's made the effort to hear their voices, he won't notice or, even worse, he won't care. To change location, consider a man in Tokyo who enters into a discussion among Japanese girls about the experience of being groped on trains. Unless he makes a similar effort to understand their perspectives, he may focus only on the chance that someday he may be falsely accused. He may fail to educate his son on the irreversible trauma often suffered by those who are assaulted, or worse, he may casually engage in surreptitiously molesting a woman himself when he feels he won't be uncovered or that she won't dare report him. Without striving to listen deeply to what people in different social positions tell us, we may end up harming not only them but ourselves as well.

C: How so?

F: We live in a time of globalization when financial structures are endowing corporations with the ability to produce goods as cheaply as possible and sell them around the world with few or no regulations. The public sphere is being privatized, corporations are paying fewer taxes and the financial sector is being deregulated. The point I am trying to make is that this economic system, which results in extreme inequality, would not be possible if we actually grasped the perspectives of those whose lives are destroyed by it. What's more, we are not only destroying the lives of people around the world, we are destroying our very own planet. The belief that we can persist in a system that brings incredible suffering to great masses of people if only it brings wealth to the few is dooming us. Now, more than ever we need to see the world as Copernicus saw it and when that happens we will have no choice but to act, to resist!

A: That's exceedingly interesting but let me return to graphic narratives for a moment to clarify your point. I know Sousanis's work too. I see what you mean now. Could you say this is a paragon of multiliteracies?

C: Multiliteracies? I am lost again. Do explain.

Multiliteracies

D: Let me step in here. Multiliteracies is a theory of literacy (i.e., reading/writing/speaking and listening) from the 1990s, that takes into account the changing nature of literacy, given, for example, the emerging digitally mediated modes of communication. Multiliteracies is a form of semiotics, that is, it analyzes the signs and symbols of this new communications environment, and relates it to pedagogy and the design of social futures.

B: I do believe Sousanis's work is a good example. It has a very interesting Deleuzian perspective regarding the sense of change and the notions of perspective and event.

D: From the multiliteracies perspective, this is an example of visual literacy, with its own set of symbols and signs involved with understanding how this visual literacy works. However, Sousanis goes further than merely presenting an example of visual literacy. His work attempts to analyze the ideas from within, something that one can do as a comic strip creator. As such, one could say that this work is philosophical, and specifically, Deleuzian.

C: A Deleuzian perspective? I am lost again. Could you unravel some ideas briefly?

D: The Sousanis cartoon goes beyond a mere representation of ideas or semiotics of visual literacy. He deliberately plays with the format of the comic strip, the ideas that are being presented, the perspective as to who is doing the drawing, and the possible interpretations of his work. This philosophical approach to representation most closely adheres to a Deleuzian position. Though this position involves too many parts to completely explain here, it is worth mentioning my multiple literacies (Masny & Cole, 2009, 2012) and cinema (Cole & Bradley, 2016) work in this area. Both of these projects attempt to bring educational approaches closer to the chaos of nature, and move away from the predominantly human-only bias in education. Similar to the work of Sousanis, this expansion of perspectivism in education is a rational attempt to make us think anew.

C: How does this apply to the language classroom and the CLIL classroom in Japan in particular, B?

B: I am interested in how to teach complex content which stimulates and motivates students, literally to the point of shaking them out of their media-intoxicated slumbers and stupor. I am opposed root-and-branch to the teaching of the lowest common denominator of content, that is to say, the content which reinforces all manner of racist, national and sexist stereotypes, and which stops students from thinking critically. The philosopher Bernard Stiegler (2015) captures the *Zeitgeist* and calls this the proletarianization of knowledge. I thought long and hard about the question of their subjectivity or, let me put it like this, what the "production of subjectivity" (Guattari, 2013, p. 1) might signify as a means to that end. We also invoked here Deleuze and Guattari's (2011) concept of the line of flight, which can be described as a connection that occurs between self and others (Deleuze & Guattari, 2011). But I had to think of how to scaffold this critical thinking approach in the CLIL class. I have been considering how scaffolding critical thinking strategies can motivate and enhance language learning. The question arises: How can we better balance scaffolding language, complexity and cognition, the latter of which I take to mean the thinking skills used to understand content (solve puzzles, reflect on learning)—(Bradley, 2015; Bradley, Hunt, & Cole, 2017)? Given the breakdown in the understanding of different conceptual strategies (feminist, post-colonial, postmodern) by the students, in the end I thought it proved vital for me to scaffold and prioritize cognition. However, because of time and the purpose of the course itself which was to teach content (modern Japanese society through documentary and film—both historical and contemporary), I could not examine at length theoretical concepts such as psychoanalysis, post-structuralism, post-modernism, cultural theory, post-colonial theory—concepts which can be used to effectively address issues such as identity and subjectivity. I had to rethink the use of non-argumentative forms. So my goal was to design conceptual scaffolding techniques and strategies in the CLIL classroom.

C: I am still struggling, could you say a little more about the connection between CLIL and multiliteracies and how it works in practice?

B: I believe the teacher should provide multimodal input in the CLIL class as much as possible because this is a means to foster different learning styles and skills in language learning. This aspect of the multimodal aids the development of new multiliteracies. The use of texts, video, commercials, documentary, film, poetry, Japanese Ukiyo-e (浮世絵), graphic novels and cartoons act as a kind of input-scaffolding. For the students to begin to discuss critically the role of the contemporary media (authentic materials), it demanded a scaffolding of concepts to enable them to comprehend the input. In the CLIL class we used an array of tasks (translation from Japanese to English, analyzing poetry and Ukiyo-e and their semantic connections, analyzing the question of fake news through TV commercials), to bolster higher-order thinking skills and authentic communication in different interactive formats (solo work, pair work, group work). The nature of the output was decided collectively as a class, with some students opting for poster presentations, others for workshop-style group activities, quizzes, video or standard PowerPoint presentation. In addition, I required a compulsory English composition. Once the tasks were agreed upon, the nature of output-scaffolding had to be designed as well. This proved relatively successful in that the methodology fostered academic language proficiency as well as learner autonomy, development of learning skills and collaborative engagement. The use of TV commercials, for example, a key component of the CLIL classroom, gave the students access to authentic language while encouraging critical thinking and higher-order cognitive skills. Finally, the CLIL class on different points of view was meaningful in the way it raised issues about the complex, media-inflected lives of the students themselves.

C: Goodness gracious me. The class sounds very experimental.

B: Perhaps so. However, I am of the view that effective CLIL classes functioning in a new paradigm of teaching and learning have to be experimental and thoroughly creative. Otherwise they may struggle to meet the design goals. On this point, I took inspiration from Michael Peters, a philosopher of education, whose embrace of "non-argumentational discursive forms" and remarks on Ludwig Wittgenstein's style(s) of thinking promoted me to tear up the format of the content class and start again by approaching language-learning and critical thinking questions from a pedagogical point of view. I have the quote in mind at hand. It is from a chapter entitled "Philosophy as Pedagogy: Wittgenstein's Styles of Thinking", in which Peters (2013) contends: "[Wittgenstein's] styles are… essentially pedagogical; he provides a teeming variety and vital repertoire of non-argumentational discursive forms—pictures, drawings, analogies, similes, jokes, equations, dialogues with himself, little narratives, questions and wrong answers, thought experiments, gnomic aphorisms and so on—as a means primarily to shift our thinking, to help us escape the picture that holds us captive" (pp. 12–13).
        I was taken aback by the way he suggests the necessity to shift thinking, to escape "the picture that holds us captive". This resonated a great deal with the graphic representations of Sousanis. I think it is necessary to combine the theory of teaching and the acquisition of English with the reality of its practice in the classroom. That would be the applied linguistic approach, I suppose. Using multiliteracies and authentic materials such as film, TV commercials, as well as graphic-form books and cartoons would be the literature aspect, albeit in a non-argumentational form.

A: I am aware that Wittgenstein is reported to have said that "a serious and good philosophical work could be written that would consist entirely of jokes" (Malcolm, Wittgenstein, & Wright, 2001, pp. 28–29). One imagines that this is consistent with Sousanis's interesting idea that Deleuze and Guattari's writing lends itself to being presented in comic, graphical form (Sousanis, 2015, p. 161).

B: I wasn't aware of that. That's an interesting point.

C: I have some further questions. I would like to know *how to do* a CLIL class. It is important to address here the educational and pedagogical implications for language learning and teaching through multiliteracies media. Please explain in concrete terms what you do in your multiperspectivism class because at the moment this is all terribly abstract!

B: Allow me to list the multiliteral resources I have used to demonstrate the necessity to adopt different points of view. Given my location in Japan and teaching a content class on Japanese society we began the thinking process with the Ukiyo-e print of Hanabusa Itchō (英一蝶, 1652–1724). It is typically called "Blind monks examining an elephant" (衆瞽探象之圖). This I used to entice students into thinking about its meaning

This was later coupled with the poem "The Blind Men and the Elephant" by John Godfrey Saxe (1816–1887), adding an important comparative cultural and historical perspective. We looked at how this story is expressed in a wide variety of literature in India and the Middle East.

A: I am familiar with this tale: it is about blind men each having a dogmatic opinion and particular perspective on the nature of the thing before them which they cannot see. It concludes with a reflection on differences and unity of parts and the whole.

B: Again using non-argumentational discursive forms in Wittgenstein's sense, from here we addressed the questions "What is the nature of postmodern media?" Concretely undertaken, we used the following award-winning TV commercials made for The Guardian newspaper: (1) *Points of View* (Weiland, 1986); and (2) *Three Little Pigs* (Ledwidge, 2012). In terms of the first, and before showing the commercial, I showed the students 20 frames taken from the commercial. This is what I designated a movie map (Bradley, 2015). Students created meaning from these frames, discussing the meaning of the flow of images, and working on the tense (this is a scaffolded language exercise). In any case as the TV commercial is for the most part silent it gave the students ample opportunity to generate language and meaning. Students then discussed the representation of youth in the scene and the unconscious assumptions and prejudices which are manifested by the frames, which we later applied to different contexts. G has some comments on how cartoons and graphic representations can help us to see things differently. He redrew Weiland's advert in graphic form

G: Thank you for inviting me to the discussion. My contribution is an attempt to create a graphic representation of the *Points of View* commercial. My first attempt was to approach the drawings as a storyboard for a scene in a movie or TV program. I tried using the original 20 frames B used in his lesson to create 8 drawings and condense the story but keep it as true to the commercial as possible. I copied the same three camera angles as in the commercial. It wasn't until I was halfway finished that I realized I was creating a storyboard for something that had already been storyboarded! I wasn't bringing anything different to the story except that it was in pen and ink.

After watching the commercial again, I decided to add some closeups and different camera angles. In panel three I portray the woman reacting with a bit of fear in her expression and in panel four relief and curiosity after the skinhead runs past her. In the final image the intent of changing the angle from above the businessman is to show a closeup of his face realizing the danger that he was saved from.

Using cartooning also places the focus on the central elements of the story: the characters, setting and props (the falling bricks). The backgrounds of the street, buildings, and cars are simplified or removed to focus on the story. The graphic representation shows the same narrative as the video but gives the observer a more involved experience regarding the characters' experience. The artist could also make the images more simplified and still convey the same experience; the observer would still be invested in the story.

B: Wow, that's incredibly fascinating. So cartoon representations can fathom emotions in a different way than moving images can.

A: Could you explain a little more about the commercial?

B: The commercial features a skinhead who appears intent on seizing a man's briefcase. The changing point of view of the camera reveals that he is in fact trying to rescue the man from falling bricks. The intent of the commercial is to act as a metaphor for understanding the truth, for getting at the truth. As for the language learning, I translated the statement (see Appendix) at the end of the short commercial into Japanese and the students translated it back into English. Before comparing the translation with the original, we did a listening exercise using the following voiceover dialogue: "An event, seen from one point of view gives one impression. Seen from another point of view it gives a much different impression. But it's only when you get the whole picture, you can fully understand, what' going on."

We then discussed the question: is it possible to understand the whole? This provides the philosophical context of the class in conformity with the class goals. Updating the exercise on different points of view, I used the 2012 commercial *Three Little Pigs* again by The Guardian. In this commercial the image, text, and audio all operate on an equal level, which reinforces the necessity for a multiliteracies dimension to language learning. As the story itself is different from the original, students were compelled to address wider social, economic and political issues in the U.K. regarding the housing mortgage crisis and fraud. In the clip, the different points of view raised across languages by users of online media (Facebook, Youtube and traditional media outlets) with different identities allowed the students to raise questions about the creation of "fake news" or simulacrum of the truth (fake news was the word of the year in 2017 according to Collins Dictionary). I again raised questions about access to the "whole truth". To undergird this point, I turned to Alfred Hitchcock's comments on the use of montage images as a way to create different meanings (Merton, 2009) and of course the majestic *The Birds* (Hitchcock, 1963) to explore the bird's-eye shot or gaze. Moreover, as our focus was on Japanese film and documentary during the course, we addressed the Rashōmon effect.

E: The Rashōmon effect? What is that?

B: This effect occurs when the same event is given contradictory interpretations by different individuals involved. The effect is named, of course, after Akira Kurosawa's film Rashōmon (羅生門; Kurosawa, 1950), in which a murder is described in four mutually contradictory ways by its four witnesses (The events of the film are based on the short story *In a Grove* by Ryūnosuke Akutagawa). Similar to Weiland's Points of View commercial, this proved heuristic in explicating the motivations, mechanisms, and occurrences of reporting an event. In other words, it addresses the essentially contested interpretations of events. Anderson (2016) describes it as "the naming of an epistemological framework—or ways of thinking, knowing, and remembering—required for understanding complex and ambiguous situations" (p. 250). There is also the film animation adaptation of the parable—*The Dermis Probe* (Williams, 1965). In the animation, inspired by a tale found in the Sufi collection of rhymed spiritual couplets known as Masnavi (Rumi, 2001) by Persian mystic Rumi (ca 13th century), a team of scientists debate the nature of an unknown material. Rumi's poem itself is a retelling of a story found in *Enclosed Garden of the Truth* (ca 11th century) by philosopher-poet Hakin Majdud Sanai of Ghazna (ca 11th to 12th century), which focuses on the mechanisms of learning and possibilities for cultural understanding (Sanai, 1910). There are many other examples of this idea too that we can find in modern science, and in Buddhism and Hinduism. In science there is Werner Heisenberg's famous view that "We have to remember that what we observe is not nature in itself, but nature exposed to our method of questioning" (Baggott, 2011, p. 109).

A: We have been talking about different points but I have a question on how to get at the truth "behind" multiple points of view. How would you demonstrate that as a form of scaffolded thinking?

B: As you know I have been using Harold Pinter in my classes. Pinter (2005) sets out his attitude on telling the truth in his Nobel Prize speech "Art, truth and politics". We hear the insistence that language is a kind of regime of order words, cliché and hearsay, often deployed to keep thought at bay and to maintain the status quo (Bradley, 2014; Chiasson, 2017).

Thoughts and counter-thoughts happen but language hides them from exposure. It is a question of truth and the maintenance of power. The public, for Pinter, is acquiescent in the maintenance of this status quo. What surrounds us, he insists, "is a vast tapestry of lies, upon which we feed" (Pinter, 2005, p. 10). He concludes his speech by discussing the role of the writer, suggesting the metaphor of the mirror. He writes: "When we look into a mirror we think the image that confronts us is accurate. But move a millimetre and the image changes. We are actually looking at a never-ending range of reflections. But sometimes a writer has to smash the mirror—for it is on the other side of that mirror that the truth stares at us" (Pinter, 2005, p. 21). Again this was consistent with the CLIL class goals of appreciating different points of view through and by using authentic literature.

C: How did you demonstrate this in multiliteracies terms?

B: We have used Pinter's short dialogue entitled *Apart From That* (Pinter, 2014a, 2014b), made shortly before his death, the BBC radio play *Mountain Language* (Pinter, 2014a, 2014b) and the original text, as well looking at his Nobel prize speech.

C: Thank you for the detailed explanation but let us return to the meta-questions that were raised in terms of the TV commercial's effect on the students.

B: From here we discussed the decline of free speech in Japan. How fake news is verified or contested, the manipulation of the public at home and abroad and the dangers of fake news, propaganda in documentaries. We examined U.S president Trump's use of Twitter. In terms of the changing contours of stereoscopic thinking, we looked at numerous multiliteral forms. For example, the Esper Photo Analysis scene in *Bladerunner* (Scott, 1982).

C: Could you possibly explain further?

B: I cannot recall in their entirety many of the conversations I had when I was a university student but there is one which sticks in my mind. I was speaking to a chemistry student who was indifferent to everything other than passing his course. Watching *Bladerunner* on video, we got into a conversation about the Esper Photo Analysis scene. Because he was a scientist I asked him innocently if such a technology existed. He replied negatively and said that it would never be realized. Those words uttered in 1991 seem somewhat off the mark nowadays as we can perform such rudimentary tasks of microscopic analysis on even the simplest photo-editing software on our PC or smartphone. I discussed this view with my students and this anecdote helped again to germinate questions about perspectives and points of view influenced by changes in technology, which can reimagine things otherwise, or destabilise and reverse the structures of relationships we adopt unthinkingly. We looked at Eames and Eames's (1977) short documentary, *Powers of Ten*, and this led to questions of the transphenomenal and metaphysical expressed in science fiction films like *Fantastic Voyage* (Asimov, 1966: Kleiner & Fleischer, 1966) the American science fiction film directed by Richard Fleischer and written by Harry Kleiner, based on the story by Otto Klement and Jerome Bixby. As you may know, *Powers of Ten* explores orders of magnitude or the relative scale of the universe. The universes that are explored are cosmic and microscopic in scale as both points of view look out to the heavens and inward of the human body until it reaches a single atom and the quarks observed. At micro and macro levels, *Powers of Ten* explores the Copernican revolutions of scale in human thinking, which underscores what F was arguing for. It demonstrates that earth-centred or anthropocentric thinking is just one mode of thought in a universe which for all intents and purposes has no centre.

C: OK, I am beginning to get this. Is there any theory which lies behind this regarding the sense of the production of subjectivity?

Production of Subjectivity

A: Might I interject at this juncture? Yes, there is indeed some very excellent work in this area. I would guide you to the recent chapter by Derek Woods on zoom and scala entitled "Epistemic Things in Charles and Ray Eames's Powers of Ten" (Clarke & Wittenberg, 2017). Woods writes of the movement of the zoom and scala across the textual. This, I think for B's purpose is a kind of textual multiliteracies: across cinema, graphic forms, visual literacies and media technologies. This, Woods says, shapes the "collective possibilities of imagination". His comments with respect to Félix Guattari are very interesting. He writes (Clarke & Wittenberg, 2017) "The broad archive of texts that use smooth zoom and scala to represent movement across scales constitute a process of subjectivation, in Félix Guattari's sense of shaping the collective possibilities of imagination in relation to social assemblages and the nonhuman environment. As these texts spread through the populations they reach, they interact with human bodies to create new forms of subjectivity. Subjectivity in this sense distributes across the media technologies and aesthetic forms that support its development across time. How we interpret it depends on the relation of text and epistemic thing" (p. 71).

Woods argues that the movement across scales constitutes a process of subjectivation. I suppose for our purposes this means that students can constitute a different point of view and different identities through changes in zoom and scala. They can generate alternative conceptual maps and recognize the existence of alternate maps. From this they can make changes to ways of thinking, which they unconsciously inherit through language and culture. The process demonstrates the contingency of one's own map of the world.

C: By Jove, that is interesting. I wonder if the *mise en abyme* is applicable here.

B: Yes, I think you are getting it. I have used a postmodern cartoon entitled "I don't get it" to demonstrate how the *mise en abyme* raises questions of where the original point of view begins and ends.

As you know *mise en abyme* is a literary concept (in our case pictorial) denoting a part of a work that resembles or is identical to the whole. It makes a double of the work within the work. In the cartoon's case, this double is reproduced ad infinitum. In the classroom, it allowed students to ask questions about the play of mirrors and multiple identities, and of virtual selves—images within images, stories within stories—again a very postmodern motif. The cartoon is very effective in provoking students to think about their relation to the cartoon and their perspective, location and situation.

A: By Zeus you're right; that's a thought-provoking way to raise questions about the role of the active, decentred, postmodern viewer as a participant in the narrative and creation of meaning. But one thing conspicuously missing from this is—semiosis.

Semiosis

C: Semiosis? Just when I thought I was getting on top of things. Not another word I don't know. Help!

B: Ah well, Professor E might help us out. I know he has been listening in. Do you have a moment to explain how semiosis might work here?

E: I do. One of my ideas is to have students create meaning in a *semiosic* way through a kind of puzzle architecture—that is, they evaluate a number of artifacts in different modalities to address questions of multiperspectivism. Students learn to piece their own semiotic puzzle together, compare with other students, and then reassemble. And then do it again. It's a kind of archaeology of contemporary society, if you will. There never is a single "correct" analysis. This is a really stimulating way of integrating authentic content from a variety of sources into a "language learning" classroom.

B: You said semiosic, not semiotic. Care to explain?

E: Semiosis has to do with meaning-making. It is a term coined by the American pragmatist philosopher Charles Sanders Peirce, who posthumously became recognized as one of the founders of the field of semiotics, or the study of signs and their significance. The other figure, who is somehow better known, was Ferdinand de Saussure. To simplify massively, Peirce's semiotics differs from Saussure's in his inclusion of an *interpretant* in the making of meaning. The *semiotic object*, Peirce would say, is not "as it is", but "as it is to me" (cited in van Lier, 2004, p. 91). So meaning is not simply a static correlation between an object and its signifier, but is in a constant state of flux. The semiotic relationship is first shaped by the person interpreting it, and then further modified by other people through social interaction, which in turn spawns new semiotic relationships. And on and on infinitely. This process is what Peirce called "semiosis", the making of meaning.

B: So learning is always up in the air?

E: Yes and no. In my view, we obviously share (or *think* we share, which might be the same thing anyway) common ideas about what something means. Without this we would have no way of communicating or creating cultures.

This shared semiosis is central even to our phylogenetic evolution. Human civilization is built on these understandings. There's a fantastic little book by Thomas Sebeok (2001) called *Signs: An Introduction to Semiotics* that describes the expansion of this "biosemiosis" into the social realm. Despite such historical continuity, however, and without getting too Derridean about the endless deferral of meaning, we have to keep in mind that semiotics—our understanding of signs—is never a settled matter. It is always and forever under negotiation. And these negotiations are, I think, an essential part of education.

B: Can you explain more about semiosis and education?

E: It's pretty simple, really. To understand "the world" is to first understand that the world is made up of myriad interpretations, perspectives, and experiences. Education is the place where these "multinesses" are allowed —or better yet, encouraged—to come up against each other, sometimes in agreement, and sometimes in discord. This is a social practice, and it is messy. Van Lier (2004) situates this social process of meaning-making at the "interconnections between the contexts that we create by our own activity and the contexts that are created by others, in which we find ourselves, either by design or by accident" (p. 40). Quite a bit like the conversation we've all been having here, isn't it?

B: And on that note I think it is time to move to the conclusion.

Conclusion

English pedagogy conducted in Japan by international teachers, who are conspicuously different in ethnic appearance from their primarily Japanese students, is haunted by irony. The apparent embodiment of cultural and linguistic alterity by such teachers inevitably reifies feelings of homogeneous nativism among their students. In other words, their presence as cultural and linguistic "others" reproduces the prejudiced assumptions that they loathe to encounter in everyday life in Japan. The role they are asked to play in the Japanese university is to confirm their ontological status as eternal aliens, detached from everything Japanese and perceived as incompetent in tasks requiring "native" knowledge, language and cultural awareness. Their English instruction renders them invisible residents, unwilling mirrors reflecting feelings of exceptionalism back onto Japanese, effectively closing students off from the multiperspectivism opened up in B's course.

How could one smash such a mirror to bits in Pinteresque fashion, throwing students' received wisdom about national and linguistic identity into doubt and fragmenting the lazily adopted "truths" on which identity positions rest? The 'pataphysical dialogue (Jarry & Edwards, 2001) employed here suggests that the solution does not lie in berating students or arguing them into imaginary submission. B rather lovingly spoons out dollops of multimodal honey to entice his flies away from their comfort zones before taking them on a non-discursive flight that destabilizes their perspectives, opening up new ways of seeing the world. Students are led not to a new perspective, but to a new way of thinking about perspectives. To put it differently, multiliteral, multiperspectival learning experiences break down ingrained binaries to produce new subjectivities. Truth becomes contingent in the unflattened world of B's classroom.

Attuned readers will have noted the ease with which the multimodal approach to scaffolded thinking can be applied to English learners of low to intermediate ability and above. Experienced foreign language teachers should have little trouble creating level-appropriate lessons around concrete images such as those found in graphic drawings, film frames, commercials and videos. What is in question, however, is their willingness to embark on such an endeavor. Is higher learning destined to be dumbed down as the Japanese university transfers increasing portions of education into English? This chapter has demonstrated that this need not be the case. By deploying scaffolded thinking exercises based on an approach grounded in research on multiliteracies and multiperspectivism, learning experiences that deal with highly complex philosophical questions related to epistemology, ontology and semiotics can be incorporated into classes with students with low to intermediate English skills. Negotiating the understanding of signs should be an essential part of every education, including language education.

Appendix

1 つの視点から見た場面は1つの印象がある。印象は観点によって異なる。 しかし、すべてを完全に理解するのは、全体を見たときだけである。

Translated from Points of View (1986), directed by Paul Weiland.

References

Anderson, R. (2016). The Rashomon effect and communication. *Canadian Journal of Communication, 41*(2), 250–265.

Ango, S. (1947/1990). Darakuron [On Decadence]. In M. Yasutaka (Ed.), *Darakuron* [On Decadence] (pp. 91–102). Kadokawa Bunko.

Asimov, I. (1966). *Fantastic voyage*. Bantam Books.

Baggott, J. E. (2011). *The quantum story: A history in 40 moments*. Oxford University Press.

Bradley, J. P. N. (2014). Pinter: Held incommunicado on the mobile. *Dialogos, 14*, 51–81.

Bradley, J. P. N. (2015). Pleasurably bepuzzled: CBI/CLIL and film. *Forum of the Center for Teaching and Learning, Teikyo University, 2*, 19–38.

Bradley, J. P. N., & Cole, D. R. (2016). On multiple literacies and language learning: Video production and embodied subjectivities. In F. Y. Sim & M. Brooke (Eds.), *ELTWO: Special issue on 5th CELC symposium* (pp. 94–105). Centre for English Language Communication, National University of Singapore.

Bradley, J. P. N., & Cole, D. R. (2017). CLIL-multiliteracies-multiple literacies theory: On the passage from active viewing to active filmmaking. *STEM Journal, 18*(2), 179–202.

Breeze, R., & Sancho, G. C. (2017). *Essential competencies for English-medium university teaching*. Springer International.

Chiasson, B. (2017). *The late Harold Pinter: Political dramatist, poet and activist*. Palgrave Macmillan.

Clarke, M. T., & Wittenberg, D. (Eds.). (2017). *Scale in literature and culture*. Palgrave Macmillan.

Cole, D. R., & Bradley, J. P. N. (2016). *A pedagogy of cinema*. Sense.

Cole, D. R., & Pullen, D. L. (Eds.). (2010). *Multiliteracies in motion: Current theory and practice*. Routledge.

Coyle, D. (2008). CLIL-A pedagogical approach from the European perspective. In N. H. Hornberger (Ed.), *Encyclopedia of language and education* (pp. 1200–1214). Springer.

De, B. E. (1985). *Six thinking hats*. Little, Brown.

Deleuze, G., & Guattari, F. (2011). *A thousand plateaus: Capitalism and schizophrenia* (B. Massumi, Trans.). London: Continuum.

Eames. C., & Eames, R. (Producers). (1977). *Powers of ten: A film dealing with the relative size of things in the universe and the effect of adding another zero* [Documentary]. Northeast Historic Film.

Elsner, D., Helff, S., & Viebrock, B. (2013). *Films, graphic novels & visuals: Developing multiliteracies in foreign language education: An Interdisciplinary approach*. Lit.

Guattari, F. (2013). *Schizoanalytic cartographies* (A. Goffey, Trans.). Bloomsbury.

Hitchcock, A. (Director). (1963). *The birds* [Motion picture]. Universal.

Jarry, A., & Edwards, P. (2001). *Adventures in 'pataphysics* (A. Melville & P. Edwards, Trans.). Atlas.

Kennedy, D. H. (2013). A social semiotic approach to content-based (language) learning. *Dialogos, 13*, 97–126.

Kleiner, H., & Fleischer, R. (Producers). (1966). *Fantastic voyage* [Motion picture]. Twentieth Century-Fox.

Koike, A. (2016). Promoting CLIL in higher education in Japan. *Journal of Development Studies, 19*, 69–76.

Kurosawa, A. (Producer). (1950). *Rashomon* [Motion picture]. BFI Video Pub.

Ledwidge, R. (Director). (2012). *Three little pigs* [Television commercial]. BBH London. Retrieved from https://www.theguardian.com/media/video/2012/feb/29/open-journal ism-three-little-pigs-advert.

MacGregor, L. (2015, November 14). *CLIL: Poster presentation*. Poster session presented at the 41st Annual International Conference on Language Teaching and Learning & Educational Materials Exhibition (JALT), Shizuoka, Japan.

Malcolm, N., Wittgenstein, L., & Wright, G. H. (2001). *Ludwig Wittgenstein: A memoir.* Oxford University Press.

Masny, D., & Cole, D. R. (Eds.). (2009). *Multiple literacies theory: A Deleuzian perspective.* Sense.

Masny, D., & Cole, D. R. (2012). *Mapping multiple literacies: An introduction to Deleuzian literacy studies.* Continuum.

Maturana, H. R., & Varela, F. J. (2008). *The tree of knowledge: The biological roots of human understanding.* Shambhala.

Merton, P. (Producer). (2009). *Paul Merton looks at Alfred Hitchcock* [Motion picture]. BBC.

Peters, M. (2013). *Educational philosophy and politics: The selected works of Michael A. Peters.* Routledge.

Pinter, H. (2005). *Art, truth & [and] politics.* Illuminations.

Pinter, H. (2014a). *Apart from that.* Bloomsbury.

Pinter, H. (2014b). *Mountain language.* Bloomsbury.

Poje, J. (2018). *The Guardian, points of view* [Original artwork].

Pullen, D. L., & Cole, D. R. (2010). *Multiliteracies and technology enhanced education: Social practice and the global classroom.* Information Science Reference.

Rumi, J. (2001). The elephant in a dark room. In E. H. Whinefield (Ed.), *Masnavi i ma'navi: Teachings of Rumi* (E. H. Whinfield, Trans., p. 185). Omphaloskepsis. Retrieved from http://rumisite.com/wp-content/uploads/ Masnavi-English.pdf

Sanai, H. (1910). On the blind men and the affair of the elephant. In M. J. Stephenson (Ed.), *Enclosed garden of the truth* (M. J. Stephenson, Trans., pp. 13–14). Baptist Mission Press.

Scott, R. (1982). (Director). *Bladerunner.* [Motion picture]. Warner Bros.

Sebeok, T. A. (2001). *Signs: An introduction to semiotics* (2nd ed.). University of Toronto Press.

Sousanis, N. (2015). *Unflattening.* Harvard University Press.

Stiegler, B. (2015). *States of shock: Stupidity and knowledge in the twenty-first century.* Polity.

Thomsen, H. (2003). Scaffolding target language use. In D. Little, J. Ridley, & E. Ushioda (Eds.), *Learner autonomy in the foreign language classroom: Teacher, learner curriculum and assessment* (pp. 29–46). Authentik.

van Lier, L. (2004). *The ecology and semiotics of language learning: A sociocultural perspective.* Kluwer Academic.

Weiland, P. (Director). (1986). *Points of view* [Television commercial]. Boase Massimi Pollitt. Retrieved from https://www.youtube.com/watch?v=E3h-T3KQNxU

Williams, R. (Director). (1965). *The Dermis Probe* [Animation, short]. Richard Williams Animation.

Becoming

Japanese English Learners on the Edge of Chaosmos: Félix Guattari and "Becoming Otaku"

How do Japanese university students learn English in Japan? Research in this field (see Gorsuch, 2001) has uncovered a host of communicative approaches, which have prioritized how English pronunciation, grammar, spelling and vocabulary have been rendered comprehensible and learnable to the Japanese subject. This paper will put forward a new approach to teaching English in Japan based on identity politics (Norton, 2000) that is mediated through the philosophical lens of Félix Guattari, and which determines the detailed subjective transformations that the Japanese learner encounters as primary to the language teaching and learning process (Kubota, 1999; Miyahara, 2000; Gilmore, 2011). Rather than positing a process of English learning on and through the Japanese learner, this study looks within the broad scope of Japanese society for learning, and at the break out points and ways in which Japan has "taken on speed" (Deleuze & Guattari, 1987, p. 268) in terms of the morphogenesis of learning values, for example, due to the affordances of technology and globalization, sometimes understood as "superdiversity" (Vertovec, 2007; Blommaert & Rampton, 2011) and "supercomplexity" (Barnett, 2000). The focus of this chapter is on the ways that language learning in Japanese society is accelerating, and how changes have come about due to the multivariant influences of technology and capitalism (see MECSST, 2002), here understood as the "chaosmos", which is defined as a composed chaos pregnant with inaugural virtuality, but one consistent with semiotic influence. Traditional Japanese connections to nature through the practice of Shinto, the native religion of Japan, now coexist alongside advanced technological innovation and global capital markets. These pressure points are access routes to forms of 21st century Japanese subjectivity and how they are presented in the contemporary context. The traditional collectivity and expression of what it means to be Japanese is undergoing a prolonged identity politics, enhanced and enacted with digital technology and capital flows (cf. MECSST, 2000). English teaching and learning in Japan must allow for and negotiate with these changes in the Japanese mindset, if the content and style of English education in Japan are to be in any way meaningful.

Embedded within recent changes to Japanese subjectivity, and which should be taken into account by a "social-cultural-affective" theory of language learning, is the nature of the English teacher. The introduction of the French theorist, Félix Guattari, into this role is in many ways a radical and playful move, which specifically questions the ways in which Japanese society conceives and respects "the teacher". The roles of the teacher and student can be reversed (according to Guattari)— through a reconsideration of the semiotic and autopoietic nature of the classroom (see Cole, 2010, 2011). Power is henceforth an attribute of the group. There are interlocking planes between the teacher, knowledge, students and learning, and these are opened up by and through exploring the unconscious (see Guattari, 1984a, 1996b). This is why this paper specifically names learning as a Japanese "*becoming-otaku*": "The otaku, the passionate obsessive, the information age's embodiment of the connoisseur, more concerned with the accumulation of data than of objects, seems a natural crossover figure in today's interface of [English] and Japanese cultures. I see it in the eyes of the Portobello dealers, and in the eyes of the Japanese collectors: a perfectly calm trainspotter frenzy, murderous and sublime. Understanding 'otaku-hood', I think, is one of the keys to understanding the culture of the contemporary world," (Gibson, 2001, p. 23). The "becoming-otaku" as learning in this paper is not an alternative means to the current English learning methods in Japan, but designates the non-representative politics and affect that this study translates into pedagogy via Guattari (see Azuma, 2001, 2009; Bradley, 2012). The English teacher's role henceforth involves working with and through the flows of desire that emanate from and in the collective Japanese audience. For example, mobile phones can be employed to navigate the educational consequences of "MSpace" (see Cole, 2012), the international fashion industry can be interrogated for the latest trends in Japanese style, the ways in which manga is read and produced can be used for English literacy purposes (see Cole & Yang, 2008). The students "become-otaku" as they engage with lessons that are guided by Guattarian pedagogy and are empowered in their learning to realize hidden and mute parts of their identities (otaku).

Félix Guattari and Language Learning

Although Félix Guattari was not a traditional linguist, in his writings, both alone and with Gilles Deleuze (Deleuze & Guattari, 1987, pp. 75–111), there is a sustained and important engagement with language through "material semiotics"—influenced by Hjelmslev, Peirce, Labov among others—and which shall be taken forward in this paper with respect to the identity politics of university English learners in Japan. The starting point for understanding Guattari's approach to language is that one cannot understand language "in-itself", as mere form only. Rather, comprehending the ways in which the language works comes about through looking at the multiple material codings of language use that a culture or society exhibits (cf. Genosko, 2008). Guattari proposed a non-signifying, a-signifying linguistics, and a pragmatics of language, that studies in depth the controls and limitation that language presents, not just in words, but in signs, images, gestures, sounds, implications, meanings and in the collective articulation of desires through identity. The idea of group enunciation, which is in contrast to individualized or subjective learning, was of paramount importance to Guattari, as he analyzed psychiatric units for the ways in which they functioned and related to mental health issues:

> There is a dimension opposite and complementary to the structures that generate pyramidal hierarchization… this dimension can only be seen clearly in certain groups which, intentionally or otherwise, try to explore the meaning of their praxis and establish themselves as subject groups. (Guattari, 1984b, p. 23)

The point here is not that we should liken language learning to psychiatric treatment, but that there is a complementary dimension to all learning that acts as a marker to allow group dynamics to work (Guattari, 1984b). The Japanese university language learners are paradoxical with respect to this promotion of the group as subject, in that they do not exhibit the ego and power-based subject hierarchies that Guattari was attending to at the *La Borde* psychiatric unit (Guattari, 1984b). Rather, the Japanese learners have a collective consciousness, based on a long history of Japanese tradition and hierarchy. This "Japaneseness" could work against the articulations of the group subject, in that the abandonment of the teacher as an authority figure in the Japanese hierarchy is unimaginable for many Japanese students. Rather, the naming of *becoming-otaku* as learning should encourage assemblages as Deleuze and Guattari (1987, p. 71) name them, which are social and political, and inclusive of non-human gatherings of forces, and that deal with the ways in which power permeates and is distributed in and by the identity politics of the group. In the context of Japanese students learning English at university, which could be reduced to a subjective performance or a passive collective rite, seen as necessary in the context of globalization, the production of the assemblages add direction and weight to group functioning. An example to use in this context might be the recent international manifestations of the "Occupy" movement (see Masny & Cole, 2012). The Japanese students could analyze and discuss what has happened with respect to the Occupy movement, and come to a group consensus that relates to the relevance of Occupy and its potential for understanding economic-spatial dynamics. Japanese students could assess their job prospects, *raison d'etre* for life at university and views from abroad regarding perceptions of Japan as a cold, death-in-life war machine (see Bradley & Cole, 2014).

The manifestation of assemblages in places of higher education as groups of learners with political messages is complexified and augmented by the use of new technology (Masny & Cole, 2012, pp. 149–179). Guattari was an activist, who founded a free radio station, and who deliberately took his intellectual concerns out of the academy and onto the streets (see Genosko, 2002).[1] This movement of thought is exemplified and accelerated by what is happening today with social media and mobile devices that have produced a ubiquitous "MSpace", whereby connectivity to electronic networks is flexible, transversal and potentially liberating (Guattari, 1995a). For example, much of the organizational work of the Occupy movement is performed online and through social networks that allow agents permanent connectivity and camouflage (Masny & Cole, 2012, p. 156). The Japanese students can organize around relevant "social-political-affective" issues such as the nuclear accident at Fukushima after the 2011 tsunami.[2] The point of the exercise is to deploy networks in meaningful and ecologically focused ways—in this case, to understand the full extent of nuclear contamination. The students can share information and map the places of contamination and explore the known and possible consequences of the nuclear disaster. The group of nuclear investigators are henceforth learning language through an engaging and relevant affective-cultural project. In other words, the students are a technological assemblage, enacting knowledge on a discursive and local level that will be of direct relevance to the future of Japan and how it functions in the "chaosmos". The point isn't that words mean more than before or have to lead to para- or meta-linguistic performance (cf. Cole, 2011), but that the group as subject now has a voice that overrides the particular concerns of individual English speakers. Another example of Guattarian pedagogy for Japanese English learners and an application of Guattari's non-signifying semiotics exists in the arrows in airports:

The airport's arrow is an asemic figure … to read the semiotic technologies of the airport itself. The arrow is both a tool and a trope for the imperatives of global transit: it turns place into passage, striates space into controlled flows, and urges the traveller to 'move on.' It is a point sign that leads the way to a consideration of the technologies, both semiotic and a-semiotic, that provide the navigational and behavioural guidance that is increasingly in evidence, not only at the airport but in all public spaces. (Fuller, 2002, p. 231)

The ways in which one reads and learns in an airport is a good example of the educative and philosophical experiences Guattari proposes. The meaning of the arrow—a type of controller of space, telling us where to go, what to do and how to get to where we are going. The airport arrow does nothing but sit in a predesignated spot, herding us into channels and creating flows. The airport arrow is not a metaphor, but, along with other signs on roads, in cities, or on the internet, is now an important part of our lives as we are increasingly herded and shuttled around public and private spaces by spectacular and cybernetic signs (Fuller, 2002). The point is to openly read and discuss these signs, and not let them become an uncritical part of our unconscious. In *A Thousand Plateaus* (1987), Deleuze & Guattari use the term order words, which are critical markers for the ways in which language works with and through the fields of power that one may encounter. The order words set up regimes of enunciation, assemblages of thought and virtual ways in which incorporeal transformations, or non-human becomings take place in and through the identity politics that the order words initiate. For example, it could be argued that we are turned into cyborg travellers in airports, obeying the signs without thinking or understanding what these actions do to our bodies. Guattarian pedagogy asks us to unpack the signs, to make maps of their influences, and to regain conscious control of ourselves in order to once again be able to use affect in depth transactions and in the "joy of living".

Guattarian pedagogy is fundamentally about excavating the presuppositions contained in identity to get to the "art of life". In the context of teaching and learning English in Japan, this means looking in detail at how the transformation of cultures in-between the East and the West is occurring and has occurred over the last decades. This clashing of cultures produces in Guattari's (1996a) terms, a form of "indirect discourse" that permeates the classroom, and activates unconscious markers that infiltrate the affective atmosphere through the order words as mentioned above. The great danger with this project as part of English language teaching and learning in Japan is that the concentration on conflict might reinstate anthropomorphic humanism, or put into place a centralisation and resubjectivation contained in the clashing of cultures. Such a subjectivating effect would have a negative impact on the classroom and the group because the students could henceforth react against English culture and mores, and centralize their characters and group identity on reactive "Japaneseness", rather than process the point of impact as dynamic articulation and the movement of affect as put forward regarding "becoming-otaku" in the "chaosmos". For this reason, the Guattarian notion of the machine is vital to ward off the reinstatement of protective humanism involved with notions such as "Japaneseness", and to keep alive the plane of otaku-becoming that generates the transversality, creativity and interaction which we are searching for in pedagogy with and through the otaku. Guattari explored notions of the machine such as the abstract machine (1996a) to work through and against a humanized notion of the self, and in particular with reference to "a-signifying" machines:

> [A]-signifying machines continue to rely on signifying semiotics, but they only use them as a tool, as an instrument of semiotic deterritorialization allowing semiotic fluxes to establish new connections with the most deterritorialized material fluxes. These connections function independently of whether they signify something for someone or not. (p. 150)

A-signifying machines are present as fluctuating, unstable, rhizomatic structures in discourse, and are present in the ways in which conversations start, evolve and finish (see Cole, 2011). The a-signifying machine provides break out points and connections between meaningful instances that define dialogic progression and relationships with "the other." In the example of Japanese students learning English at university, one could say that the other is the unresponsive student, unable to process the Guattarian pedagogy and identity politics as proposed by this paper. A route into the psychology of the potentially closed student, and the ways that they could be subjectivated by the expectations of Japanese schooling and obeying authoritarian lines of flight (see Cole & Hager, 2010) is through dance. The student who has been conditioned into robotic and predictable responses by schooling, and is not open to the experimentation of investigating conflicts between East and West as a machine, could potentially be opened up by dance:

> This suggests to me the position of a Butoh dancer such as Min Tanaka when he completely folds in on his body and remains nevertheless hypersensitive to all perceptions emanating from the environment. But more simply it will suffice to remark here that we see such intrinsically structured objects every day and that they do not work with the exterior environment any less. (Guattari, 1994b, p. 133)

The othered student has been turned mute by the conditioned environment and the machinic influences of the Japanese education system and culture in relation to the "chaosmos". Yet there is, simultaneously, opportunity here, as this othering can be explored and unpacked, or perhaps the internalization of learning mores is an interiority that can lead to art. Butoh dancing is an art form that inspires a form of aesthetics of silence, or understanding of how muteness is also an extreme type of listening and sensitivity to the aural environment. Deleuze and Guattari (1987) analyzed the works of Franz Kafka and Samuel Beckett in this context. Literature that includes such minor becoming would be useful in teaching Japanese students English in Japan. The next section of this paper takes the philosophy of Guattari and applies it to technology and language learning.

Guattari, Japanese Language Learners and Technology

Guattari (1995a, p. 97), who was concerned with the ambiguous effects of technology on subjectivity and thought, conjectured that the era of the digital keyboard would soon be over. Quite presciently, after its demise, humans would speak into their machines rather than type in instructions. As a critic of the political abandon of postmodernism, and a witness to the sweeping techno-scientific mutations already underway in the early 1990s, Guattari envisaged the emergence of new social, political, aesthetic and analytical practices aiding the production of transversalist plural and polyphonic subjectivities in the "chaosmos", which he saw as liberated from the shackles of empty speech and any ensuing erosion of meaning, e.g. by introducing "becoming-otaku" for the collective language learning practises of Japanese students. Guattari was opposed to the mass media's "infantilising subjectivity" (Guattari 1996b, p. 272), and to what he termed as the will to "neuroleptise subjectivity" (Guattari, 1996b, p. 215), that is to say to make subjectivity treatable by antipsychotic drugs. Guattari described how the textuality of machinic ontology decentres the idea of the subject and moves the emphasis to the question of subjectivity and its production in semiotics. This focus has clear pedagogical import for Japanese language learners at university as processes of subjectification permeate, work upon and transgress the "subject"—for better or worse. Aspects of life traverse the "subject" and are constitutive of memories, desire and the mind. As such, this transversal relay and operation is relational, network specific and affective in nature. Guattari argues that it is impossible to consider such machinic evolution in any simple binary fashion—that is to say either straightforwardly positively or negatively—because one must, first of all, situate its articulation within *collective assemblages of enunciationa*—in the case of this chapter, Japanese students at university, their "becoming-otaku" and in relation to the "chaosmos". Communication and information devices produce subjectivities on both signifying and affective registers, prepare new modulations of expression, and engender "new universes of reference". These universes are what Pierre Lévy (2001) describes as "dynamic ideography". Guattari foresaw the emergence of a post-media era, in which informatic subjectivity is capable of breaking writing away from old script forms to inaugurate hypertextualities, or new cognitive and sensory writings. For Genosko (2002), Guattari breaks fresh ground in thinking the shift from scriptural semiotics to hypertext and is thought-provoking in explicating the nature of a-signifying part-signs and how they function in relation to the machinic phylum. For Guattari, "unprecedented" plastic universes offer the possibility of new modes of living as well as more deadends: "more death-in-life, more of the same from the *steamroller of capitalistic subjectivity*" (1995a, p. 91). Through the prism of the ethico-aesthetic paradigm, Guattari saw potential in tearing asunder the relation of sign and signified in identity construction, in deterritorializing the domain of signification to approach the plane of machinic consistency, in leaving behind a free-floating sign adrift of context and territory, and in the context of this chapter such a movement in thought involves "becoming-otaku" in the "chaosmos". Whence coupled and connected with other a-signifying signs, Guattari saw the possibility of generating and being creative with material flows and fluxes.

On the matter of the machinic phylum, or technological lineage, and the machines to come, Guattari (1995a) argues that the universe of reference pertaining to the word-processing machine *completely* changes humanity's relationship to expression—whether it is in writing, the alphabet, printing, computing, image banks or telecommunications. As machines inform universes of reference, Guattari (1995a) claims that students learning languages with a word-processor are thereby situated in incipient universes of reference, which are distinct cognitively and affectively from previous formats. It follows that students attuned to use new media and technological devices are learning in singular universes of reference. Enthused by this idea, Guattari in a short piece entitled *On Machines* (1995b) suggests that the "autopoietic" and "hypertextual" position of the machine possesses a pragmatic potential to challenge "the ontological iron curtain"—also an expression deployed by Lévy (2001)—in separating the subject and things. The notion of the machinic phylum is made clearer here by understanding the futural way in which different generations of machines open up the lines of machinic alterity and virtualities of other machines to come. As a general trend, computers and technologies aid learning through connectivity—for example, a Japanese English student unable to speak in English can connect with machines through online multigame environments. Here, the Japanese student forges a subjective composition according to the consistency of different online gaming assemblages, and he or she henceforth engages with "becoming-otaku" in the "chaosmos". Each new technical machine carries latent possibilities to transform existential territories and engender new universes of reference. In other words, the mechanosphere, represented here by the virtual multigame, constantly reengineers the situation as the Japanese student learns English through gaming and articulates through this gaming context.

Writing in the late 1980s and early 1990s, Guattari goes so far as to claim that humanity, sited at an "unavoidable crossroads" (Guattari, 1995b), must confront its fetish with technology to extract the positive momentum from it or risk entering into cycles of repetition of a more deathly variety—the being of the machine in inertia, or a machine in nothingness. While balking at a romantic return to some form of primate territoriality, Guattari (1995b) claims it is important to think the mechanosphere through the prism of "meta-modelization", as this model does not signify as such, but rather produces "diagrams". Such a move aids the understanding of *agencements* in ontological heterogeneous universes, in which allopoeitic machines, built from the outside in, and, autopoietic, self-creating machines—"live together in the chaosmos". Comprised of the ontogenetic, which pertains to the developmental history of an organism within its own lifetime and phylogenetic elements—the evolutionary history of a species—technological machines are caught in a "phylum", that is to say, preceded by some machines and succeeded by others. New universes of reference can help reorganize existential corporeality and promote creative possibilities, but they are equally at risk of being appropriated by the peddlers of the "deadening influence" (Guattari, 1995b, p. 5), i.e. the mass media. For Guattari (1995a, 1995b), the vital question is how to escape the repetitive impasses so as to resingularize singularity, which is here termed through learning about "becoming-otaku". Guattari envisaged a post-media era affirming the reappropriation and re-singularization of the use of media. But the question arises: How does one extricate oneself from the perceptual fascination with the luminous, "overexposed" (Crary et al., 1988), almost hypnotic animations on our TV screens, computer screens or tablet devices?—a question also discussed by Sylvère Lotringer (2009). To paraphrase Virilio in *War and Cinema* (1989), weapons are tools not just of destruction but also of perception. Moreover, they are stimulants in chemical and neurological processes, which affect human reactions and the perceptual identification and semiotic differentiation of objects. We read or decode images and composites of mental imagery in the "blink" of an eye. This is important, because, according to Lotringer (2009), were it not for the "blink", TV viewers would become so intimate with the present noological field, that they would hallucinate images in the "chaosmos". While the explanation for such phenomena is partly found in understanding the refrain that fixes the subject in front

of the screen, Guattari (1995b) argues that computers, expert systems and artificial intelligence also contribute to, assist, and relieve thought of redundant or
inert schemas. Furthermore, computer-aided design can lead to the production
of images opening onto unprecedented plastic universes, and enabling Japanese
students of English to study technologically mediated modes of expression as
"becoming-otaku".

Whereas Guattari in his book *The Three Ecologies* (1996b) welcomes the
"technological development of mass media, especially their miniaturization, the
lowering of their costs, and the possibility of using them for non-capitalistic ends"
(p. 65), he nonetheless warns of the "age of planetary computerization" (p. 103)
which is seemingly accelerating headlong into an era of "a monstrous reinforcement of earlier systems of alienation, an oppressive mass-media culture and an
infantilising politics of consensus" (p. 103), and these statements define the ambi-
guity of technology in the chaosmos. The obverse of this is, for Guattari (1996b),
to view forms of thought assisted by computers as laden with mutant possibilities,
relating to universes of reference such as rap music, and the modulations, variations and the becomings of minor patois and creoles. In corollary, further questions
that one needs to ask with respect to the Guattarian-based identity politics of
Japanese university students learning English with technology are: (1) How and
why do events take place when groups wire themselves to machines in terms of
identity, subjectivity and learning? (2) How does the engrossment in "machinic
funk" and addiction to machines lead to social reclusion (hikikomori), and to a
kind of tearing away of consciousness, a *Zerrissenheit* of subjectivity or absolute
dismemberment?[3]

Conclusion

Guattari's (1984a, 1995a) two-fold messages about the effects of the mass media
and the machinic enslavement from watching too much TV or surfing the internet without critical intent, are relevant and concise with respect to the Japanese
university English language learners. The students at university use technology
to communicate their messages about the stimulus material to learn English in a
manner that is driven by the "political-social-affective" energies of the assemblage.
The groups of students became assemblages through the mediation of mobile and
technological devices, with the idea of communicating their responses and when
mobilizing their desires in what may have been perceived by them as external
forces. This is where the "becoming-otaku" comes to the fore, and the character
traits of the Japanese—such as the ability to organize themselves effectively in

groups, and to effectively use sophisticated, technological means for communication in complex manners—is an aid and benefit in terms of English language learning. This aspect of the study is in opposition to, for example, writing a set piece, the English essay as an assessment exercise, or completing an English examination based on linguistic understanding. The Japanese university students progress in their studies due to the hybrid mixture of intercultural communication, technological mediation, the affective and conflictive stimulation of the material (affect) and an identity-based understanding of "Japaneseness" with respect to the assemblages produced and the pedagogy deployed. The quality of "being Japanese" is understood here not in terms of an essential attribute of the subject, or a form of "resubjectivation", but as being able to handle the potentially alienating and disavowing influences of capitalism, here termed as the "chaosmos". In other words, Guattarian pedagogy trusts the strength and reserves of the Japanese collective character to overcome the effects of contemporary everyday life. The Japanese subject is encouraged to overcome any negative influences that may have been thrust upon them by chaotic yet universal globalization and the individualistic and competitively driven task of learning English, and to surge ahead in terms of the contiguities of affect, technological networked augmentation, and the transversal means to become a coordinated underground of effective, Guattarian, "otaku agents".

Notes

1   Guattari was also interested in the free radio movement in Italy and Japan. See Tetsuo Kogawa's Translocal website: http://anarchy.translocal.jp/guattari/index. html.

2   On the notion of Guattari and technological devices as mediating thirds connecting the individual, school and community see Bradley (2012).

3   A particularly striking example of an obsession with English testing and social reclusiveness is Takehiko Kikuchi, a self-classed hikikomori, who scored a maximum 990 points in the Test of English for International Communication (TOEIC), an international English test for non-native speakers, 27 times.

References

Azuma, H. (2001). *Dōbutsukasuru posuto modan: Otaku kara mita Nihon shakai*. Tōkyō: Kōdansha.

Azuma, H. (2009). *Otaku: Japan's database animals*. University of Minnesota Press.

Barnett, R. (2000). *Realising the university in an age of supercomplexity*. The Society for Research into Higher Education & Open University Press.

Blommaert, J., & Rampton, B. (2011). Language and superdiversity. *Diversities*, *13*(2), 1–23.

Bradley, J. P. N. (2012). Materialism and the mediating third. *Educational Philosophy and Theory*, *44*(8), 892–903.

Bradley, J. P. N. (2013). Is the otaku becoming-overman?. 東洋大学人間科学総合研究所紀要, *15*, 115–133.

Bradley J. P. N. & Cole, D. R. (2014). On conjuring the pea-and-thimble trick. *Journal of Engaged Pedagogy*, *13*(1), 1–9.

Cole, D. R. (2010). The reproduction of philosophical bodies in education with language. *Educational Philosophy and Theory*, *42*(8), 816–829.

Cole, D. R. (2011). The actions of affect in Deleuze: Others using language and the language that we make… *Educational Philosophy and Theory*, *43*(6), 549–561.

Cole, D. R. (2012). Doing work as a reflection of the other: Notes on the educational materialism of Deleuze & Guattari. In D. R. Cole (Ed.), *Surviving economic crises through education* (pp. 165–182). Peter Lang.

Cole, D. R., & Hager, P. (2010). Learning-practice: The ghosts in the education machine. *Education Inquiry*, *1*(1), 21–40.

Cole, D. R., & Yang, G. Y. (2008). Affective literacy for TESOL teachers in China. *Prospect*, *23*(1), 37–45.

Crary, J., Feher, M., Foster, H., & Kwinter, S. (1988). *Zone 1*. Urzone.

Deleuze, G., & Guattari, F. (1987). *A thousand plateaus: Capitalism & schizophrenia II* (B. Massumi, Trans.). The Athlone Press.

Fuller, G. (2002). The Arrow—directional semiotics: Wayfinding in transit. *Social Semiotics*, *12*(3), 231–244.

Gibson, W. (2001, April 1). Modern boys and mobile girls. *The Observer*. https://www.theguardian.com/books/2001/apr/01/sciencefictionfantasyandhorror.features

Genosko, G. (2002). *Félix Guattari: An aberrant introduction*. Continuum.

Genosko, G. (2008). A-signifying semiotics. *The Public Journal of Semiotics*, *2*(1), 22–35.

Gilmore, A. (2011). "I Prefer Not to Text": Developing Japanese learners' communicative competence with authentic materials. *The Modern Language Journal*, *91*(1), 15–30.

Gorsuch, G. (2001). Japanese EFL teachers' perceptions of communicative, audiolingual and yakudoku activities. *Education Policy Analysis Archives*, *9*, 10–10.

Guattari, F. (1984a). Fromanger, 'la nuit, le jour. *Eighty Magazine*, 62–69.

Guattari, F. (1984b). *Molecular revolution: Psychiatry and politics*. Penguin Books.

Guattari, F. (1994). The architectural machines of Shin Takamatsu (T. Adams & C. Howell, Trans.). *Chimères*, *21*, 127–141.

Guattari, F. (1995a). *Chaosmosis: An Ethico-aesthetic Paradigm*. Indiana University Press.

Guattari, F. (1995b). On machines. *Complexity*, JPVA 6, 8–12.

Guattari, F. (1996a). Semiological subjection, semiotic enslavement. In G. Genosoko (Ed.), *The Guattari Reader* (pp. 141–148). Blackwell.

Guattari, F. (1996b). *The three ecologies*. Athlone Press.

Guattari, F., & Rolnik, S. (2008). *Molecular revolution in Brazil.* Semiotext(e).

Kubota, R. (1999). Japanese culture constructed by discourses: Implications for applied linguistics research and ELT. *TESOL Quarterly, 33,* 9–35.

Lévy, P. (2001). *Cyberculture.* University of Minnesota Press.

Lotringer, S. (2009, Oct. 31). *Paul Virilio: The itinerary of catastrophe* [Lecture]. The New York Academy of the Arts, United States.

Masny, D., & Cole, D. R. (2012). *Mapping multiple literacies: An introduction to Deleuzian literacy studies.* Continuum.

Ministry of Education, Culture, Sports, Science and Technology (MECSST). (2000). *The education reform plan for the 21st century: The rainbow plan.* http://www.mext.go.jp/english/topics/21plan/010301.htm.

Ministry of Education, Culture, Sports, Science and Technology (MECSST). (2002). *International exchange and cooperation: Promotion of foreign language education.* http://www.mext.go.jp/english/org/exchange/10b.htm

Miyahara, A. (2000). Toward theorising Japanese interpersonal communication competence from a non-Western perspective. *American Communication Journal, 13*(3), 20–34.

Norton, B. (2000). *Identity and language learning.* Longman.

Vertovec, S. (2007). Superdiversity and its implications. *Ethnic and Racial Relations, 29*(6), 1024–1054.

Virilio, P. (1989). *War and cinema: The logistics of perception.* Verso.

CHAPTER EIGHT

Becoming-Literature: Deleuze and the *Craquelure*

Zigzagging across literacy, the literary and literature, break-through and break-down, cracking times and the crack-up, processes of becoming, transformation and dead-ends, I endeavor to introduce the "image" of literature developed by French philosopher Gilles Deleuze (1925–1995). As we shall see, reading and writing literature will be considered a question of transformation or becoming—a fragmentary process, always haphazardly in the midst of things, and importantly, destined for "a missing people," for those "yet to come" as Paul Klee and Franz Kafka are wont to say. The point to be made is that teaching transformation or indeed the transformation of teaching ought not to be construed as the sole preserve, or militant pursuit, of sad pedagogues, as a dogmatic indoctrination thrust upon pre-formed identities, but rather a curious happening—serendipitous even, in-between—part of a process of creative involution or entangling, forming a block of sensation on which its own lines of experimentation run "between" the terms in play and beneath assignable relations—a-parallel evolution, a becoming other for the other: transformation and experiment as a futural orientation, a line of flight without destination or inclination. Where this creativity or transformation begins or ends is bracketed from the outset to avoid dogmatic determination. Why? Like children's play, the love of literature—how machinic bodily desire affirms the joy of reading and writing—implies the impossibility of forecasting how things will work out, for good or worse. Hence, we shall refrain from declaring that some becomings are more preferable than others. For some this a perilous ethical gambit but for others it is a risk worth taking. Against the familiar approach of: "*Grow up! There is only one model for reading and writing. And it is the one I decree!*" perhaps it is better to pause for reflection when challenged—in my view unethically and fascistically—to choose between the becomings which emerge from reading the sacred texts of this or that literature or those becomings which take on a real material and machinic order during "play." This is a question of the innocence of becoming and *amor fati*. The trajectory of this paper therefore suggests—through a stark reading of schizoanalysis[1]—that it is only in pushing through or accelerating delirium or schizophrenia *qua* process that creativity can become unleashed from repetitive, immiserating cycles of commodification, consumption and exchange.

Let's start with three quotes which will serve as guides. The first two are by Deleuze. The first reads: "The ultimate aim of literature is to set free, in the delirium, this creation of a health or this invention of a people, that is, a possibility of life" (1997, p. 4). The second: "Learning a foreign language means composing the singular points of one's own body or one's own language with those of another shape or element, which tears us apart but also propels us into a hitherto unknown and unheard-of world of problems. To what are we dedicated if not to those problems which demand the very transformation of our body and our language" (2001, p. 241)? The first makes a direct link between health and literature and "the people to come." The second says learning is founded in and through what is beautifully described as a "voluptuous apprenticeship of the senses" (Cole, 2012, p. 4). From this point of view, and concerning the image of thought as such, the learning process *qua* semiotic inquiry takes place "in and through the unconscious" (Deleuze, 2001, p. 165) because only that can be considered the true engine of desire. The third quote is from Bernd Herzogenrath, Professor of American Studies at the University of Frankfurt, who, while discussing the films of David Lynch argues:

> There is an almost "ethical imperative" to devote time and energy exactly to such works of art that challenge and subvert the "mainstream" (of thought), that experiment with other than the established ways of seeing, thinking, and feeling. (p. 199)

From these quotes certain observations can be derived, one of which is that "we"—as *privileged* deliverers of truth—teach not to "liberate" wretched, repressed souls but to create and transform ourselves and others through an embodied, affective pedagogy. This view is derived from a schizoanalysis of the unconscious, which, contra the dogmatic and caricatured readings of the psychoanalysis of Freud and Lacan, has little truck with pre-formed structures or outcomes. But this perspective, while sharing the intellectual genealogy of schizoanalysis, also attempts to think afresh the material problems facing young people in our contemporary age.

Through the prism of Multiple Literacy Theory (MLT) developed within the singular and collective works of Masny and Cole—the so-called "third way" between New Literacy Studies and multiliteracies—I shall outline the *intensive* rather than extensive nature of reading literature, undertaking an *applied Deleuzianism* in the field of education, to account for the conception of reading and writing as *processual, transformative* and indeed *deterritorializing*—described elsewhere as "the breaking up of order, boundaries and form to produce movement and growth" (Sutton, 2008). Inspired by Deleuze's transformational pragmatics (Semetsky, 2013, p. 220), which combines the work of John Dewey and Paulo Freire, the event of reading is encountered as an uncanny and experimental one, that is to say, a singularity. Intensive or machinic reading assesses how texts work, what they produce, "for me" or "for us," akin to what the English poet and novelist Malcolm Lowry says of his own work: "it's anything you want it to be, so long as it works" (qtd. in Deleuze & Guattari, 1983, p. 119). Of course, while reading is a fundamental component of learning and education, reading, here, has less to do with esoteric, philological exercises obsessed with signifiers and signifieds, and is more of an opening to the world rather than a dogmatic representation of it. Put in the words of Deleuze, it is like extracting from texts a power, a revolutionary force.

Perhaps there are two ways of reading a book. The first one searches for essential and stable subjectivities, the interiority of the author and so on. The other is interested in experimental perspectives. This second point of view considers the book as "a little non-signifying machine" (Deleuze, 1995, p. 8)—text as part of a wider extratextual vitalist practice. One picks up a book and discovers how one can connect with it *machinically,* how one can hook up with one's life-world, immediate environs, existential comportment. If nothing is produced, so be it, one tries another book. Thinking the book as part of a wider, complex set of assemblages that continuously connect, bifurcate and combine leads to a more emergent pedagogy. There is nothing to explain, understand, or interpret; it is more a matter of simply plugging into an electric circuit. It is a question of what works, and the *work* which must be done together as a praxis of thought. This second, intensive way of reading differs from the first as it questions how a book operates hydrodynamically, which is to say that writing and reading become *a flow* or "delicious flux" as D. H. Lawrence insists. Writing enters into relations of "current, countercurrent, and eddy with other flows" (Deleuze, 1995, p. 8). Writing and literature are affairs of becoming (*devenir*), unfinished, always in process and *in situ*, a metamorphosis, as Deleuze says. Why? Because, as Deleuze insists, *l'ecriture* itself is metamorphosis.

Similarly, we could describe the *intensive way of teaching* in terms of contact with the outside. This intensive format is "a flow meeting other flows, one machine among others" (Deleuze, 1985, p. 9). If reading through experimentation and affectivity is embroiled in the maelstrom of life—amidst events that are alien to the stifling prose, and idle, pious talk sometimes found in imperial edicts—the reader may extract joys and affects and, for Deleuze, this transformative reading is affirmative, joy-ous, in love with life—after all, *what else is there?*

Although a philosopher by trade, Deleuze was passionate about this experimentation with thought and the love of teaching. On the subject of his own classes, he says his seminars were akin to "moving matter" like music, "with each group taking from it what suits them at the time" (qtd. in Dosse, 2010, p. 354). Taking a slightly skew-whiff view regarding the notion of intensity, and, as T. S. Eliot says of genuine poetry—that is to say, it *communicates* before it is understood—Deleuze says there is no difficulty in understanding the ideas in books because "concepts are exactly like sounds, colours or images" (Deleuze & Parnet, 2002, p. 10); they are intensities which either suit or do not. The reader simply takes from the encounter what enhances his or her everyday materiality. And through the micrological, imperceptible comportment of the body, what is affected can be a new spring in one's step, a change in worldview. What is incorporated then is what enlivens, what embraces the secret of *joie de vivre*. This way of reading grants to the book the ontological equivalence of art, a record, play, film or TV show. Literature in the form of film or philosophy is a distinct embodied thought process. In this radical democracy of objects, the pragmatic question pertains less to significance or place in the pantheon, and more to how literature works, what thoughts or feelings manifest—what sensations and perceptions interact with the body—or what transforms, often imperceptibly. Perhaps we can put the point thus: Writing does not emanate from the self-assertion of a rationally ordained, pre-fabricated, shrink-wrapped subject, but rather involves its eviction and dissolution. It is thus a process of emptying out the "I," "opening it up to possible encounters with a number of affective outsides" as Rosi Braidotti says (qtd. in Parr, 2010, p. 310). Explaining the point, Braidotti writes: "Writing is an orientation; it is a skill that consists in developing a compass of the cognitive, affective, and ethical kind. It is quite simply an apprenticeship in the art of conceptual and perceptual colouring" (Parr, 2010, p. 311). On this very point, Deleuze would interject to insist that "great" writing and aesthetics whence wedded in a variety of domains, can go beyond the world of the everyday:

The great aesthetic figures of thought and the novel but also of painting, sculpture, and music produce affects that surpass ordinary affections and perceptions, just as concepts go beyond everyday opinions. (Deleuze & Guattari, 1994, p. 65)

The great novelist is thus an artist who invents "unknown or unrecognized affects and brings them to light as the becoming of his characters" (Deleuze & Guattari, 1994, p. 174).

Humming *ritornellos*

Becoming-literature can be described as a *ritornello* or refrain; one hums it in a *collective agencement of enunciation* as one becomes-otherwise, in that moment of imperceptible metamorphosis. This becoming-otherwise is what the philosophers also call becoming-nomadic, a desire of the self as a process of transformation, a desire for *qualitative* transformations as Braidotti claims. The reader draws short-term *ritornellos* from the literary canon to make intensive reading *an experience of difference*—an uncanny encounter, as the event never passes where one thinks, nor along the rightful prescribed paths. In *A Thousand Plateaus*, Deleuze and Félix Guattari describe the refrain—which they claim is *their own* fully-fledged philosophical concept—thus: "The refrain moves in the direction of the territorial assemblage and lodges itself there or leaves … *We call a refrain any aggregate of matters of expression that draws a territory and develops into territorial motifs and landscapes*" (Young, Genosko, & Watson, 2013, pp. 254–255). Explaining the importance of the concept in Deleuze and Guattari's philosophy, Deleuze answers the question "do you think you have created any concepts?" posed by Didier Eribon in an interview entitled *We Invented the Ritornello*, thus: "How about the ritornello? We formulated a concept of the ritornello in philosophy" (2006, p. 381). And in the essay *On Philosophy*, Deleuze continues: "We tried to make the ritornello one of our main concepts, relating it to territory and Earth, the little and the great ritornello" (1985, p. 137).

Like hairline fractures across molar aggregates of job, school, family, sexuality, the *ritornello* is that little tune—"tra-la-la-la"—sung when one moves in a territory. This is performed when solace is sought in the dark or when one travels—again this is about transformation and the problem of deterritorialization (one can stand or sit still to do this); it is about understanding what one becomes when one reads—what powers are intensified.

Taken into our context here, refrains are at work when students read and think. Let me try to explain this with an example from Leander and Boldt's research on youth multiliteracies (2013). In the case of Lee, a 10-year-old Japanese American boy, in love with manga, martial arts, all things Japanese, we can say, from a Deleuze-inspired literacy perspective: What Lee desires is not reducible to reductive, dogmatic, standardized, psychoanalytic formulae, as in the desire for a fetishized object like a Japanese sword—that is to say, the desire for possession of its phallic hardness, gleaming destructiveness, its cold aesthetic; rather it is desired as a partial object in a composition of desire. He desires in aggregate. His desire flows in and across assemblages (*agencement*). His becoming-Japanese is a constructivism, a desire engineered. His desire-aggregate encompasses manga reading, kimono wearing, kanji writing, video game playing, Japanese speaking, the martial arts body, the flying kick, samisen music, the mysterious other, the Far East as a world so very far away yet constructed in his own territory or milieu. In terms of place, time, and movement, Lee *is* becoming-literature, becoming-manga—his joy is one of body, movement, the production of sensation, the unfolding of possibility. Think about first watching *Karate Kid* (1984): how many of us did the famous crane kick for years afterwards? Think about watching *Karate Kid* with your first girlfriend, or performing a whole repertoire of popular refrains in the school playground—"Paint, the fence!", "Wax on wax off, wax on wax off." Mimicking heavily accented Japanese-inflected English—"No such thing as bad student, only bad teacher." Or in another time and place, through *Saiyuki*, the Japanese TV series from the 1970s, derived from the original Chinese classic, *Hsiyu-chi*, penned in the 16th century—dubbed and broadcast as *Monkey Magic* in the UK. Think about becoming-Monkey and the refrains which ensue—"Primal chaos ruled the Worlds before Monkey. Monkey was born of time, of Heaven and Earth, of Sun and Moon, out of a stone egg"—"The nature of Monkey is irrepressible!"—both etched indelibly in the collective memory.

Can we not say, then, that affect and pedagogy are part of the same assemblage; that "the materiality of change, the act of learning" is identical with the passage between bodies which affect one another? If so, and in a not altogether and manifestly nutty sense, children are Spinozists because their bodies are made up of affective relations which occupy planes of becoming, desire and creativity. Borrowing language from Deleuze and Guattari, Leander and Boldt make the case for a non-text-centric approach, which rejects the over-rationalization of youth engagement in texts and instead explores the different experienced sensations; in other words, how individuals feel "differently, read differently, experience [themselves] or the narrative differently" (2013, p. 36). As Leander and Boldt say, the rhizomatic element in learning pertains to the ongoing present, "forming relations and connections across signs, objects, and bodies in often unexpected ways" (p. 26). And as Jacobs insists in *Reimagining Multiliteracies* (2013), because the design element focus of the New London Group,[2] for example, appears to exclude notions of movement and surprise, it is Leander and Boldt's work which instead homes in on the individual in a state of becoming or flux. Indeed, what matters for Leander and Boldt is to utilize materials in a composition of desire, to consider fluidity and indeterminacy as a key element in any epiphany in the classroom, to "recognize difference, surprise, and unfolding that follow along paths that are not rational or linear or obviously critical or political" (2013, pp. 43–44), to affirm notions of imagination, play, and the unknown itself.

The Student of Literature

Just as Lee in Leander and Boldt's study becomes other when he reads manga, adorns a kimono, when he flails his arms and legs to emulate the imagined balletic movement of the fighting samurai, the same could be said of the Japanese university student or students from overseas living in Tokyo, all in love with literature—with foreign languages and peoples, smells, tastes, sonic matter, the flows of exotic cities. With book in hand, the student of literature frequents cafes, listens to the jazz of John Coltrane or the songs of the Beatles, shops for retro clothes—perhaps even adorns a black French beret, affects a Liverpool accent, sits sullen in empty parks freezing to death waiting for something to happen, walks and walks in the pouring rain alongside the Chuo line entranced by the lyrics of Radiohead, dreams of romance in all manner of strange couplings; finally "kops off" or falls in love—dances, reads more and more, learns more and more, enjoys more and more. "Yeah! This is what it is about!"—he or she might say once the affected cool exterior crumbles. Or, perhaps, in another assemblage of desire and with refrains to orient becoming otherwise, he or she may assume the mannerisms, proclivities, the gait and affectations of lonely and hermetic characters that, for example, slowly and majestically take shape in a good Murakami Haruki novel. So here is youth in movement and experimentation: playful, expressionistic—operable and embedded in a collective assemblage of enunciation—a real transformation. Moving amid affective intensities—with friends, strangers, colleagues, teachers and lovers, the student makes a conjunctive circuit of desire—book *and* song and language and weather and milieu and dream—an ethology and ecology of learning, a virtual *chaosmos*. In-between and amidst this is a becoming-literature—a kind of foreign language within language—a "vector of deterritorialization"—where lands and cultures are sold, autochthonic territories are left behind to embrace imaginary worlds that undermine ancient regimes and strata. Everything is up for grabs because a new earth beckons! Here reading literature is an engineering problem—a question of how to hook together sign-machines of desire and fantasy with other concrete, immanent assemblages—productively. Tra-la-la-la—to give life life.

There is another model also. One where the refrain turns out badly—exhausts itself even. This is the refrain which resists becoming-otherwise, which reterritorializes on the familiar, the safe, striated order of formalized rules and obligations. This is the refrain which dare not desire otherwise or embark on the unknown. It is found, for example, in French writer and social critic Azouz Begag's work (1989, 2007) on Algerian immigrant communities in Lyon, France. Begag discerns a strong sense of resistance to becoming-French. Immigrants, retaining a fixed way of doing things from their homeland, construct a simulacra of what they have left behind. To ward off the existential anxiety and alienation of being away from home, desire turns to nostalgia and withdraws. A false feeling of security is gained in the fictional spaces of cable TV programs imported from home. Soap operas act as a reterritorializing literature (Conley, 2012). Desire turns to rust or rot (*rouiller*). Foreign teachers in Japan from predominantly rich countries may at times follow this model—a fixed way of life, a simulacra of the homeland. Think of the ex-pat lifestyle, resistance to local languages, to the habits and ways of life of the other; conformity with stereotypes which may serve the purpose of linguistic and cultural hegemony and the preservation of their own dominant *lingua franca*. One makes a territory of imported TV shows, Skype, SNS—to ward off the possibility of becoming otherwise. The antidote or refrain to this is perhaps Žižekian and optimistic in inspiration. In the documentary entitled "The Possibility of Hope" which accompanies the film *Children of Men* (2006), Slavoj Žižek says that one must be set adrift, from land or identity, to renew or become otherwise. One must cut ties, from all securities and safe havens. In other words, if there is no sanctuary, one must negotiate the *spatium* of intensive desire. Discussing the concept of the boat and reflecting on the ecological crisis facing mankind, Žižek suggests the boat as an adequate metaphor for describing the current state of being for vast swathes of humanity. As he says:

> We must really accept how we are rootless. This is, for me, the meaning of this wonderful metaphor, boat. Boat is the solution; "boat," in the sense of, you accept rootless, free floating. You cannot rely on anything. You know, it's not a return to land. Renewal means you cut your roots. (qtd. in *Children of Men*)

If renewal means one must consider severing the roots to one's ancestral home, then homesickness is the lot of *Dasein*; *we are indeed all adrift.*

Committed Teachers

Committed teachers, for Deleuze, are those who encourage their students to partic-ipate along with them. We learn to swim or learn a foreign language only through understanding practice "as signs"—a semiotics. As Deleuze says: "Everything that teaches us something emits signs; every act of learning is an interpretation of signs or hieroglyphs" (2008, p. 4). Furthermore, Deleuze outlines his paragon of the teacher. He says that students learn little, almost nothing, from those who say "do as I do." Rather, it is better to listen to those teachers who ask to "do with me," whose practice emits heterogeneous signs rather than proposing gestures to reproduce. From this perspective, while demonstrating what or how to do some-thing the teacher must also *become other for the other*. The class, for example, is processually a becoming-other in relation to itself—de-familiarizing, decentring, a transformatory force. *If you want to teach literature, you must decentre the classroom, you become other for the other*. This is something more than the translation of one imperial code into another, but rather a corporeal and indeed incorporeal trans-formation, an imperceptible moment of alterity. This model critiques the peda-gogical and one-dimensional model of the relay of knowledge from bequeather to bequeathed and contests the conventional model of the school teacher who "poses" problems to which the pupil must discover solutions. Such a model imprisons each party, Deleuze says, as both are kept "in a kind of slavery" (Deleuze, 1988, p. 15). Adopting a more radical view, Deleuze goes on to say that freedom truly lies in the power of students to decide and to constitute problems in their own way.

In recent decades, attempts have been made to redefine the learning of literacies in order to incorporate different understandings of plurality and the influence of new technologies, including multiliteracies. The main argument in this research claims that young people engage in a multitude of social communication practices that exceed the boundaries of simple text encoding and decoding. Adding another dimension to this new world of literacies is the work of Masny and Cole in *Multiple Literacies Theory* (2009). This Deleuzian-informed MLT contests pre-ordained so-cial, cultural, historical and physical assemblages. Building on the work of Deleuze and Guattari, MLT views literacies learning as a process of constant, indetermi-nate becoming—a process of moving, extending, creating difference and differing literacies, where learning is taken as an immanent, uncontrollable, unpredictable process. The spectator's fluid creation of meaning is part of this process. MLT is a paradigm of educational materialism, exploring dissonance, affect, assemblage, and transversal creative processes (Bradley, 2012, pp. 892–903; Bradley & Cole, 2015, pp. 1–9), through its examination of breakthroughs, breakdowns, and blockages in literacies learning. Think about film, for example, as a kind of playful reading of sense rather than absolute conclusiveness of representation. Moreover, MLT helps to rethink the idea of "translingual and transcultural competence" and the ability to "operate between languages" (Gibaldi, 2007, p. 3). Masny and Cole contend that reading is construed as an immanent, intensive and inherently interesting process, "a mapping of events of experiences on different planes" (Masny & Cole, 2012, p. 78).[3]

MLT advocates such as Masny and Cole adopt an epistemology without closure; theirs is more an ad hoc theory that tolerates experimentation and courts *aporia*. Distrustful of closed systems of thought, MLT aims to engineer non-teleological futures, different methods of transformation. Such a practice affirms a journey into difference, an experience of embodied transformation. This becoming-chaosmos— a composed chaos, which James Joyce introduces in *Finnegan's Wake*—cannot be explained through orthodox subject/object relations. The becoming-otaku of Japanese students (Bradley & Cole, 2015), becoming-Canadian of immigrant communities (Waterhouse, 2011), resistance to becoming-Australian in Latino communities in Sydney (Cole, 2012), Koreans attending English-as-second-language classes in Australia (Masny, 2014), and the creativity in Michelangelo Antonioni's work (Beighton, 2015) are some examples of research which discloses how transformation occurs in unexpected ways. This form of teaching is inherently political in the sense that it explores those moments that create "ruptures and differences," which lead the class, the project, the student or teacher to a new site of learning and becoming. It is fundamentally concerned with becoming and breakthrough and contests the blockages, the dead ends of education. In this way, and according to Braidotti, through thinking and employing affective literacy, such a pedagogy may help formulate a new trajectory towards the transformation of culture and the splitting and dispersion of false identities and binaries.

Conjunctive Syntheses—Deleuze and Guattari and Literacy and Literature and ... and ...

Lest we forget that to be radical is to grasp the thing in question by the root, as Marx suggests—let us return to one of the guiding threads of this paper which is that the root is youth—in Nietzsche's parlance, the child as innocent becoming. Expressed in light of the concept of the rhizome in Deleuze's work, and with the root understood as youth as such—reading is less about an invariant, totalizing, or dogmatic representation—less about closure and completeness—because the act of reading is an immanent and never-ending process of becoming or transformation or deterritorialization. Thinking beyond technology-dominated approaches to multiliteracies, the Deleuzean approach to literacy and literature cares little for pre-established design or outcomes. It thinks *immanently* as it relates and connects across signs, objects, and bodies in undreamt of ways. Reading, to repeat, has two senses. One is the aforementioned orthodox mode of interpretation. The other is more radical as it courts a critical pedagogy through reading the self, world and the object of analysis *qua* text. The self is text. It is an experiment with uncertainty, complexity, the futural incalculability of systems and the open-endedness of becoming.

Intermezzo and the Crack (*fêlure*)

Discussing learning and its relation to affects, Semetsky (2004) in "The Role of Intuition in Thinking and Learning" highlights the positive role the rupture or crack plays in the classroom. On this point, she suggests that the breakdowns, crack-ups and frustrations in the classroom are not always omens of failure and lines of flight that turn inward, implode or immolate, but may remould subjectivity as affective events.

Hannibal: From Crack to *craquelure*

During a post-mortem, in Season 2, Episode 2 of the TV show *Hannibal*, Hannibal, the arch-villain, standing in front of a grotesque corpse full of striated lines and in full poetic mode, suggests the presence of trace evidence in the *craquelure,* a word which derives from the French *craquelé.* To the nonplussed post-mortem expert, Hannibal explains that the *craquelure* is the crack that appears on an oil painting as it dries and becomes rigid with age. And importantly for our purposes, Hannibal notes that cracks are not always weaknesses, as he says, "A life lived accrues in the cracks." Deleuze takes a slightly different line and insists that art itself is a path between the cracks. As he says: "There is no work of art that does not indicate an opening for life, a path between the cracks" (Bogue, 2004, p. 9). This is a voyage which enjoins with the life that has amassed over time.

Baby, et Up All Her Spinoza?

Indeed, in an autobiographical essay "The Crack Up" (1936), originally published in *Esquire* magazine, F. Scott Fitzgerald traces his own death instinct and fall into alcoholism. We can understand this sense of the crack as a matter of bodies and affects. Fitzgerald ends the essay with an imagined conversation with a character who speaks to him in the wise, Spinozist words of a friend:

> So she said: "Listen. Suppose this wasn't a crack in you – suppose it was a crack in the Grand Canyon."

> "The crack's in me," I said heroically.

> "Listen! The world only exists in your eyes – your conception of it. You can make it as big or as small as you want to. And you're trying to be a little puny individual. By God, if I ever cracked, I'd try to make the world crack with me. Listen! The world only exists through your apprehension of it, and so it's much better to say that it's not you that's cracked – it's the Grand Canyon." (p. 74)

The reply "Baby, et up all her Spinoza?" (p. 74) leaps out of the page because the crack is always a question of affect and the capacity to be affected. Spinoza is central for Deleuze because of the timely questions "what can a body do?" and "of what affects is it capable?" Indeed, in the 22nd series of *The Logic of Sense*, entitled "Porcelain and Volcano," Deleuze discusses how self-destruction comes out of left field. Something happens that shatters the image and sanctuary of a perfect life— "looks, charm, riches, superficiality and lots of talent"—like "an old plate or glass" (p. 154). This is what he describes as the "terrible *tête-à-tête* of the schizophrenic and the alcoholic" (p. 154).

"The Crack-Up" is used by Deleuze to explain the three different kinds of transition from one state or stage in life to another: The first pertains to the large breaks: youth and adulthood, poverty and wealth, illness and good health, success or failure in your job. The second, the almost imperceptible cracks or subtle shifts of feeling or attitude, sometimes insidious, which involve molecular changes in the affective constitution of a person—so an imperceptible rupture rather than a signifying break. Fitzgerald asks: "Whatever could have happened for things to have come to this" (Deleuze & Guattari, 1987, p. 194)? The third constitutes the abrupt and irreversible transitions through which the individual becomes otherwise. This tripartite structure is a matter of lines—lines of rigid segmentarity (molar breaks), lines of supple segmentation (molecular cracks) and lines of flight or rupture (abstract and deadly yet teeming with intensity; alive). Indeed, for Fitzgerald, and, likewise Deleuze, all life is a process of breaking down; Fitzgerald speaks of his own self-immolation as something sodden and dark, of how an optimistic young man experienced a "crack-up of all values"—a molecular crack which came all of a sudden changing everything and nothing. Again as Fitzgerald says, the crack-up happens almost without you knowing it but then comes suddenly indeed. Discussing his indebtedness to Fitzgerald, in *Dialogues II* Deleuze says:

> The great ruptures, the great oppositions, are always nego-tiable; but not the little crack, the imperceptible ruptures, which come from the south. We say "south" without attaching any importance to this. We talk of the south in order to mark a direction which is different from that of the line of segments. But everyone has his south—it doesn't matter where it is—that is, his line of slope or flight. (pp. 131–132)

In the work of Fitzgerald (2009), Lawrence, Miller, Kerouac and similar ilk, Deleuze finds nothing but departure, becoming, passage, leaping, a relationship with the outside. Such writers create "a syntax that makes them pass into sensation that makes the standard language stammer, tremble, cry, or even sing" (Deleuze & Guattari, 1994, p. 176). They contort language, to "wrest the percept from perceptions, the affect from affections, the sensation from opinion" all for that "still-missing people" (Deleuze & Guattari, 1994, p. 176). In summa: they create an absolute deterritorialization or new Earth—one might even say they write for a transvaluation of all values. Explaining this elsewhere, Deleuze and Guattari say the relation of the crack to the rhizome is always a question of micropolitics:

> This time, there are outbursts and crackings in the immanence of a rhizome, rather than great movements and breaks determined by the transcendence of a tree. This molecular line, more supple and disquieting, is not simply internal or personal: it also brings everything into play, but on a different scale and in different forms, with segmentations of a different nature, rhizomatic instead of arborescent micropolitics. (1987, p. 119)

Thinking the relation of signs, health and the crack, Deleuze in *Logic of Sense* notes how the crack, despite the risks, is vital for creativity. He writes: "If one asks why health does not suffice, why the crack is desirable, it is perhaps because only by means of the crack and at its edges that thought occurs, that anything that is good and great in humanity enters and exits through it, in people ready to destroy themselves—better death than the health which we are given" (1990, p. 182). Deleuze thinks literature and the practice of writing are an orientation towards "a health yet to come." It is here that becoming and writing suggest resistance to the present. The fabulating function of literature for Deleuze implies that writing is concerned with health and the construction of a missing people. Putting the above remarks back in the education context and thinking the crack-up in the classroom and its relation to youth and transformation, Silvia M. Grinberg explains:

> It is no longer, then, a question of the indifference of these young people and their unwillingness to learn, but of the complexity of their desires, the hints of affirmation as well as the tensions that they express when they say "I want." The question ... is to what degree ... are they able to resist or transform current forms of domination. (2013, pp. 214–15)

So while the crack may indicate poor health, as it is the accompanying pain to the intensities one feels in a life held in permanent precarity. In *Transpositions: On Nomadic Ethics*, regarding a discussion on the nomadic processes of transformation, Braidotti, following Deleuze, maintains the point is to learn how to refuse the sad passions which one feasts upon on "the crest of the wave of cracking-up" (2006, p. 208). If one toils in "the long deep crack" of life, the question is how to learn to ward off the sad affects "of orchestrated demolition of the self" (Braidotti, 2006, p. 213). In Braidotti's essay "Affirmation Versus Vulnerability: On Contemporary Ethical Debates," (2009) she suggests that from the experience of and recovery from the crack up, what returns is a new force of health, resistance, adaptability, even ethical transformation, which is productive of difference. As she says, "[p]aradoxically, it is those who have already cracked up a bit, those who have suffered pain and injury, who are better placed to take the lead in the process of ethical transformation .... They know about endurance, adequate forces, and the importance of Relations" (2009, p. 156). For Deleuze, and indeed Nietzsche, the question is how to live in and on the surface of the crack, to traverse it, delicately, like the tightrope walker, balancing as ever over the precipice, yet learning all the while how to avoid headlong, hell-for-leather suicidal collapse and thus to resist the perilous descent into nihilism and decadence.

Schizoanalysis/Metamodelling/Symptomatology

As Deleuze and Guattari's schizoanalysis can be taken as a question of metamodelling or symptomatology, according to Janell Watson (in *Diagrammatic Thought*, 2009), D. H. Lawrence and Fitzgerald become important for Deleuze. Why? Because they think differently from psychoanalysis: they search for greatness and its relation to health and illness.[4] As a *symptomatologist* of his age, Fitzgerald discloses the forces, modes of existence that animate or suppress the present state of things. While rejecting any hope of forging a political project based on schizoanalysis on the immediate horizon, Guattari nonetheless suggests practices to sustain health while becoming-otherwise. In an interview with Jacques Pain, he states: "Without pretending to promote a didactic program, it is a matter of constituting networks and rhizomes in order to escape the systems of modelization in which we are entangled and which are in the process of completely polluting us, head and heart" (1996, p. 132). This point connects well with the aforementioned question of health and illness and how the latter link up with the process of creation and transformation through embodied and affective pedagogies. This is taken up more recently by Ian Buchanan, Tim Matts and Aidan Tynan in their introduction to *Deleuze and the Schizoanalysis of Literature*, in which they stress the importance of transformation: "Schizoanalysis is itself a practice, but one that operates alongside other practices in order to help us better understand—and in some cases to challenge and transform—the relations between theory and practice in any given field" (2015, p. 4).

Conclusion

Yet, scepticism regarding the socially transformative nature of play and becoming exposes an important problem for schizoanalysis. The pessimism and the ease with which some dismiss a crucial dimension of becoming otherwise is worth considering in greater detail because there is a lingering question as to what extent schizoanalysis can differentiate transformation from creativity. The problem for schizoanalysis is how to build a research paradigm which does not operate *in vacuo* but connects with other practices to ensure enduring, and yes, even successful, transformation. The dilemma has been explored recently by Buchanan, who reaches a conclusion which is in sharp contradistinction to Leander and Boldt's study. Speaking at the Crisis and Un/Making Sense—Art as Schizoanalysis symposium, in New Delhi, India, in January, 2015, Buchanan argued that the becoming-other by young people through technology (or in play acting, as in the case of Lee) may well be creative but it is not strictly speaking transformatory. He is clearly right to challenge the difference between the two but his conclusion appears unduly pessimistic. In his keynote address, he argued:

> Cultural critics who sing the song that popular culture and all its new devices and toys are liberating are simply singing from capitalism's hymn sheet. I never kinda understood the idea you often hear in cultural studies that young girls (are) watching *Buffy* and then going out and thinking Buffy is empowering. I don't buy that for a second. When you hear young kids say I watched an episode of *Buffy* and then I hacked it and cut it up and made my own version of *Buffy* so it is all about me, I don't think that is empowering either. It might be creative but it is not empowering. It hasn't changed

their social position in the world. I think we need to be pretty careful about what we think of and understand by the idea of empowering. Simply making a video is not empowering. It is maybe creative but it hasn't changed your social reality. (Buchanan, "Introduction")

While one can clearly see Buchanan's point regarding the type of lowest common denominator material that young people are often exposed to—the kind painstakingly marketed and advertised aggressively to them—and one should equally be cautious at affirming all forms of play as creative and/or transformatory, there is nevertheless some ground for arguing that the matter at hand is more complex than to draw a dogmatic distinction between the process of creativity and the point of transformation. Buchanan's scepticism here is striking because it highlights the apparently different *habiti* of cultural critics and education theorists. Why is it that education theorists such as Masny and Cole and not cultural theorists such as Buchanan are more optimistic about the ability for transformation? Moreover, one may also wonder why the division between creativity and empowerment/transformation is dogmatically defined because one of the hallmarks of schizoanalysis is to zigzag across the boundaries, to think the becoming between different terms.

Contra Buchanan, one might have some justification for insisting that if new forms of schizoanalysis are to have any lasting impact and effect, the apparent incommensurability between these two paradigms needs to be rethought and considered alongside Deleuze's concept of counter-effectuation. This notion will surely help us to understand transformation as an event which breaks loose from itself "as it is incarnated" (Spindler, 2011, p. 261).

Why is it that at the very moment that schizoanalysis shows the potential for breakthrough, its prophets and scribes condemn its revolutionary potential? If foreign language learning is this abstract line of flight and rupture, a clash and collision of worldviews, if it can be described as the dumbfounding of molar aggregates—a zigzag across job, family, class, nationality, sexuality—the extraction of a revolutionary force—then perhaps we can say that this is the ultimate aim of literature, to engender new modes of health, the invention of a people, a missing people, a minor language, a language within language. Literature then is a writing for a readership in becoming—"an oppressed, bastard, lower, anarchical, nomadic, irremediably minor race" (Deleuze, 2001, p. 109). It is the search for "a possibility of life" and a future people who resist the intolerable and the shame of the present. And it is for them that we teach and write in the hope that we may become them someday.

Notes

1 Based on the materialist psychiatry of R.D. Laing, schizoanalysis probes revolutionary *breakthrough* rather than psychological breakdown. The function of schizoanalysis is to engineer subjectivity *qua* creative process, while also working on the metamodelling of systemic malfunction. For Holland, schizoanalysis can be described as an "extraordinary venture in experimental thinking and writing" (qtd. in Deleuze and Guattari, 1983, viii), or in the words of Deleuze and Guattari themselves, at the end of *Anti-Oedipus* they write: The task of schizoanalysis is that of learning what a subject's desiring machines are, how they work, with what syntheses, what bursts of energy, what constituent misfires, with what flows, what chains, and what becomings in each case. [And] this positive task cannot be separated from indispensable destructions, the destruction of the molar aggregates, the structures and representations that prevent the machine from functioning. (p. 338)

2 Multiliteracies is widely linked with a group of scholars who formed in 1996 to discuss the effects of technology on the learning process. The members came to be known as the New London Group. The NLG published a seminal article, "A Pedagogy of Multiliteracies" in the *Harvard Educational Review*, in which they made the connection between the multiplicity of literacies present in learning contexts, and the wider plane of social change. Their philosophy was to inform teachers of this multiplicity of literacies and utilize different and innovative pedagogies that matched diverse learning options such as evolving technological applications. Multiliteracies theory envisages language and other modes of meaning as dynamic and unstable representations, subject to constant redefinition by users as they function. The NLG addresses how emergent meanings are generated online, in video captioning, in interactive multimedia, in desktop publishing and so on. The NLG's philosophy states that the role of pedagogy is to develop an "epistemology of pluralism." The NLG analyses how globalization and technology impact upon literate practices and how literacy teaching links up with issues such as local diversity and global connectedness. The task ahead is to understand the interactions among users of multiple languages and multiple Englishes, and communication patterns that seemingly transcend culture, community, and national boundaries.

3 For Masny, reading is the probing of how a text functions. Reading here carries a heterodox sense of the uncanny, for that which is *untimely* is a challenge to the already-thought. This form of *Unheimlich* points to the "fraying of language" (Spivak, 1993, p. 181) and the limits of "sense." MLT asks after the affects produced and the connections and collisions of worldview. Reading intensively therefore is a line of flight, of deterritorialization, a disruption in the territory one inhabits. Interested in the immanent process of affective becoming, MLT, following Freire, traces the transformative effects produced in strange encounters.

4 On this point, Deleuze compares his own repertoire of artists to philosophers and claims their fragile, "little health" is a consequence of viewing "something in life that is too much for anyone, too much for themselves," which, he says, has put on them "the quiet mark of death" (1994, p. 175).

References

Begag, A. (1989). *North African immigrants in France: The socio-spatial representation of "Here" and "There"*. European Research Centre, Loughborough University.

Begag, A., Hargreaves, A. G., & Wolf, N. (2007). *Shantytown Kid (le Gone Du Chaâba)*. University of Nebraska Press.

Beighton, C. (2015). *Deleuze and lifelong learning: Creativity, events and ethics* [Doctoral dissertation, Canterbury Christ Church University]. Springer.

Bogue, R. (2004). *Deleuze's wake: Tributes and tributaries*. State University of New York Press.

Bradley, J. P. N. (2012). Materialism and the mediating third. *Educational Philosophy and Theory, 44*(8), 892–903.

Bradley, J. P. N., & Cole, D. R. (2015). On conjuring the pea-and-thimble trick. *Journal of Engaged Pedagogy, 13*(1), 1–9.

Braidotti, R. (2006). *Transpositions: On nomadic ethics*. Polity Press.

Braidotti, R. (2009). Affirmation versus vulnerability: On contemporary ethical debates. In C. V. Boundas (Ed.), *Gilles Deleuze: The intensive reduction* (pp. 143–160). Continuum.

Buchanan, I. (2015, January 10). *Introduction to Schizoanalysis* [Keynote address]. Crisis and un/making sense: Art as schizoanalysis symposium. New Delhi, India. https://khojstudios.org/event/crisis-and-un-making-sense-art-as-schizoanalysis/.

Buchanan, I., Matts, T., & Tynan, A. (2015). Introduction: Towards a schizoanalytic criticism. In . I. Buchanan, T. Matts, & A. Tynan (Eds.), *Deleuze and the schizoanalysis of literature* (pp. 1–22). Bloomsbury.

Cuaron, A. (Director). (2006). *Children of Men* [Film]. Universal Pictures.

Cole, D. R. (2012a). Latino families becoming-literate in Australia: Deleuze, literacy and the politics of immigration. *Discourse: Studies in the Cultural Politics of Education, 33*(1), 33–46.

Cole, D. R. (2012b). Matter in motion: The educational materialism of Gilles Deleuze. *Educational Philosophy and Theory, 44*, 3–17.

Conley, V. A. (2012). *Spatial ecologies: Urban sites, state and world-space in French cultural theory*. Liverpool University Press.

Deleuze, G. (1988). *Bergsonism* (P. Habberjam & H. Tomlinson, Trans.). Zone Books.

Deleuze, G. (1990). *The logic of sense* (C. V. Boundas, Trans.). Columbia University Press.

Deleuze, G. (1995). *Negotiations, 1972–1990* (M. Joughin, Trans.). Columbia University Press.

Deleuze, G. (1997). *Essays critical and clinical* (D. W. Smith & M. A. Greco, Trans.). University of Minnesota Press.

Deleuze, G. (2001). *Difference and repetition* (P. Patton, Trans.). Continuum.

Deleuze, G. (2008). *Proust and signs: The complete text* (R. Howard, Trans.). Continuum.

Deleuze, G., & Guattari, F. (1983). *Anti-Oedipus: Capitalism and schizophrenia* (R. Hurley, M. Seem, H. R. Lane, Trans.). University of Minnesota Press.

Deleuze, G., & Guattari, F. (1987). *A thousand plateaus: Capitalism and schizophrenia* (B. Massumi, Trans.). University of Minnesota Press.

Deleuze, G., & Guattari, F. (1994). *What is philosophy?* (G. Burchell & H. Tomlinson, Trans.). Columbia University Press.

Deleuze, G., & Lapoujade, D. (2006). *Two regimes of madness: Texts and interviews 1975–1995* (D. Lapoujade, Ed., and A. Hodges, M. Taormina & M. Taormina, Trans.). Semiotext(e).

Deleuze, G., & Parnet, C. (2002). *Dialogues II* (B. Habberjam & H. Tomlinson, Trans.). Columbia University Press.

Dosse, F. (2010). *Gilles Deleuze & Félix Guattari: Intersecting lives.* Columbia University Press.

Fitzgerald, F. S. (2009). *The crack-up* (E. Wilson, Ed.). New Directions.

Gibaldi, J. (2007). *MLA handbook for writers of research papers.* Modern Language Association of America.

Grinberg, S. M. (2013). Researching the pedagogical apparatus (*Disposi-tif*): An ethnography of the molar, molecular and desire in con-texts of extreme urban poverty. In R. Coleman & J. Ringrose (Eds.), *Deleuze and research methodologies* (pp. 201–218). Edinburgh University Press.

Guattari, F. (1996). *The Guattari reader* (G. Genosko, Ed.). Blackwell.

Herzogenrath, B. (2013). On the *lost highway*: An encounter. In D. Elsner, S. Helff, & B. Viebrock (Eds.), *Films, graphic novels & visuals: Developing multiliteracies in foreign language education: An interdisciplinary approach* (pp. 185–200). LIT Verlag.

Jacobs, G. E. (2013). Reimagining multiliteracies: A response to Leander and Boldt. *Journal of Adolescent & Adult Literacy, 57*(4), 270–273.

Leander, K., & Boldt, G. (2013). Rereading "A Pedagogy of Multiliteracies": Bodies, texts, and emergence. *Journal of Literacy Research, 45*(1), 22–46.

Masny, D. (2014). Disrupting ethnography through rhizoanalysis. *Qualitative Research in Education, 3*(3), 345–363.

Masny, D., & Cole, D. R. (2009). *Multiple literacies theory: A Deleuzian perspective.* Sense.

Masny, D., & Cole, D. R. (2012). *Mapping multiple literacies: An introduction to Deleuzian literacy studies.* Continuum.

Parr, A. (2010). *The Deleuze dictionary.* Edinburgh University Press.

Semetsky, I. (2004). The role of intuition in thinking and learning: Deleuze and the pragmatic legacy. *Educational Philosophy and Theory, 36*(4), 433–454.

Semetsky, I. (2013). Deleuze, *Edusemiotics*, and the logic of affects. In I. Semetsky & D. Masny (Eds.), *Deleuze and education* (pp. 215–234). Edinburgh University Press.

Spindler, F. (2011). Event, crack-up and line of flight. In H. Ruin & A. Ers (Eds.), *Rethinking time: Essays on history, memory, and representation* (pp. 257–268). Södertörns.

Spivak, G. C. (1993). *Outside in the teaching machine.* Routledge.

Sutton, D., & Martin-Jones, D. (2008). *Deleuze reframed: Interpreting key thinkers for the arts.* I.B. Tauris.

Waterhouse, M. C. (2011). *Experiences of multiple literacies and peace: A rhizoanalysis of becoming in immigrant language classrooms* [Doctoral dissertation], University of Ottawa.

Watson, J. (2009). *Guattari's diagrammatic thought writing between Lacan and Deleuze*. Continuum.

Young, E. B., Genosko, G., & Watson, J. (2013). *The Deleuze and Guattari dictionary*. Bloomsbury.

CHAPTER NINE

Latino Families Becoming Literate in Australia: Deleuze, Literacy and the Politics of Immigration

What does it mean to become literate? Certainly, in the context of Australia, literacy has much to do with learning the English language to speak, read and write. Yet this study looks to broaden and expand upon such a focus, as learning the English language brings with it a host of divergent factors that include first language learning, cultural and social mores about education and specific contextual matters such as the ways in which individuals and groups are being acculturated and schooled in Australia (Brown, Miller & Mitchell, 2006; Rennie, 2006). Furthermore, in contemporary society, reading and writing technology has moved on to include a plethora of mediated digital formats that the migrants also must negotiate (see Kress, 2003). The expanded notion of becoming literate is represented here through the conjunction, "becoming-literate", that implies a simultaneous convergence and divergence of factors involved with English language learning, rather than an outcome-based understanding of what immigrants must do to learn English or to fit in with the mainstream (cf. Dias, Arthur, Beecher, & McNaught, 2000). Becoming-literate is therefore a conceptual construction that does not simply involve the change from being illiterate to literate but is a multi-directional and dimensional notion that is a convergent assemblage of parts that often chaotically collide in language learning spaces. These spaces may be schools, adult literacy classes, social situations, the home, work, or watching Australian media. Becoming-literate does not prioritize the subjectivity or agency related to individuals or groups undertaking English language learning but draws socio-cultural maps of the changes that are taking place in the families, and these maps are intended to indicate the directions in which the lives of the immigrants are moving (Ferdman, 1999) both to demonstrate the physical reality of Latino family life in Australia and to show how their needs are evolving.

This notion of "becoming-literate" relies on the socio-semiotic work of Deleuze and Guattari (1987) that appears in their second Capitalism & Schizophrenia opus, *A Thousand Plateaus*. Such socio-semiotics foregrounds becoming as a process that includes relationships with external factors of change that are simultaneous with those that are patterned in the construction of multiple selves such as self-determination, the will, motivation and attitude. This research paper, which is based on the Deleuzian notion of becoming, therefore importantly bisects the psychology of changes involved in literacy with those that may be constructed through understanding the sociology of the situation. The notion of becoming that one may derive from Deleuze (cf. Colebrook, 2002) is purposely designed to inhabit a different space from mainstream psychology or sociology, not to diminish either activity, but as a way of construing becoming as a potentially chaotic and indeterminate other that is crucially multiple.

In terms of education, the notion of becoming has been characterized as a type of constructivism (Semetsky, 2006), or micro sociology (Ringrose, 2010) that addresses the fluctuations of the self and other through learning. Yet migrant learning is also importantly open to the new social conditions that the immigrants must understand and reconstruct from their perspective as they start to participate in contemporary Australian life. This process of change implies that the Latino families' desires, intentions and actions are entwined with the ways in which capital is affecting them (see Bourdieu, 1997). In effect, they are redrawn as human capital through their move to Australia, and their reactions to the penetration of capital into their personal life will determine much of their future in the new society, including their educational horizons. This study of family literacies is therefore critically concerned with the politics of immigration and the ways in which it determines social life. The immigrants bring with them ways of coping with Australian conditions from their previous lives in South America. Yet they will also have to evolve new strategies for working with unfamiliar social and cultural factors, including divergent experiences of discrimination, isolation, racism, the English language and capital.

Two Case Studies

Two Latino families in western Sydney, NSW, were studied for a period of four months in 2010. These families were chosen through a series of social networks between the researcher/author and the research assistant. The research assistant was a bilingual South American who was chosen to work with the families in English and Spanish, as she would not take a non-interested position on the data. The case studies were constructed as pieces of social science (cf. Anyon, 2009), with open-ended interviews, observation, triangulation of the data where possible and full ethical approval for the project. Yet the writing of this chapter uses the poststructural positioning that educational research may derive from Deleuze and Guattari (see Hodgson & Standish, 2009). This positioning indicates that the two case studies are not structurally distinct data sets, solely one dimensional and purely qualitative in nature, or presented as being potentially representative of ideal or privileged Latino families. The writing of this report demonstrates the rhizomatic or schizoanalytic paradigm for social science that Deleuze and Guattari (1987, pp. 3 26) suggest. Subtle, sometimes disparate, connections are henceforth made between data sets through examination and (re)presentation, and key aspects of the data are subsequently analyzed for questions that relate to immanence, confluence and potentially conflictive affective change. This questioning is not to suggest that anything may now pass as poststructural social science, but that the combined consciousnesses of the researcher and writer are not imposed upon the data without intense scrutiny and analysis.

This writing is therefore pivotally suggestive of the often-relative power relationships that happened in and through the research and will attend to latent power relationships that are currently shaping the literacies of the two families in Australia. This work follows on from the discussions of qualitative analysis as they appear in Maxwell and Miller (2008), where the figure of Deleuze & Guattari's rhizome is positioned as encapsulating a poststructural extension of Hume's distinction between resemblance and contiguity as modes of association of ideas (1739/1978). Saussure (1916), Jakobson (1956), and Barthes (1968) subsequently took up Hume's distinction as expressing the difference between paradigmatic and syntagmatic relationships. Deleuze & Guattari's (1987) rhizomatics adds another level of qualitative distinction to the analysis of the case studies, one that ultimately comes about through the specific writing of the report and provides a bridge between the multiplicities inherent in the data (i.e., life) and the linguistic and imagined sense of the analysis. The rhizome adds a non-spatial, anti-hermetic element to the work of research that is suggestive of inter-corporeal and transformative affect.

The qualitative data in this study is organized and presented through Deleuze & Guattari's rhizomatic lens.

La Familia Flores[1]

The first family that was researched are from Uruguay. They moved to Australia in 2007 and live in the Penrith district of Sydney. The family consists of a father, Raul, 42, a mother, Edith, 37, and they have two boys, Mati, 10 and Nico, 8. The mother had been born in Australia, but went back to Uruguay when she was 11 after her family decided that they missed South America. The Flores family came to Australia to seek greater economic opportunities, and to create a better future for their sons. They initially lived with Edith's brother but had an acrimonious "falling out" with him that has left a bitter scar. They currently rent a small flat in Penrith, the father works as a forklift driver at a local furniture warehouse; the mother recently trained as an early-childhood worker but is presently unemployed. The two boys go to a local state-run primary school, and are engaging individuals who make friends easily, but are not interested in study. The mother is bilingual, and the father relies on her to translate from English to Spanish. Raul is struggling to learn English, has attended various adult language courses, though he finds English pronunciation difficult, and does not consistently study English on his own. He misses his last job in Uruguay, which was as a chauffeur to the Dutch ambassador. He reminisces at length about this job and speaks derisively about his current post in the warehouse. The family keep in touch with their relatives in Uruguay daily via Skype and by using satellite telephone cards. The dominant language in the home is Spanish, though they are developing networks in English and Spanish. The boys speak English at school with Spanish accents, Mati is particularly sociable, and Edith has made friends with several English-only speaking mothers at the school.

La Familia Smith

The second family that was studied are from Chile. The father, Bob, 38 was born in Alabama, and met the mother, Reina, 42, who is from Valdivia, Southern Chile, on a scientific cruise. Reina had one daughter, Rose, 12, from a previous relationship, and the couple have a second daughter together, Violeta, 6. The family arrived in Australia in 2008, and came because Bob had gotten job with a company that sells and installs large scientific machines. His job involves the installation and setup of the machines. The parent company that controls this business was recently replaced in a hostile corporate takeover that has caused family stress in terms of job security. Reina is a trained geologist and wants to carry on with her studies or get a job in this area, though she is currently doing only part-time courses such as permaculture to get out of the house. The family presently live in a rented house on a mountain that overlooks the Sydney basin. The eldest daughter is quiet and studious and enjoys her new state high school. Rose speaks English with an American accent, as the family had previously lived in Texas, where Bob had also found work. Violeta is an incredibly energetic young girl, and the family recently moved her to an alternative Montessori-style school because she did not respond to the state school system. Reina chooses not to speak English if possible. Both girls are bilingual, and Bob speaks a little Spanish. Reina considers their time in Australia to be limited before they go back to Chile, though Bob openly contradicts this opinion as he states that he has little chance of finding suitable work in Chile. The family are beginning to develop networks of English and Spanish speaking individuals around their home.

Nomadic Family Literacies

Much of the work in the literacy knowledge field has come from the United States, where the immigration of Latino families is commonplace (see Tejeda, Martinez & Leonardo, 2000). Predominantly ethnographic, qualitative and narrative research methods have been deployed to understand the ways in which the families and their resultant literacies change once they arrive in their new country. These studies have looked at the success or otherwise of the migrant children in schools (Peterson & Heywood, 2007), the adult migrant literacies (Norton, 2006), bilingualism (Volk & de Acosta, 2001) and the ways in which the immigrants negotiate educational life in America by using Spanish (see Moll & Gonzalez, 2004).

The difference that this study brings to the knowledge area is that the two families of the case studies were set into motion as nomads even before they migrated to Australia. The knowledge of this study comes through the grounding of the research in the Deleuzian concept of becoming. Becoming lends the families a type of nomadism that is derived from *A Thousand Plateaus*. In the book, social theory is mitigated through the behaviours of sedentary communality and nomadism. In and through sedentary accumulation and the consequent modes of living, the societies of Europe built a form of organization that was vulnerable to attack from flighty and rapid nomadic invasion. A good essential example of this is the Mongol hordes, which swarmed from Asia to assail medieval feudal Europe in the 13th century. Deleuze and Guattari (1987) contend that these nomads marked European history, not only as invaders, but also in terms of reorganized and renegotiated forms of warfare (Chambers, 1985). Before the invasions of the nomads, sedentary communities had been built around agrarian-serf types of accumulation that had dominated European society. Post-nomadic invasion, Europe began to be based around expansionary capitalism. Braudel (1967) put the beginnings of the European market economy at around 1500 C.E.; the point from Deleuze and Guattari (1987) is that the nomadism of the Mongols fundamentally changed the velocity and trajectory of European conquest over time through new social organization. The Europeans began to incorporate the nomadism of the Mongols into their armies, and in so doing left behind the aristocratic formalism of knights and serf-territories. Departing from landlocked feudalism, the Europeans set out in boats, and went to explore and conquer new territories. Armies became lighter, quicker, better organized and more able to adapt to new conditions. In short, Deleuze and Guattari sum up the influence of the nomad invasions on sedentary European society through the phrase, "the war machine" (1987, pp. 351–423) which is a conjunction that explains the working of nomadism in defence-orientated society.

The war machine could take us a long way from the Latino families becoming-literate in Australia. Yet the confluence of terminology here indicates the ways in which the Latino families have absorbed the lessons of the Mongols in their passage to Australia. Such learning is not a result of coming from South America but happens in the change from one place to another, or by becoming "other-than" (e.g., Cole, 2009) according to Deleuze. The nomadism of this study is about the "othered" and "othering" movement of two families' literacies and indicates characteristics that relate to the findings of the case studies.

Economic Literacies

Both families came to Australia for economic reasons. The Flores family is convinced that the poverty of South America is insurmountable and growing. Australia is on the other hand a rich country, where there is a good chance of making money. The Smith family came due to Bob's new job, which he describes as the best that he has ever had. The tax system, benefits, the price of groceries and presents for the children all take up a lot of thought and conversation of the two families. They are also aware that they are placed in a market system in Australia, where qualifications, skills and labor are priced. The Flores family adheres more closely to economic rationalism, whereas Reina in the Smith family does question this financial sea of change in thought and language. She prefers to consider notions of community and values as they relate to her home in Chile, and she has reproduced these ideas as a shield in her new home in the mountains outside of Sydney. The

Flores family are preparing to be actively engaged in entrepreneurial enterprises, such as trying to set up a mobile coffee-van, which they see as a possible way out of economic servitude. The children are not directly involved in these economic literacies but act as receptors and consumers of the ideas. For example, the Flores boys are fascinated by video games; Violeta has mountains of toys that are piled up on the lower floor of their house. Meanwhile, the research assistant noticed a marked increase in tension in the Smith household during the hostile corporate takeover and the consequent possible loss of income.

Bureaucratic Literacies

Parallel to and overlapping with the economic literacies, the families have had to engage with new bureaucratic systems because of moving to Australia. The design of the health system, the benefit and rebate system, housing, the tax systems and visa/citizenship statuses are all based on application forms and require evidence for claims, which the Latinos must negotiate. In the Flores household, Edith has been put in charge of these literacies due to her English ability, and she feels this responsibility is a burden. Bob looks after the bureaucratic affairs in the Smith family but is unsure about whether to apply for permanent residency with the resultant lowering of tax and improved health coverage, due to the complexity of the process. These bureaucratic literacies are daunting for Spanish speakers as the application forms and associated technical documents contain a large array of new vocabulary and notions that do not exist in South America. Again, the children do not directly partake in these literacies, but feel the results of the tension and frustration that these systems can produce. In particular, the bureaucratic literacies have produced an imbalance in the Flores family, in that Edith feels under pressure to understand the bureaucratic system fully to apply in the correct way for available benefits. In the Smith family, the bureaucratic literacies have a latent power effect on the family, due to the understanding that their current work visas give them a continuing inferior status in Australia that they must eventually negotiate.

Emotional Literacies

Deleuze and Guattari (1987) use the notion of affect rather than emotion, but on a normative level, and with reference to the two case studies, the families have both had to deal with huge emotional upheavals. For example, the Flores boys miss their dog that they left behind in Uruguay—there is a picture of him, prominently placed in the cramped front room of their flat. Reina's mother is experiencing early onset of Alzheimer's disease, and Reina feels that she should be back in Chile helping to care for her. Her eldest daughter, who misses the family connections and close, communal lifestyle in Chile, perhaps most keenly feels Reina's emotional literacy. Bob was in the US military for ten years before he met Reina, and is used to coping on his own, and in fact seems to enjoy the isolation of their mountain home. The Flores family are in an ambiguous situation with respect to emotional literacies. They compensate for the distance between themselves and their family in Uruguay by using Skype and telephone communication. They are also positioning themselves as potential trailblazers for more family members to come to Australia and to leave behind the difficult South American situation. The two boys are perhaps most affected by the Flores' emotional literacies and demonstrate this by consistently acting in a childish manner.

Adaptive Literacies

This subtle aspect of the families' nomadic literacies works underneath the other literacies as a powerful contiguous and disjunctive force. An example from the Flores family is an event that took place in a supermarket, where they experienced disgruntled annoyance from another shopper in the checkout queue. They had misunderstood the boxing arrangements, and because they were discussing this in Spanish, the next shopper decided to intervene on their behalf. An argument ensued, the family consequently learnt about shopping-line etiquette in Australia, and the possible ways in which using Spanish in public places can be interpreted. The difference between the Flores family and the Smith family is that Reina is not actively engaging in adaptive literacies (and their potential conflicts). She is fully capable of doing so, yet her embedded thought that she will soon be going back to Chile makes her less open to these potential lesion and displacement points. Reina's daughters and husband are more congruent and aligned with adaptive literacies.

These four literacies that the case studies have discovered are not exhaustive and cross over in various complicated ways. In contrast to studies that have placed cultural discontinuity as being a prime mover in immigrant literacy learning (e.g., Markose & Hellsten, 2009), this study represents the nomadic literacies as being simultaneous, emergent and continuous, yet indicating forms of entwined otherness. In Deleuze and Guattari's (1984) first work on Capitalism and Schizophrenia, the Oedipal family comes in for close attention, and is disrupted as a source of molar power. The nomadic approach that is used in their second volume sets the family amongst a series of interconnected qualitative flows or multiplicities. These flows had already started before the South American immigrants came to Australia, and live on in their memories, actions and dreams. The four literacies as listed above show the ways in which the families are crossing over and "becoming other" in Australia. They also represent a map of affect that sits within the literacies to create and be created by atmospheres that inhabit the same spaces as the families. The representation of the nomadic family literacies does not valorise or prioritize the family as a particular unit of organization but shows the ways in which the families are changing and are fully permeated by relative power concerns (see Masny, 2005).

Language as Surface Effect (MLT)

How do these nomadic family literacies translate into linguistic phenomena? Diana Masny (2009) has explained this aspect of the study in her work on multiple literacies theory (MLT). Masny explored the development of writing amongst school-age children working in more than one language in Canada. She found that the act of writing is a surface effect that results from a series of loosely connected accidents. For example, a first-language Spanish speaking girl in Canada, who is also navigating Portuguese with her father and French at school, will linguistically skip between the three syntactical systems when writing (Masny, 2009). The girl also demonstrated strong emotional content in her writing and related much of what she articulated to her powerful family environment. In the terms of the nomadism of this study, the girl is negotiating between emotional and adaptive literacies through her writing, whilst performing within bureaucratic literacies in terms of the designated French curriculum at school. Masny interviewed the girl and shows how the imagination of the child is fully activated in and through these writing activities, that are in many ways the final acts of entwined thought processes. The girl shows how she is associative in her thinking and can make imaginative leaps when talking about her writing, as she explained that much of the sense of her language comes from extra-terrestrials (2009, pp. 25–27). The point here is that being trilingual is "othered" in mainstream schooling, and the child feels that her sense of language comes from a far-off galaxy, very different from her present reality. In terms of MLT, the surface-effect of language has been produced after the "othering" environment at school has been experienced and internalized. The girl reacts to the French mainstream with recourse to the emotion of her maternal Spanish, which for her is safe and homely. In terms of this study, Reina's daughter Rose demonstrates otherness at school when asked about Australian citizenship during a routine reading comprehension exercise.

The teacher raised the topic of citizenship through the classroom pedagogy and reading comprehension, and this action has had deep ramifications for Rose. Rose expressed her desire not to become Australian; in the terms of nomadic family literacies this reaction is related to the emotional, adaptive and bureaucratic literacies. The emotional and adaptive literacies are activated via the mention of Australia as home, and the ways in which Rose and Reina miss Chile. The bureaucratic literacies of this idea involve the curriculum that is being followed and the ways in which citizenship education is integrated into mainstream knowledge. The teacher may or may not have been aware of Rose's sensitivities as she is a quiet and inward girl. Yet giving her this exercise has stirred up profound memories and thoughts about transitioning into Australia, where she currently feels out of place. In terms of MLT, the unconscious is full of qualitative detail (cf. Cole, 2010) that swirls and buckles with the forces of the nomadic family literacies. Roses' writing suggests a point of rupture that comes through the words and leads to a maelstrom of indeterminate affect. Rose positions herself as an American Chilean, and in doing this she removes herself from Australia, and through this gap she may possibly find happiness. In contrast, Mati's English writing-book does not demonstrate any personal commentary, but a wealth of cartoon doodles

The becoming-literate in the nomadism of the Flores family comes through Mati's doodles in terms of emotion and identification. Mati loves watching cartoons and playing video games, he is highly sociable and wants to fit in with the other children. His school writing as a surface effect of these forces is stilted and conformist. In contrast, his doodles are expressive and represent a throughline to the ways that he is learning in Australia. In terms of MLT, the inculcation of cartoons, video games and peer socialization in Mati's life has created a means of expression that reproduces these effects through drawing. His cartoons show us the ways in which the multiple literacies come together through doodling, yet also remain distinct. The cartoons depict little action figures holding guns, diving and standing upright, ready to engage with the viewer. Mati's unconscious plays with emotional and adaptive literacies through these cartoons, whereas the bureaucratic literacies of the mandated curriculum reproduce power effects such as finishing the exercise or correctly answering a question. Mati sees power for himself in watching cartoons, playing video games and in making friends. The schoolteacher wants Mati to write in a way that he finds far less interesting. A rupture point has therefore been created between cartoon watching, playing video games and making friends, and his school-based literacy. This rupture point leads to affect, that is visible in Mati's temperamental emotional states and unstable powers of concentration at school. In this case, one might discern how one child's careful doodles are indicative of the affect produced through nomadic family literacies.

The Politics of Becoming

This study may be understood as a series of overlapping frames. One frame is shaped by the nomadic family literacies, another through language as surface effect or MLT. The third frame comes about due to the politics of becoming involved with the research project. Deleuze (1987) stated that his notion of becoming was derived from Nietzsche's will to power, and this pivot runs through the research, both in terms of the aspirations of the two families and the rationale for investigation. In the US, the politics of immigration involving Latino families crossing the border has created a broad polemic and defines a south-north axis upon which people, money and goods travel. In Australia, the Latinos have mostly come by plane; this migration has been largely ignored politically as attention has been focused on boat arrivals and the north-south axis from Asia to Australia. This research therefore opens a new front for discussion by examining the ways in which the Latino families are becoming-literate in Australia. Their respective wills to power are indicative of a set of changes that are happening to them as they settle and merge into the Australian populace. These immigrant changes may be spoken about and discussed, creating a dialogue and political discourse for education. The characteristics of the politics of becoming that emerged from the two case studies were:

Money

Both families were very concerned about money. The economic problems in South America and the perception that Australia is a rich country are important drivers for both families. This aspect of the case studies translates into education through the ways in which the families can support their children's progress or otherwise. The Flores family did not seem to be readily supportive and considered educational materials for the boys to be an unnecessary expense.

Networks

The Latino families are making networks of friends and contacts in their respective locations. This part of the changes that are happening to them sits within the shadow of the friends and families that they have left behind. South American society relies on these networks, and the families are attempting to reproduce these relationships in Australia by having barbecues, going to social events, and proactively talking to neighbours. In educational terms, this networking translates into the social necessity of turning the school into a learning community. The Latinos flourish in networks of connective identities, and this aspect of social life is not strong in some parts of urban Australia. The Latino family's sense and act on this separation, which translates into the politics of the situation through oscillations in perceived and real exclusion and inclusion, closeness, and distance.

Status

The question of one's place in society is important for the Latinos. The two families relate this question to income and work, and Raul often reminisces about his important role as a chauffeur in Uruguay. Reina adds an interesting twist to this element of the politics of becoming as she considers herself and her family to be part of an indigenous community. Bob has Native American ancestry, and she identifies with indigenous Chileans. Reina therefore associates indigenous heritage with dignity, values and the position of her family as being antagonistic to colonials; and such positioning has important ramifications for living in Australia. Educators need to be sensitive to status concerns when addressing the Latinos.

Fun

Beyond the serious elements of the politics of becoming as listed above, the Latinos have a profound sense of fun. This fun underlies much of what they want to do in Australia. For example, dancing is almost obligatory in every South American celebration, yet in Australia dance is not so centrally placed in one's life. There is an underlying flirtatiousness that mediates much of South American society that hardly exists in Australia. The South Americans are therefore likely to interpret standoffish behaviour as lacking in affection, as they are used to physical ties being demonstrated. Latinos can be caught out in educational situations by the strict moral rules around touching and physicality in Australian schools.

These four characteristics of the politics of becoming cross over and change given the fluctuations of life. The Latino immigrants are caught in this power matrix; yet can escape from it in unexpected and singular ways (Cole & Hager, 2010). For example, this research project has included giving the families tokens to buy books for their children, and this act works through the politics of becoming of the families by positioning the university as aiding their cause. The related associations of research, the university, education, and the Australian system are connected through the bureaucratic literacies of the nomadic families, and merge into the politics of becoming through money and status. The families feel privileged to be part of this research, and the chance to purchase free books for their children is one less expense to worry about. These case studies found less direct expressions of discrimination and prejudice than expected; rather, the four elements of the politics of becoming straddle the lives of the families like the marbling in an elaborate cake. Perhaps this is because the recent immigration of the Latinos fits in with previous post-war waves of Mediterranean Greeks and Italians, who are now accepted parts of Australian culture (Collins, 1991). The Spanish accents when speaking English do mark out the Latinos to an extent, yet their friendly and sociable manner eases paths to inclusion in multicultural Australian life.

Conclusion

The politics of immigration that this research has discovered involves the specific lives of two Latino families, and their settlement in western Sydney. In tandem with all qualitative research, one should be sceptical about the generalization of these findings. Yet the Deleuzian platform for this paper gives the researcher and analyst new tools to understand and articulate the facts of qualitative data. By focusing on the multiple literacies that run through the stories of the two families, one can extract planes of emergent data that interact and clash through their representation in such an article format. Deleuze's precise political framing of his ideas has been much debated in the scholarly literature (Garo, 2008), yet here it does extend to colouring the politics of immigration. For example, the Deleuzian framing does not make one focus exclusively or preferentially on issues of social justice. Rather, the "real life" of the immigrants comes through the paper as a definite, shifting backdrop for any analytic remarks that have been made above. Deleuze (1987) was concerned about the normative power of his work, and this concern meant that he rarely sided with one simple position in a political debate.[2] He therefore retains his politics as fluid and fluctuating, able to pick up on and use either side of a political debate in a novel and creative way. Doing social research through a university is not value-neutral, yet by employing Deleuze's philosophical position, one is able to attend to many of the power markers in research that could potentially pinpoint or demarcate the research participant as "other". The Deleuzian position, if applied, should help the immigrants and educationalists with literacy learning projects in Australia through the explanations of their otherness.

Notes

1 All names that appear are self-selected pseudonyms.
2 The famous exception to this was when Deleuze commented about the injustices that have been committed against the Palestinian people in Le Monde.

References

Anyon, J. (2009). *Theory and educational research: Towards critical and social explanation.* Routledge.

Barthes, R. (1968). *Elements of semiology* (A. Lavers & C. Smith, Trans.). Hill and Wang.

Bourdieu, P. (1997). The forms of capital. In A. H. Halsey, H. Lauder, P. Brown & A. S. Wells (Eds.), *Education, culture, economy and society* (pp. 46–58). Oxford University Press.

Braudel, F. (1967). *Capitalism and material life: 1400–1800* (M. Kochan, Trans.). Harper and Row.

Brown, J., Miller, J., & Mitchell, J. (2006). Interrupted schooling and the acquisition of literacy: Experiences of Sudanese refugees in Victorian secondary schools. *Australian Journal of Language and Literacy, 29*(2), 150–163.

Chambers, J. (1985). The devil's horsemen: The Mongol invasion of Europe. Athenaeum.

Cole, D. R. (2009). Indexing the multiple: An autobiographic account of education through the lens of Deleuze & Guattari. In D. Masny & D. R. Cole (Eds.), *Multiple literacies theory: A Deleuzian perspective* (pp. 119–133). Sense Publishers.

Cole, D. R. (2010). Multiliteracies and the politics of desire. In D. R. Cole & D. L. Pullen (Eds.), *Multiliteracies in motion: Current theory and practice* (pp. 124–139). Routledge.

Cole, D. R. (2012). The actions of affect in Deleuze: Others using language and the language that we make. In Graham, L. J., & Cole, D. R. (2012). *The power in/of language.* Wiley-Blackwell.(pp. 1–12).

Cole, D. R., & Hager, P. (2010). Learning-practice: The ghosts in the education machine. *Education Inquiry, 1*(1), 21–40.

Colebrook, C. (2002). *Deleuze.* Routledge.

Collins, J. (1991). *Migrant hands in a distant land: Australia's post-war immigration* (2nd ed.). Pluto Press.

Deleuze, G., & Guattari, F. (1984). *Anti-Oedipus: Capitalism and schizophrenia* (R. Hurley, M. Steem, & H. R. Lane, Trans.). Athlone Press.

Deleuze, G., & Guattari, F. (1987). *A thousand plateaus: Capitalism & schizophrenia II* (B. Massumi, Trans.). Athlone Press.

Deleuze, G., & Parnet, C. (1987). *Dialogues* (H. Tomlinson, & B. Habberjam, Trans.). Athlone Press.

Dias, C. J., Arthur, L., Beecher, B., & McNaught, M. (2000). Multiple literacies in early childhood: What do families and communities think about their children's early literacy learning? *Australian Journal of Language and Literacy, 23*(3), 230–247.

Ferdman, B. M. (1999). Ethnic and minority issues in literacy. In D. Wagner, R. Venezky & B. Street (Eds.), *Literacy: An international handbook* (pp. 95–101). Westview.

Garo, I. (2008). Deleuze, Marx and revolution: What it means to "remain Marxist". In J. Bidet & S. Kouvelakis (Eds.), *Critical companion to contemporary Marxism* (pp. 605–624). Brill.

Hodgson, N., & Standish, P. (2009). Uses and misuses of poststructuralism in educational research. *International Journal of Research & Method in Education*, *32*(3), 309–326.

Hume, D. (1978). *A treatise of human nature* (2nd ed.). Oxford University Press. (Original work Published ca. 1739 C.E.).

Jakobson, R. (1956). Two aspects of language and two types of aphasic disturbances. In R. Jakobson & M. Halle (Eds.), *Fundamentals of language* (pp. 55–82). Mouton.

Kress, G. (2003). *Literacy in the new media age*. Routledge.

Markose, S., & Hellsten, M. (2009). Explaining success and failure in mainstream schooling through the lens of cultural continuities and discontinuities: Two case studies. *Language and Education*, *23*(1), 59–77.

Masny, D. (2005). Multiple literacies: An alternative or beyond Freire. In J. Anderson, T. Rogers, M. Kendrick & S. Smythe (Eds.), *Portraits of literacy across families, communities, and schools: Intersections and tensions* (pp. 171–184). Lawrence Erlbaum.

Masny, D. (2009). Literacies as becoming: A child's conceptualizations of writing-systems. In D. Masny & D. R. Cole (Eds.), *Multiple literacies theory: A Deleuzian perspective* (pp. 13–31). Sense Publishers.

Maxwell, J. A., & Miller, B. (2008). Categorizing and connecting strategies in qualitative data analysis. In P. Leavy & S. Hesse-Biber (Eds.), *Handbook of emergent methods* (pp. 461–477). Guilford Press.

Moll, L., & Gonzalez, N. (2004). Engaging life: A funds-of-knowledge approach to multicultural education. In J. Banks & C. Banks (Eds.), *Handbook of research on multicultural education* (2nd ed.) (pp. 699–715). Josey-Bass.

Norton, B. (2006). Not an afterthought: Authoring a text on adult ESOL. *Linguistics and Education*, *17*(1), 91–96.

Peterson, S. S., & Heywood, D. (2007). Contributions of families' linguistic, social, and cultural capital to minority-language children's literacy: Parents', teachers', and principals' perspectives. *The Canadian Modern Language Review*, *63*(4), 517–538.

Rennie, J. (2006). Meeting kids at the school gate: The literacy and numeracy practices of a remote indigenous community. *Australian Educational Researcher*, *33*(3), 123–140.

Ringrose, J. (2010). Beyond discourse? Affective assemblages, heterosexually striated space, and lines of flight online and at school. In D. R. Cole, & L. J. Graham (Eds.), *The power in/of language* (pp. 48–67). Wiley.

Saussure, F. de (1916/1986). *Course in general linguistics*. Open Court.

Semetsky, I. (2006). *Deleuze, education and becoming*. Sense Publishers.

Tejeda, C., Martinez, C., & Leonardo, Z. (Eds.). (2000). *Charting new terrains of Chicana(o)/Latina(o) education*. Hampton Press.

Volk, D., & de Acosta, M. (2001). Many differing ladders, many ways to climb: Literacy events in the bilingual classrooms, homes and community of three Puerto Rican Kindergartners. *Journal of Early Childhood Literacy, 1*(2), 193–224.

Pedagogy

CHAPTER TEN

On Conjuring the
Pea-and-Thimble Trick

Who speaks and who acts? It's always a multiplicity, even in the person that speaks or acts. We are all groupuscles. There is no more representation. There is only action, the action of theory, the action of praxis, in the relations of relays and networks. (Deleuze, 2004, p. 207)

Mediating Third

In his essay "Materialism and the Mediating Third", Joff Bradley (2012) set out a theoretical model for engineering a *mediating third* in foreign language classrooms. Sadly, and despite the effort and care put into the essay, the result was overly abstract. In truth, he fears few will ever read it or take the time to understand its implications. This is a clear example of how one writes *in vacuo*, of how one spins on one's own axes, of how one produces black holes and cycles of deadly repetition—a central theme in the essay. The shortcomings of the paper were many but chief among them was a paucity of concrete application. This is a regular criticism leveled at research which is excellent theoretically but poor practically, thin on the ground, as it were. The obverse is equally true. When research is focused solely on practice in itself, the findings invariably are one-dimensional, or simply anecdotal and boring. Self-criticism aside, wedding theory and praxis is never an easy task as the dialectical unity of theory and praxis—that pea-and-thimble trick as Orwell called it—is one few ever or care to master. This paper is thus a reflection on the shortcomings in Bradley's essay and how he set about remedying them. It is the outcome of a research paradigm incorporating multiliteracies, multiple literacy theory (MLT) and critical theory, and one which widens the scope of what Guattari (1995) calls "the ecology of the virtual".

My research is focused on a pedagogy which identifies and isolates cartographically the blackholes of machinic répétition mortifère (social reclusivity, addiction to technologies, education for any absurd purpose!). Its remit is to isolate, germinate and agitate moments of n-1 "plus three" creativity (joy, intensity, desire, a relation to the outside). Using an experimental assemblage initially forged by Célestin Freinet (1896–1966), his idea of the mediating third object, Guattarian schizoanalysis, and MLT (Masny & Cole, 2009), it is contended that a progressive critical pedagogy is one that ultimately searches out circuit breakers or vacuoles of communication which interrupt the immolating cycle of repetition or eternal return of the same. Other components of this assemblage include the production of new modalities of subjectivity, existential territories (modes of becomings) and incorporeal universes of reference (found in music and the plastic arts in institutional and ethico-ethological level contexts which affect subjectivity and the body in varying ways). On this account, learning is a semiology to signs and events; a question of sensitivity to affects, and how in turn to affect them (Masny, 2013).

This reconstructed pedagogy is directly related to affective and critical models of literacy and how they can be taught and learnt (Cole & Pullen, 2010). Critical literacy practice situates the text in socio-cultural contexts and probes the meanings of the text vis-à-vis the reader; in the case of this paper, how Japanese students relate to the "chaosmos" of everyday capitalist life—social precarity, refugeeisation, the end of the Bubble economy, solitude, depression, and ultimately suicide.

Using the language of schizoanalysis, what is sought after is the understanding of the cognitive and semiotic ecologies which govern social, cultural, environmental or technological assemblages. Like Freinet, Guattari (Genosko, 1996) was focused on creating de-Oedipalizing institutional contexts, to escape the stifling cocoon of the state-controlled classroom and the prefabricated, shrink-wrapped ideas found in textbooks. Concerned with engineering a virtual ecology of institutional life, creativity, for Guattari was a way to transcend dogmatic institutional practices, which might preclude the emergence of heterogeneity or fresh becomings. Through triangular experiments, which used a mediating object (for example, a collectively produced monograph), the purpose of learning was to create progressive scenes of subjectification, which is to say the construction of new forms of subjectivity, to overcome what Guattari's mentor Fernand Oury (1920–1998) designated the *encaserne scolaire* or school-as-barracks. Simply put, the third object opens students to the world. Two becomes three plus n. It is with the triangle and threes that micropolitical pedagogies manifest. The schizoanalytic reading of a subject-group envisages it formulating its own projects, speaking in its own name—never an easy task—and being heard by those outside the classroom. Freinet encouraged students to trace their material connections to the world, through objects, machines, people and places. Through reading, discussion, performance and reflexive journal writing, Freinet viewed the classroom as a space for collective imagination and engagement.

Bradley concluded his 2011 essay with Guattari's question, "how one can make a class operate like a work of art?" Bradley implicitly agreed with the idea that teachers should seek out techniques of rupture, paths to resingularization or ways to engineer a new "purchase on existence" (Guattari, 1995, p. 133). The question is how to transform the infernal machine. How can one stop students "spinning in the void"? From turning into pulp (Stiegler, 2012)? If teachers want students to engage critically in literature, ideas and the world then their contributions must go somewhere—they must have a relation to the outside, a relation to the desires, hopes and fears of the students. Teaching must mean. It is a form of pedagogic suicide to have ideas and projects left unread, circulating impersonally and meaninglessly as mere data sets between computers, phones, or attachments to email. Their productions must belong to a wider circuit of becoming, desire, change and transformation.

In subject-groups (comparable to Sartre's treatment of the group-in-fusion), Guattari found a way to formulate a creative pedagogy through transversal elements, by which relations to the institution are subverted through play, that is to say, the subject-group is mobilized to throw existing academic divisions of labor into question. A creative and critical pedagogy raises awareness of the microphysics of affect in the classroom. How do teachers and students operate across molar aggregates? The subject-group is formed in its own making, speaks and is heard and tested against these goals and ends. The situated knowledge of the students forms a group identity and delinks itself from a common spatiotemporal subjugation to institutional power. There is a shift of power relations away from the teacher/leader towards the more diffuse, situated knowledges of the students— a relation to the outside, a relation to the different worlds and experiences that students bring into the classroom—to what MLT theorists call reading the self and the world in creative flux.

Practice

In the autumn semester of the 2012–2013 academic year at Toyo University in Tokyo, Japan, (class size=n=38) third-year undergraduates, aged between 20–22 (29 female and 9 male), taking a year-long course in advanced English writing, responded to and researched the current social and political woes assailing Japan, with especial attention given to the lives and work-situations of Japanese youth in the wake of the 2011 earthquake and nuclear meltdown in Fukushima. Students were also asked to respond to several Western perceptions of Japan (外圧). Lesson plans for the course were based on the affective and intellectual reaction and response to an academic journal article by Professor Anne Allison of Duke University (Allison, 2012). The theoretical direction of the class was grounded in the aforementioned interpretation of Guattari's pedagogy (1984) and informed by the notion of affect in Spinoza's *Ethics* and elaborated through Deleuze and Guattari's (1987) notion of abstract machines, which view affects as disruptive and transformative of subjectivity. Affect, according to Deleuze and Guattari (1987), following Spinoza, is "puissance: or the power to affect and be affected".

All of the students in the study were at university full-time and many had tentatively started attending workshops and company introduction meetings (setsumeikai 説明会), as part of the intrusive albeit institutionalized job hunting season (shūshoku katsudō 就職活動). In Japan, usually beginning in the autumn semester of the third year of an undergraduate degree, sometimes sooner, students begin the arduous task of finding a job for life after graduation. Their fledgling individuality vanishes in a flash. Outwardly their hair returns to matte black, and spotless black suits and white shirts are adorned by all. Perhaps inwardly too, their hopes turn from literature and the world of ideas and dreams to the world of work and reason: the madhouse awaits.

The research was affectively-led as it compelled the students to think about their immediate futures, about their desires, about what they bring to the class-room. As part of their course, students were asked to critique a 2012 paper by Allison entitled "Ordinary Refugees: social precarity and soul in 21st century Japan". Writing in the *Anthropological Quarterly*, Allison's exposition notes a raft of endemic social problems in Japan. She finds a series of social maladies such as a loss of home-base (ibasho 居場所), net cafe refugeeisation (nanminka 難民化), the relationless society (muenshakai 無縁社会), social precarity in the form of irregular work (freeta フリーター) and disposable labor (hiseiki koyo 非正規雇用). According to Allison, the young and old in Japan suffer a sense of hopeless-ness and futurelessness—a precarity of soul (see Franco Berardi, 2009). Allison justifies this statement with evidence taken from the current state of Japan such as the growing number of people dying alone, social recluses (hikikomori ひきこも り), bullying (ijime いじめ), and the rise of what she calls the desperately lonely (kodoku 孤独). On top of this, there is the NEET phenomenon, i.e., those who have a part-time or no job, and have little to almost no stake in society. Assaulted by growing hardship, a low birth rate, and the ageing population, structurally and endemically, Japan is increasingly polarized, according to Allison—a society on the slide (suberidai shakai すべり台社会).

The outcome of this experiment in the English writing classroom was fruitful for both students and teachers alike in several respects, because, on the one level, the students in the group could find something meaningful to say about Allison's argument and although her dense vocabulary proved to be particularly daunting, the academic style and overall direction of the paper fostered an emotional perturbation in the readership. Moreover, students wrestled with the "truth" of the article, and whether the author had successfully extrapolated and correlated the social facts about the current state of Japanese society to the subjective feelings of Japanese people. For example, one student wrote: "I don't know what she is talking about, we [the Japanese] are a very hardy and creative people, we will find a way out of the current problems. I have hope for the future." An example of the psychological distress vis-à-vis the current economic realities facing students across the planet upon graduation is found in the following remark: "We [in Japan] are a strong economy that is undergoing a prolonged period of hardship. But when we look at other countries such as Greece and Spain, we know that we are not alone in our suffering, but the current global economic problems should make us more likely to organize ourselves into self-help networks that express our desires to live a good life." Several other responses included below emerged in letters sent to Allison, after the professor of social anthropology kindly replied to the questions posed in my students' final essays. On the whole, students were unanimous in condemnation of the general direction of Allison's article. One student wrote that Japan would overcome its current economic problems through "intelligence, hard work and the Japanese ability to adapt to new living conditions".

| Student 1: | Your essay was very difficult to read for me, but it was a good opportunity to deliberate about Japanese realities. I also think there is hope that things will be better in the near future. |
| Student 2: | In Japan, the nuclear meltdown incident occurred in March 11, 2011 and the outlook for revival is still vague. We mustn't avoid solving this problem, but in fact we Japanese can't find steps to revive. We have a lot of issues of politics, economies and societies, however we need to treat them one by one and settle them. I'm glad to hear your precious |

	opinion and I thought we Japanese have to take some actions without just so much talk.
Student 3:	I thought all of young people from all over the world need to know the situation of other country. If we don't know about it at all I think the world will be worse. So I really want young people to know how to change the world. I really thank you for your essay because it gave us good chance to think about the place where we are.
Student 4:	The Government in Japan has to solve this problem at once. I worry about the radioactive contamination problem. I think many foreigners worry about it, too.
Student 5:	The Olympics will be held in Japan at 2020. And I begin to get united by preparations to perform a meeting of people of the world. You said, Japan was a dark country, but, surely this impression of Japan will change.
Student 6:	I agree with your opinion "The future of Japan is in the hand of young people like yourselves." I think that young people have to study and know about present situation of the world.
Student 7:	We have one problem is Fukushima's nuclear power plant. I think this is a today's biggest problem in Japan, and most of people around world think so. We have to solve this problem as soon as possible. Anyway, we can get hope from the Olympics.

Many students used the article as a prompt for introspection and psychoanalytic self-diagnosis, which sometimes took on a negative tone if the students felt pangs of recognition in aspects of Japanese society that the article explored. The article successfully managed to provoke the students into reflection about their own situation as well as the wider consequences of the 2008 global financial crisis in countries such as Greece, Ireland and Spain. The teacher prepared documentary materials which helped students to see the plight of other young people in the world. The students therefore connected the social malaise in Japan that the article describes to the ways in which the global economy ebbs and flows. Students could therefore make a connection with the economic climate and social life, rather than writing about anything essential or fundamental with respect to the Japanese personality. Students were provided with several documentaries regarding Japan's problems with *hikikomori*, as well as documentaries focused on the plight of young people in Italy, France and Ireland. From this exposure and with the guidance given in several lesson plans, the teacher felt confident that students developed critical visual literacy skills along the way. What the teacher found was a becoming-global or becoming-Other of the student.

Conclusion

The class essays were completed before news broke of the decision to nominate Japan for the 2020 Olympics. Allison's reply to the students also came after the uplifting news. The decision generated a new series of questions, concerns, and hopes from my students. It also put their essays and Allison's too into context. Over the course of the year, the university students progressed in their studies through a hybrid mixture of intercultural communication, technological mediation, the affective and conflictive stimulation of the material (affect) and an identity-based understanding of "Japaneseness", with respect to the assemblages produced and the pedagogy deployed. Students responded enthusiastically to Prof Allison's thank you note, which can be read in the appendix. They all agreed that while they disagreed with the overall tone of the essay and while the research was hard slog, not only English skills but also their critical faculties as well were put to the test.

It has been shown that the mediating third experiment principle Bradley invoked and applied was empowering for both himself and his students. The fact that students saw their work effecting and influencing critics on the other side of the planet encouraged them to see themselves as agents of change and transformation. It set in train a transversal movement between molar aggregates, a way to foster dissensus and difference in education—a way to connect critically with the world of work and reason. The process also began to contest ossified curriculum and instruction and unleashed micro-becomings, the becoming-global of the student and teacher alike (Aoki, 2005). It would seem that the students are already on the way to forming critical thinking war-machines to contest received truths and explanations.

Appendix

September 17, 2013

Dear students of Professor Joff Bradley's class at Toyo University,

Professor Bradley has shared with me your essays and letters generated from reading my article on social precarity in Japan. Thank you for taking my essay so seriously and for engaging with the issues I raise there. I have given you all short responses to your own essays and notes. But I'd like to add just a few comments that came up in a number of your remarks.

The issue I call social precarity is indeed something that is not limited to Japan or Japanese. People around the world are struggling with the same problems of un(der)employment, social disparity, and hopelessness about the future. Youth are particularly hard hit and precarious and have been behind a number of social movements and protests around the world from Arab Spring to Spain, Italy, and Greece. Here, as in Japan, young people want secure jobs and reasonable hope that they can have the kind of lives that their parents did, or what they have been led to believe constitute "good life."

That people like myself (someone called me a "critic" but I'm actually more a scholar and anthropologist who works on social conditions in Japan—that's my speciality, hence the reason I concentrate on Japan rather than elsewhere) examine issues like *hikikomori* and *kodokushi* in Japan doesn't mean that we are looking down on Japan or criticizing Japanese. A "critic" in one sense of the word means a social critic who critically examines social conditions of a country. This is what I attempt to do as an anthropologist of Japan. But to critically examine a place doesn't simply mean to criticize. It means to understand the roots of behaviour (like employment and underemployment) and, as one of you put it so nicely, to also think of possible solutions to problems.

The future of Japan is in the hands of young people like yourselves. Those of us who point out problems and pressure-points are mere observers. And we point out the shift—in attitude, fortunes, and orientation—between the era of high economic growth in the 1970s and 80's and now: the two decades following the bursting of the bubble economy that has been accompanied by "lost decades" and "lost generations" of youth. Times have changed and it's true that many westerners find this surprising. A book written by a famous Harvard sociologist, Ezra Vogel, in the 1980s, was called *Japan as Number One*. And there he suggested, among other things, that America should adopt an educational system like Japan's because economic productivity and competitiveness was so high in Japan. Today, journalists and scholars who study Japan point out different phenomena like the high suicide rate and freeter. In part, the world is seeing its own future reflected in what is happening today in Japan.

I end my own article thinking about hope. I find it interesting that not many of you mentioned this. But Japanese are known the world over for their resilience in the face of adversity. After the earthquake, tsunami, and nuclear meltdown on March 11, 2011, Japanese responses were reported with awe and admiration across the globe. This too bears promise for responses to the kinds of social precarity I point out in my article.

I wish you all the best in leading Japan into a future beyond social precarity. A post-precarious Japan?

Best,
Anne Allison

References

Allison, A. (2012). Ordinary refugees: Social precarity and soul in 21st century Japan. *Anthropological Quarterly, 85*(2), 345–370.

Aoki, T. (2005). *Curriculum in a new key: The collected works of Ted T. Aoki* (W. F. Pinar & R. L. Irwin, Eds.). Lawrence Erlbaum Associates.

Berardi, F. (2009). *Precarious rhapsody: Semiocapitalism and the pathologies of the post-alpha generation.* Minor Compositions.

Bradley, J. P. N. (2012, October 01). Materialism and the mediating third. *Educational Philosophy and Theory, 44*(8), 892–903.

Cole, D. R., & Pullen, D. L. (2010). *Multiliteracies in motion: Current theory and practice.* Routledge.

Deleuze, G. (2004). Intellectuals and power [an interview with Michel Foucault]. In D. Lapoujade (Ed.), *Desert Islands and other texts: 1953–1974* (pp. 206–213, M. Taormina, Trans.). Semiotext(e).

Deleuze, G., & Guattari, F. (1987). *A thousand plateaus: Capitalism and schizophrenia.* University of Minnesota Press.

Genosko, G. (Ed.) (1996). *The Guattari reader.* Blackwell Publishers.

Guattari, F. (1984). *Molecular revolution: Psychiatry and politics.* Penguin.

Guattari, F. (1995). *Chaosmosis: An ethico-aesthetic paradigm.* Indiana University Press.

Masny, D. (2013). *Cartographies of becoming in education: A Deleuze-Guattari perspective.* Sense Publishers.

Masny, D., & Cole, D. R. (2009). *Multiple literacies theory: A Deleuzian perspective.* the Netherlands: Sense Publishers.

Stiegler, B., & Ross, D. (2012). *Uncontrollable societies of disaffected individuals.* Polity.

CHAPTER ELEVEN

Woe Betide You the Truth Be Told: Linguistic Corruption as a Pedagogical Tool

It is the responsibility of intellectuals to speak the truth and to expose lies. This, at least, may seem enough of a truism to pass over without comment. Not so, however. For the modern intellectual, it is not at all obvious. Thus we have Martin Heidegger writing, in a pro-Hitler declaration of 1933, that "truth is the revelation of that which makes a people certain, clear, and strong in its action and knowledge;" it is only this kind of "truth" that one has a responsibility to speak. (Chomsky, 1967)

What does it mean to rise above the corruption of language to teach the corruption of corruption itself? What does one become as a consequence? Is it conceivable or merely the conceit of the pedagogue? I am going to draw on several resources from literature and philosophy to think about corruption as a pedagogical tool and will think about this in the sense of undermining one own's position or right precisely through the undermining of one's own language. I am keen to think about the nature of the corruption of language, especially the English language, and how one can come out of trauma and grief to find a path to reconciliation, because, simply, I am faced with this question, is English the right language to reach truth and reconciliation? With the role of the teacher in mind, I am to discuss corruption as a pedagogical tool concerning young people and the desperate need to "corrupt the corruption" as Badiou says in The true life (Badiou, 2017). I am looking at the language of grief, violence, the violence of words and the dangerous, malignant, venomous, infective, virulent affects that sometimes enshroud or cloak words, and by which and through which transform words into weapons with sharp, penetrating, piercing and deadening or malignant effects. Not to think this way, seems a betrayal of one's duty as a teacher and a disavowal of one's position of power.

On the master's dominant narrative

Truth be told, I have peered long and hard into the dark, loathsome abyss of my language, its history and culture, to look at words and their apparent meaning, to understand what envelops them and to know what sticks to them like tar. Since these words are English words, I draw on Nobel Laureate and British playwright Harold Pinter (1930–2008) to understand the corruption and the rot of words (see "Pinter: Held Incommunicado on the Mobile" in Bradley & Kennedy, 2020) and ask a range of questions: What does it mean to speak the master's dominant narrative? What is the nature of the complicity with this tactic? Is English—a language battered black and blue by its own historical violence and legacy—the right language to teach peace, empathy, cosmopolitanism and global citizenship? What does it mean to use English to respond to a world in strife and violence? (see Bradley's essay "Deleuze and Globish" in Bangou, Waterhouse, & Fleming, 2020). What can or should be another lingua franca for global citizens within this catastrophic morass? Must protest, resistance and refusal always be in the master's dominant voice? How can trauma be expressed otherwise than the dominant code and how can barriers be overcome and empathy spread in a language of not one's own belonging?

Addressing this admittedly long series of questions, it is instructive to consider Pinter's thoughts on menacing silences and precarious resistances alongside the phenomenology of American philosopher Alphonso Lingis in which we find an understanding of reconciliation and hospitality and perhaps a fitting response to the hell of worlds or spaces excluded by the hyper-order of urban technopoles, that is, those spaces in-between languages where nothing is said but everything is nevertheless understood (Lingis, 2008). Again, I concern myself with telling the truth, with fearless speech, with the Greek notion of Parrhesia (παρρησία) [franc-parler in French] and the question of corruption as such as I am interested in exploring the uses of truth-telling as a Foucauldian-, Badiouan-, Deleuzian-inspired pedagogical tool. Here I ask myself and with these resources to hand: What is my own truth telling? What does it mean to speak authentically against a backdrop of trauma and violence? How can one situate truth-telling in terms of social justice and what is the nature of virtue in this truth-telling?

Those interested in the structural violence inherent in language should and must be concerned with the imperialism of words and speech, the "language of the capital" (Chiasson, 2017, p. 50), the language of military might, the dominant code of order words (*mots d'ordre*) and passwords. English, the language of planetary capitalism, the de facto instrument of imperialism, is the war machine of communication. Bearing this in mind, it is a fair question to ask whether English is the right language to teach peace, empathy, cosmopolitanism or global citizenship. What does it mean to use English to respond to a world suffering war and violence if one is deeply concerned with the telling of truth, with fearless speech (Foucault, 2001)? Faced with these questions, it seems to me that what I am searching for is a new pedagogical sense of self-subverting authority, a self-subverting exposure and subversion of power relations and structures, a way to constantly undermine one's own person as a legitimator of power/knowledge. How does one renounce one's own dominating trend?

I agree with Gilles Deleuze that we must hijack speech, corrupt speech, to create "vacuoles of noncommunication" or circuit breakers that elude control but how to do it? I shall use Pinter's work to explore this. In any event, and as a constant refrain, I ask myself what is my own truth telling? Should I and how do I corrupt others to take a risk, to speak truth to power? Do I reproduce power relations in this act and what is changed as a consequence? Against a continuing backdrop of war, trauma and violence, how can I undermine myself and my role if, by definition, by speaking English I am acting in bad faith? To answer these questions, I draw on philosophy and literature to understand my own lot, my own station, my own furrow of thought, as it seems to me profoundly clear that not to think about language without this repertoire of self-subverting tools is tantamount to a dereliction of duty.

Performative uncomfortable utterance
My refrain

> I'm English. I'm from England. I speak English, you speak my language. I mean I'm English but I'm not in England. But I'm English. I often don't feel very English and in fact I don't think I've ever felt very English, I mean English English. You know what I mean, don't you? But I teach English. I know English. People expect me to be English. I'm English period (assertive). Maybe not. Maybe I'm not English English.

The frustration of being different or of speaking another language or having to learn this imperial tongue of mine must be maddening for you. It's maddening for me to tell the truth as the world in the last few years has heard much of Donald Trump who speaks "degenerate" statements or énoncés (Guattari, 2000, p. 43). His world of Twitter digests is English but not English English. The late Bernard Stiegler follows and recognizes Félix Guattari in The Three Ecologies in the 1980s for understanding presciently the dangers of toxic power and its ecological effects, and speaks of Donald Trump in the following critical manner:

[L]e président Trump incarnant le destin suicidaire global que se révèle être l'ère Anthropocène lorsqu'elle atteint ses limites, à savoir: maintenant.

President Trump embodies the global suicidal destiny that turns out to be the Anthropocene era when it reaches its limits, namely, now.

Guattari writes of Trump and the like and their "degenerate" statements:

Just as monstrous and mutant algae invade the lagoon of Venice, so our television screens are populated, saturated, by 'degenerate' images and statements. In the field of social ecology, men like Donald Trump are permitted to proliferate freely, like another species of algae, taking over entire districts of New York and Atlantic City; he 'redevelops' by raising rents, thereby driving out tens of thousands of poor families, most of whom are condemned to homelessness, becoming the equivalent of the dead fish of environmental ecology. (Guattari, 1989)

Truth be told, I think such English cannot be a fitting medium for the language of reconciliation. And even more than this, I wonder if English English is the right tool for reconciliation. My English English is not a tool for reconciliation. I am sure there are other languages which have qualities more suitable for reconciliation. It might be Urdu, a beautiful language. It might be Japanese with its exquisite elements of keigo or honorifics. It might be Tamil, one of the world's oldest languages. It might be the Korean language or the Chinese language, which at their most lofty, you might say, do not take to direct antagonism easily, preferring instead subtly, evasion and circumspection, that is implicit communication which avoids confrontation.

Performatively, and to confound matters, do allow me to continue this ever so slightly uncomfortable Pinteresque anecdote. I am here speaking my tongue, speaking a "performative contradiction of enunciation" (Derrida, 1998, p. 3) in a language, which is not my own. I speak a monolingualism which is not my own. "I only have one language, yet it is not mine." Derrida writes:

Because language is not [the master's, or the colonist's] natural possession, he can, thanks to that very fact, pretend historically, through the rape of a cultural usurpation, which means always essentially colonial, to appropriate it, to impose it as 'his own.' That is his belief; he wishes to make others share it through the use of force or cunning; he wants to make others believe it, as they do a miracle, through rhetoric, the school, or the army. (1998, p. 23)

I think there is something important at work here in this existential and linguistic aporia. Let me put it like this drawing on my own experience. As a boy, I was told by numerous teachers not to speak my dialect, a dialect that I grew up with as my parents, working-class parents, are from Northern England, from Lancashire to be exact. In Northern England, my teachers since I was a wee boy scolded me for speaking the way my parents spoke. The dialects found in Bolton and Burnley and those industrial towns in-between are raucous, playful and beautiful, cocky and splendid, but teachers told me not to speak with a dialect, told me to speak a master language, a master argot, if you like, the artificial and fabricated language of the BBC, the dialect of the British Raj—now the dominant mode of planetary-wide communication. Again, and performatively, I repeat, I only have one language, and yet it is not mine.

The English language itself is being taken away from the English

At this juncture, it is worth exploring Slovenian philosopher Slavoj Žižek's argument on the use of English as it has an interesting twist connected to the above declaration. Exploring the ambiguities and paradoxes of the dialectic of linguistic and cultural colonization, and challenging the notion that to win power one must imitate and adopt the code of the colonizers, Žižek contends that a space of liberation is precisely cleaved open from the social disintegration which ensues from the colonization process. Against the complaint that resistance to colonization is formulated detrimentally in the language of the colonizer, we could say that the glottophagy of "English" (Calvet, 2005; Chiti-Batelli, 2003, Lecercle & Riley, 2005) does not so much imperil local and cultural identities but rather offers a tool of resistance, a pedagogical and pharmacological tool—a poison and a cure. Speaking on India's experience of colonization at the hands of the British Empire, Žižek insists that in the very use of an imposed alien tongue there inheres the spectre and possibility of a new universalist, democratic state, a new radical possibility in contradistinction to a precolonial, mythical or pristine past. In other words, there is a kind of futural utopia of language at work. This possibility is created through colonization itself as the adopted new language symbolizes the absence of a primordial, autochthonic identity. In the long search for origin, there is no more mythical "India" or mythical "England" to be found. The universalist language and like global capitalism itself means there are no roots, places, originary pure, virgin identities or territories—no belonging or origin or nationhood. Against critics who question any sense of a priori alienation which manifests in the use of the language of the colonizers, and other forms of cultural colonization, Žižek (2015) outlines what he designates as the Malcolm X factor, the Hegelian "absolute recoil," which is to say, in the very loss of something one creates a lost dimension. In Hegelian-Žižekian terms, there is parallax "shift in perspective," a way to perceive the uncanny in the everyday field of vision. The overcoming of a crisis is a shift of perspective, a passage from what has gone to what will become. For Žižek, reconciliation can be radically immanent in that a shift of perspective occurs vis-à-vis what first appears as disintegration. Immanence emerges as the shifting of transcendence. In the shift of perspective, we find what previously appeared as conflict or a problem already appears as its own solution, its own reconciliation. This is not taken in the sense of a pure, unadulterated, reclaimed pristine past, a nostalgia for the good old days, for roots, for imperial domain and its codes, but rather the possibility of something new coming into being.

As a universal language, English is "stolen from British people themselves" whose own claims to universality are exposed as particular interests of the ruling imperialist class (English English). Instead, we must search for a new universality as Žižek says (2013):

> [C]olonialism is not overcome when the intrusion of the English language as a medium is abolished, but when the colonizers are, as it were, beaten at their own game—when the new Indian identity is effortlessly formulated in English, i.e., when the English language is 'denaturalized' when it loses its privileged link to 'native' Anglo-Saxon English-speakers.

And again

> This is what is beautiful in global capitalism, what I really love: Even the English language itself is being taken away from the English.

That English is being taken away from the English themselves suggests a new dimension to the question of reconciliation and the overcoming of trauma. It suggests a shared language or code for the overcoming of particular interests. It suggests a way out of the aporia myself and others toil from within. From the disruptive and transformative experience of trauma, there is a self-subverting of the meaning of history, memory, and language. A new series of affects emerge.

The language of the capital

To examine war narratives which depict violence and trauma, I chose Pinter's play Mountain Language (2013) as it explores the psychological factors of both victors and victims. The play was arguably inspired by Pinter's trip to Turkey with Arthur Miller and concerns over the torture and the fate of the Kurdish people. But Pinter insists the play is not solely about the Turks and the Kurds but the banning of languages throughout history, such as Irish, Welsh language, Urdu or the Estonian language. In the distortions of everyday language Pinter, throughout his career, questioned whether permanent peace is possible when the language used remained coded with violent affects. I agree with him that the exploration of hostility, fear and violence remains timely and urgent. Why? Our time is pockmarked by a sinister, fascistic, corrupting micropolitics, a politics of distortion and fragmentation of desire, an implosion of meaning. Our time is tainted by an oppressive and authoritarian operation of state power both in reality and in our mental life. Pinter is essential for understanding the corrosive effects of power and the affects which insinuate themselves stealthily within the language games of legitimacy of both the dominant and the dominated.

In the play Mountain Language women from the mountains have been granted permission to visit their imprisoned relations, inmates one surmises who have resisted state or military authority. A dehumanizing regime denies oppressed groups the right to use a native tongue, a language which would ground their subjectivity. The women are imprisoned and tortured. A prison officer announces they are not allowed to speak in their language to their men. It is a military decree that their language is outlawed and forbidden, their language no longer exists. The "language of the capital" is imposed on mountain people to impose cultural hegemony and homogeneity.

> Now hear this. You are mountain people. You hear me? Your language is dead. It is forbidden. It is not permitted to speak your mountain language in this place. You cannot speak your language to your men. It is not permitted. Do you understand? You may not speak it. It is outlawed. You may only speak the language of the capital. That is the only language permitted in this place. You will be badly punished if you attempt to speak your mountain language in this place. This is a military decree. It is the law. Your language is forbidden. It is dead. No one is allowed to speak your language. Your language no longer exists. Any questions? I do not speak the mountain language. (Pinter, 2005, pp. 255–256)

At the end of the play and without rhyme or reason a new law comes into force allowing the suppressed language the permission to utter its own code. Here Pinter shows us the precarious, arbitrariness and absurdity of power. The guard tells the mother and daughter to speak their own language which they refuse to do. But why refuse? On whose orders must one refuse? The mother's ambiguous silence could stem from the trauma and terror at the hands of the guards or it could be an act of resistance, a refusal to speak a language now granted official recognition but allowed by those who are without an ethical mandate; in other words, it could be a subversive refusal to respond to the ideological coercion of the master language. This for me offers a transferable pedagogical tool for understanding the relay of hegemony and resistance. Pinter explores how language games are indeterminable and interminable.

> Mountain Language lasts only 20 minutes, but it could go on for hour after hour, on and on and on, the same pattern repeated over and over again, on and on, hour after hour. (Billington, 2007, p. 794)

The final dénouement to the play is striking because it shows that fearless speech cannot be ordered but itself must arise from the subject itself, from the swelling of subjectivity itself, from subjectivation, that is, the coming into being of the subject. One cannot demand that the Other must speak fearlessly, one cannot demand that the Other be free. We can say that the words of the guards "shock, strike, jab, bite, pick on, harass, lacerate" bodies (Lingis, 2019, p. 14). Lingis says of words that we subject ourselves to them, to those "oppressive, words, abrasive words, stinging words, biting words, cutting words." Such words "construct us, lacerate us, humiliate us, sicken us, mortify us" (see Lingis in Jones, 2019, p. 88). Words are said not for their representational form but for their condensing, intensifying force. Lingis describes the relationship with alterity as a bond, of being "commanded, contested, having to answer to another for what one does and for what one is. It is also finding oneself addressed, appealed to …" (Lingis in Lévinas & Lingis, 2002, p. xxii) but in the dialogue between the prisoner and the guard, one senses the limits of the phenomenological description as those affects enveloping the words take on a more material reality and force. The affects generated by the words of the guards mean there is great risk in rising against them. A striking dialogue proceeds:

> Prisoner: Mother, you can speak, Mother, I'm speaking to you. You see? We can speak. You can speak to me in our own language. You can speak. Mother, can you hear me? I am speaking to you in our own language … Do you hear me? It's our language … Can't you hear me? Do you hear me? Mother? …
>
> Guard: Tell her she can speak in her own language. New rules. Until further notice.
>
> Prisoner: Mother?
>
> Sergeant: Look at this. You go out of your way to give them a helping hand and they f**k it up. (Pinter, 2005)

Alphonso Lingis wonders how truth is held by people whose different perceptions and judgments led them to war. He asks: "What kind of truth can be established? How much of the truth about their violent past is necessary for communities to begin to coexist and build a common future?" (p. 145). He writes:

> Greatly traumatic events are not simply retained by memory; they are integrated in a course of mental life that continually opens upon a future of new events and actions. In some cases they block access to the future: the victim lives in his or her trauma and cannot live in a now that is different and envision a future that arrays new possibilities. In other cases the reverse happens: the trauma is closed off to consciousness, cannot be recalled, cannot be understood or interpreted. In every case, as the years pass, what

one has undertaken and lived through modifies what one remembers of a traumatic aggression and how one remembers it. (2019, p. 146)

In First Person Singular, Lingis insists that the duty to speak in one's own name is demanded by the rational collective (2007a, p. 91). The duty to speak in our own name is imposed under threat of exclusion or effacement by a specific social machinery. Summoned to speak, we are circumscribed, called to account, by a force within discourse, a death within language, a death sentence. Lingis says: "The order, prompt, or cue that orders us to speak in our own name is already... a verdict, a death sentence" (2007a, p. 91; see George & Sparrow, 2014). This summons is a subjectification, a subjection, a death sentence. What the phenomenology of Lingis renders clear is how the "cues, watchwords, and passwords order how we are to speak and when we are to speak" (2007b, p. 115) are enveloped and penetrated by power relations and therefore resistance to them carries its own dangers of seduction, collusion and complicity. He writes: "If the constitution of a subject, subjected to and subjugated by the face that orders us to stand on our own and speak in our own name is a death-sentence, the release of becomings in all directions could well become destructive and self-destructive" (2007b, p. 119). This is where Lingis and Pinter work together well for it is Pinter's dialogue which demonstrates how power corrupts the articulation of the truth—and there lies its pedagogical lesson. In his essay Truth and Reconciliation, Lingis asks how truth is determined among people whose different perceptions and judgments led them to war.

He asks to what extent is truth required for the reconciliation of peoples in conflict: "What kind of truth can be established? How much of the truth about their violent past is necessary for communities to begin to coexist and build a common future?" (Lingis, 2018, p. 437). It is worth quoting Lingis in full and he clarifies Pinter's point brilliantly:

> And there are times when we are to speak in our own name. We are enjoined under oath to tell the court just why we kept pit bulldogs and what we did when they attacked the victim. The paramedic is required by the medical staff to say just how he saw the accident victim when he arrived on the scene and how the victim reacted in the ambulance on the way to the hospital. The student is asked to write down on the exam just what he has understood. The researcher is required to report exactly her methodology, her data, her verifications, or her work will be rejected by the journal and she may be dismissed from her position and from the profession. The prisoner is ordered to identify himself and recount his activities under threat of torture. It is not some inner compulsion to authenticity, but a collective, a social machine, that orders me to speak in my own name. (2007b, p. 115)

And in Deleuze's work, in his critique of the dominant image of thought, we find a sustained critique of the philosophical practice of representation, of the majoritarian thought that functions as representative of, that speak for, that speaks the truth of every minor, babbling, stuttering or immigrant tongue. This is the indignity in speaking for others which Pinter's play Mountain Language exposes so brilliantly. The idea of fearless speech and the act of parrhesia, that is "to speak candidly or to ask forgiveness for so speaking," for me raises the question of the task of philosophy, namely the corruption of youth. Badiou writes profoundly on this matter:

> Philosophy is a movement, the goal of which is to transform subjectivity, a subjectivity which is corrupted by dominant opinions. [T]he definition of philosophy must be, effectively, the corruption of the youth: to destroy the true corruption of youth by the ordinary world and to corrupt the corruption. That is, to save the youth from the heavy presence of the corrupted world. (Badiou, Bartlett, & Clemens, 2018, pp. 33–34)

Žižek, a fellow traveller with Badiou, also speaks of the task of a philosopher as one of corrupting the youth of today, which is to say to make them understand their freedom in capitalism is not what it seems:

> [T]he task of a philosopher is no longer to undermine the hierarchic symbolic edifice that grounds social stability but... to make the young perceive the dangers of the growing nihilist order that presents itself as the domain of new freedoms. (Žižek, 2019)

To be young is to be caught in an aporia, a difficult quandary, "a principal contradiction" insists Badiou. To be young is to prepare for integration into society, yet, all the while the social itself is imploding. In this context, it is fair for youth to ask why they must defer gratification, why study, why undergo an apprenticeship, why waste youth. Why speak the master's argot? Badiou speaks to youth from the perspective of an old man. He tells them it is necessary to change the world, to take risks and confesses his aim is also to corrupt youth, to make youth think of another way of living; he suggests they look for something worthwhile, something to live for, something that may break, one may say, the bad infinity of capital (money, pleasure, and power), perhaps even search out a new universality and language. In his book True Life, Badiou explicated upon the meaning of corruption further: "to corrupt youth means only one thing: to try to ensure that young people don't go down the paths already mapped out, that they are not just condemned to obey social customs, that they can create something new, propose a different direction as regards the true life" (Badiou & Spitzer, 2017, p. 8). Elsewhere, in a discussion on the question of the rupture, Badiou says that "[t]o corrupt the youth is to become a part of an immanent exception" (Völker, 2019, p. 16). He explains:

In fact, a great work of art, an invention, a creation, is something that, within particular conditions, necessarily transcends those particular conditions. This is what I've called an immanent exception. It's an exception that's internal; it's not an external exception. And so if particular works are capable of having a universal value it's because they are not entirely reducible to the particular conditions of their creation but are also an immanent exception within these conditions. (Badiou, Engelmann, & Spitzer, 2015, p. 63)

This "immanent exception" is when the truth wells up and bursts forth, when it emerges from the depths of one's own subjectivity or collectivity. This is when one speaks in one's own name but in a language which is not one's own but a universal and futural language.

Conclusion

After all that has gone on, I remain doggedly interested in English words and their apparent meaning. I remain a student of what envelops them and belongs to them like cancerous wounds. In this respect, Pinter is vital to understanding the corruption and the decay of words. He is important for understanding the exhaustion of everyday speech and its pathological depths. From studying his work we can better grasp the affective impact of invective, misogynous words, homophobic slurs, hate speech, injurious slander. One finds that language is a kind of regime of order words (*mots d'ordre*), cliché and hearsay, often deployed to keep thought at bay, to maintain the status quo. Here, there is much work to do to understand the pragmatics of illocutionary speech acts (acts which subtend the locutionary) and their perlocutionary effects, that is, effects which persuade, cajole, frighten and inspire (Lecercle, 2002, 2006). And for Lecercle (Lecercle & Riley, 2005, p. 74), interlocution is agonic and expressive of rapport de forces (power struggle or differential relation between forces). Indeed, for Lingis, it is when we speak in our name (Lingis, 2007a, 2007b; see Bradley, 2013, 2014), when we take responsibility for what is said and connect with intensities and the otherness of the other, that we set in motion passwords which evade control. In this respect, it is important to ask the following questions: How can one speak otherwise than everyday chatter of "the they" (Das Man) and of everydayness? How can one resist? How can one perform the act of truth-telling because thoughts and counter-thoughts occur imperceptibly as language hides them from exposure? This is a play of truth and the maintenance of power. We are not innocent in this and there is much disavowal at work to conceal the real state of affairs. Indeed, the public, for Pinter, is acquiescent in the maintenance of this status quo. What surrounds us, he insists, "is a vast tapestry of lies, upon which we feed."

> Political language, as used by politicians, does not venture into any of this territory since the majority of politicians, on the evidence available to us, are interested not in truth but in power and in the maintenance of that power. To maintain that power it is essential that people remain in ignorance, that they live in ignorance of the truth, even the truth of their own lives. What surrounds us therefore is a vast tapestry of lies, upon which we feed. (Pinter, 2013, p. 288).

It seems to me that to write a Marxist philosophy of language one must take up the everyday world that for the young is not only putrefying, poisonous and overcome with existential doubt, but desperately pervaded by a deep sense of ecological trauma and grief. Such a philosophy would demand praxis, to transform the world for the better, for youth coming into the world of power and its abuses, for it is youth we must guide in earnest. Yet, performatively, what language should I use to express this? Resistance to domination begins in the intersection between trauma and world-making. That is why we too must speak of that emotion which wells up within. And we must let it come out. This is not to serve the rich and spoilt who clamour to polish off their upbringing and to protect and continue their privilege and interests but to call the present to account, to call to account those who deny and blemish the world; in so doing we have a duty to fabulate the world afresh for the sake of youth, for the sake of a youth to come. This is to corrupt youth and corrupt the corruption. This is the perennial response to the "intolerable" and shame of the present as Deleuze says. In the broken middle of our times, our task is to find in utopias and heterotopias, imagined spaces and inaugural sites of voyage, journey and transformation—a new universal language of liberation. One task is to cut through the reifications of cliché, stereotype and habit in everyday speech to regain the intensity and warmth of words, to enhance the capacity to live, to reconcile ourselves with others. We are tasked with putting ourselves in question, of subverting ourselves, because we, in our most desperate of ages, simply must offer answers to youth who see the world without future or open horizon (Stiegler, 2018, 2020). I suspect what we are aiming for is the corruption of power by and through the corruption of youth. This would be an act of counter-power to burst asunder the protective chatter and hypocrisy that enshrouds social corruption.

References

Badiou, A., Bartlett, A. J., & Clemens, J. (2018). *Badiou and his interlocutors. Lectures, interviews and responses.* London: Bloomsbury Academic.

Badiou, A., Engelmann, P., & Spitzer, S. (2015). *Philosophy and the idea of communism: Alain Badiou in conversation with Peter Engelmann.* Oxford: Wiley

Badiou, A., & Spitzer, S. (2017). *The true life.* Cambridge, UK; Malden, MA: Polity Press.Bangou, F., In Waterhouse, M., & In Fleming, D. (2020). *Deterritorializing language, teaching, learning, and research: Deleuzo-Guattarian perspectives on second language education.* Leiden; Boston: Brill Sense.

Billington, M. (2007). *The life and work of Harold Pinter.* London: Faber.

Bradley, J. P. N. (2013). On the materiality of thixotropic slogans. *Dialogos, 12.* 71-100.

Bradley, J. P. N. (2014). On imperatives of coexistence and communication. *Dialogos, 13.* 127-152.

Bradley, J. P. N., & Kennedy, D. (2020). *Bringing forth a world: Engaged pedagogy in the Japanese university.* Leiden; Boston: Brill/Sense.

Calvet, L.-J. (2005). *Language wars and linguistic politics.* Oxford: Oxford University Press.

Chiasson, B. (2017). *The late Harold Pinter: Political dramatist, poet and activist.* London: Palgrave Macmillan.

Chiti-Batelli, A. (2003, August 20). Can anything be done about the "glottophagy" of English?: A bibliographical survey with a political conclusion. *Language Problems and Language Planning, 27*(2), 137–153.

Chomsky, N. (1967). A special supplement: The responsibility of intellectuals. *The New York Review of Books*, 23.

Derrida, J. (1998). *Monolingualism of the other, or, the prosthesis of origin.* Stanford, CA: Stanford University Press.

Foucault, M. (2001). *Fearless speech.* Los Angeles: Semiotext(e).

George, B., & Sparrow, T. (2014). *Itinerant philosophy: On Alphonso Lingis.* Brooklyn: Punctum Books.

Guattari, F. (2000). *The three ecologies.* London: Athlone Press.

Jones, D. E. (2019). *The philosophy of creative solitudes.* London; New York: Bloomsbury Academic.

Lecercle, J.-J. (2002). *Deleuze and language.* Houndmills, Basingstoke, Hampshire: Palgrave Macmillan.

Lecercle, J.-J. (2006). *A Marxist philosophy of language.* Leiden: Brill.

Lecercle, J.-J., & Riley, D. (2005). *The force of language.* Basingstoke, Hampshire: Palgrave Macmillan.

Lévinas, E., & Lingis, A. (2002). *Otherwise than being or beyond essence.* Pittsburgh, PA: Duquesne University Press.

Lingis, A. (2007a). *The first person singular.* Evanston, Ill.: Northwestern University Press.

Lingis, A. (2007b, January 01). Subjectification. *Continental Philosophy Review, 40*(2), 113–123.

Lingis, A. (2008). Conflict resolution and reconciliation of peoples. In P. Rothfield, C. Fleming & P. A. Komesaroff (Eds.), *Pathways to reconciliation* (pp. 41–52). Hampshire: Ashgate.

Lingis, A. (2018). *The Alphonso Lingis reader*. University of Minnesota Press.

Lingis, A. (2019). *Irrevocable: A philosophy of mortality*. Chicago: The University of Chicago Press.

Pinter, H. (2005). *Plays 4*. London: Faber and Faber.

Pinter, H. (2013). *Various voices: Sixty years of prose, poetry, politics, 1948–2008*. London: Faber & Faber.

Stiegler, B. (2018). *Qu'appelle-t-on panser?: 1*. Paris Éditions Les liens qui libèrent.

Stiegler, B. (2020). *Qu'appelle-t-on panser?: 2*. Paris Éditions Les liens qui libèrent.

Völker, J. (ed) (2019). *Badiou and the German tradition of philosophy*. London: Bloomsbury Academic.

Žižek, S. (2013). Love as a political category. Subversive Festival, 6. *Zagreb, Croatia*. Retrieved July 18, 2019, from http://www.youtube.com/watch?v=b44IhiCuNw4

Žižek, S. (2015). *Absolute recoil: Towards a new foundation of dialectical materialism*. London: Verso.

Žižek, S. (2019). *Like a thief in broad daylight: Power in the era of post-human capitalism*. New York: Seven Stories Press.

CHAPTER TWELVE

The Power of Emotional Factors in English Teaching

Teaching English in secondary schools brings together internal and external influences. The most pressing external influence is often the curriculum design that is being used in the zone that places and contextualizes English within a knowledge system. Animating this design are social forces such as the importance of English to the community and the ways in which English may explore identity through literature (Doecke et al., 2006). Internal influence on the English teaching that happens in the classroom is more complex, as particular teachers will bring their own motivations and conceptual understandings about English to bear on their teaching (Kress, 2006).

This chapter puts the field of knowledge about English teaching into play through the curriculum changes that have recently been happening on the island of Tasmania, Australia due to the introduction of a framework called *Essential Learnings* and explanations from secondary practitioners about the emotional aspects of teaching English. It aims to connect the internal and external dimensions of English teachers' professional lives to the benefit of the student trainee teachers undertaking the research, and the main researcher who has brought this evidence and thinking together. This joining exemplifies the value of research as a nexus for understanding complex aspects of English teaching (Cole, 2007a) and exploring the ways in which this complexity may be represented to challenge power concerns that might separate emotion from identity and change.

Methodology

The Bachelor of Teaching course that pre-service trainee English teachers follow in Tasmania is a postgraduate qualification—and includes aspects of educational research training. This project was designed for them as part of this training and is a form of action research (Martin et al., 2006). The student teachers learn through doing—in this case talking to in-service English teachers and gauging their opinions and ideas with respect to curriculum change and emotion. Fifty-eight secondary English teachers were interviewed for this project in their place of work for up to an hour and a half at a time. These teachers constitute a random sampling of different ages, ethnicities and gender. The student teachers were required to write up their research in the manner of a mini-thesis, building literature reviews, coding, analysis and critical evaluation of the themes that emerged from the semi-structured interviews and any observations that they undertook in the schools. In this way, the quality of their research was monitored and evaluated by the main researcher, who marked and discussed the results with the students. This project gained full local ethics clearance, both in terms of the students using the data for their own projects, and the aggregation of the evidence that is represented. Students supplemented their data with self-reflective diaries and notes from teaching in four practicum experiences over two years.

The teachers who were interviewed read an information sheet about the research and signed a consent form to take part. The students designed an appropriate research instrument, which included open-ended and informational questions about emotion and curriculum change (Gubrium & Holstein, 2002). Specific questions that ran through the research designs included: "What is the reaction of the teachers to curriculum change in Tasmania?" and "Discuss the emotional factors that permeate your English teaching". The students' analysis of the data depended on their ability to make qualitative distinctions in the transcripts (Upton, 2005), and to isolate themes in the research that corresponded to curriculum change and emotional proclivity. This research has been organized by the lecturer and main researcher running the course with the consent of the students and teachers, and provides an overview of the results obtained by them over four years.

The sections that follow differentiate between different English teacher types. This set of categories relates to curriculum change and the effects of the *Essential Learnings*. These teacher types are not sketchy characterizations of typical English teachers (Marshall, 2000) or crude stereotypes, but constitute a discourse analysis (Fairclough, 1992) of the complex identity resources available to English teachers in Tasmania during the research and time of change. The resultant Discourses are wholly interrelated and may coexist in the same subject, yet for the purposes of representation have been separated by the main researcher from the evidence as it was presented by the students and after intense discussion. The data that is included in the Discourses serves as evidence, and is also related on many levels to the power and identity structures that are present (Cole, 2005) in the English teaching system of Tasmania. The distinction used here between Discourses and discourses works to pinpoint those governmental forms of communication—Discourses—that carry power concerns and identity constructions, and everyday forms of language use—discourses (Gee, 2003). The overall research question for this section is: What are the categories of English teacher identity that one might discern after the introduction of the *Essential Learnings*?

The Essential Learnings (ELs)

The *Essential Learnings* was implemented in the Australian state of Tasmania in 2002 after many years of public consultation and debate (Watt, 2005) and is parallel to other Australian curricula such as the *Victorian Essential Learnings* (VELs). It is a knowledge framework based on constructivist and integrated curriculum principles (Dowden & Nolan, 2006). According to the ELs, the teaching of English is henceforth integrated into the "Essential Learning of Communicating".

As one might discern, the teaching of English is reorganized through this model—*Being literate* is valued alongside numeracy, information and arts literacy. Teachers should design units of exercises according to generative themes, and include communicative opportunities under these themes through which the students will improve their literacy skills. The ELs is assessed through standards that relate to each element in the framework; for secondary English teachers, the standards of *Being literate* are of primary concern. For many years, English was taught in Tasmanian secondary schools in a traditional manner, without a fixed curriculum model. This teaching constituted the study of classic and contemporary English texts for years 7–10, and marked against a set of state-wide English standards. According to the guidelines of the ELs, English teachers are now expected shape their lessons to suit communication goals, and this has resulted in three distinctive reactions that one can use to understand English teacher identities (Discourses) with respect to this curriculum change. The following categories were arrived at through rigorous discussion and debate between the student researchers and the lecturer.

Essential Learners

These teachers are thoroughly convinced that the ELs is a step in the right direction. They agree with it because it restructures the teaching of English in the context of social and cultural factors. According to this perspective, English in the secondary context becomes more aligned and integrated with the primary area of literacy, which enables learners to communicate effectively using words whilst thinking critically about text. For example:

> *Teacher A*: The ELs has given me the chance to really start planning some relevant lessons for the kids. I work in a school with a severely disadvantaged cohort. They have no money, and they come from families with no money. Now we don't have to go through the motions of studying a novel or planning gap-fillers to use up the time. We can do work that will help this group in the real world—to earn money!

It could be argued that the ELs provide continuity and scaffolding between primary and secondary language learning. Essential learners may well be sympathetic to whole language philosophy, and integrate critical literacy into their everyday English teaching through interdisciplinary units of work. The new knowledge framework (ELs) fits in with a socially constructed view of English teaching.

Neutral Pragmatists

The in-service English teachers in this group identify curriculum changes as exterior to their personal beliefs about English teaching. As such, they will take on board some of the tenets of the ELs without being overly concerned about implementation. Neutral pragmatists will go about their business of teaching English through text and organizing the curriculum according to traditional definitions of English education such as teaching the classics, while also being able to fit in their lesson ideas with the ELs. For example:

> *Teacher B*: I'm most familiar with Communicating, Being Literate and Being Arts Literate. I've sat down, and wrote my own rubrics – and that takes a lot of time, and it takes a lot of time to assess, 'cause you sit there with your school's understanding of it, and the actual ELs folder understanding of it, and whatever you've done with the rubric, and it takes probably five times as long to mark things. We are progressing, and getting there. I will work my way through this new system. It's hard to hand down to the kids as well, because they look at these numbers and they're not exactly sure what they mean.

The pragmatists will use aspects of critical literacy and child-centred learning—and yet will not articulate a specific overarching mandate with which to make any changes in the curriculum through their teaching and learning. These teachers perceive the new knowledge framework to be an outside influence, to be tolerated and worked with, but without transformative power, which is in *their* classroom practice and the agreements that they come to with their students.

Defenders of the Canon

The third reaction to the introduction of the ELs that this research has uncovered is that it is a threat to subject integrity. These English teachers not only consider this reform as interfering in their teaching practices, but they also believe it to be wrong. This is because the ELs impinges on their beliefs about the canon of English literature, and the appropriate pedagogies to get this body of work across. Teachers in this group are vocal opponents of the ELs, perhaps supporting other, more traditional curricula, where the subject disciplines are rigidly differentiated into subject areas. For example:

> *Teacher C*: I'm worried about social engineering, and I'm worried about that in ELs and critical literacy … in the ELs, for example, there are these world futures and personal futures. Now, somewhere, someone's decided, if you're going to assess someone on world futures, someone's obviously got an idea about what they would like the world to be like … but if I buy that teachers are able to sell a worldview – what happens when it's not one I like?

These teachers may hold a cultural heritage or skills-based approach to teaching English that is shaped by direct instruction and the pivotal role of the English teacher in passing on truths about English cultural life.

Interdisciplinary Subject Area

One of the most prevalent educational issues that this research has identified is the contrast between interdisciplinary knowledge, and the preservation of the subject disciplines in the secondary context (Shulman, 1986). The ELs framework lends itself to working across subject areas, and developing integrated units of work around generative topics. The intense discussion and analysis of the transcripts has shown that English teachers fall into two Discourse categories with respect to interdisciplinary work.

Vocational Project Managers

These teachers fully embrace interdisciplinary working. The reorganization of English into communication studies suits them as they enjoy the real-life contexts and the freedom to explore the media. Such teachers approach pedagogies from the perspective of multiliteracies (Mills, 2005) so that students use research and critical analysis to examine social phenomena through reading and writing projects (Mills, 2006). For example:

> *Teacher D*: We were doing a unit of work on autobiography. The issue of motorbikes came up! We decided to follow this theme, and did research into the sales and branding of motorbikes. We looked at the gender stereotypes around motorbikes. Students found out about biker gangs, we looked at where they lived, what they believed in and what types of people they were. We did market research and critical analysis of the image of bikers and the associated gender stereotypes.

It could be argued that opening English up to the interdisciplinary style of planning and teaching is a response to new cultural conditions. Students will have to become literate in different ways in the 21st century, and their repertoires of literate activities should be aligned with these changes (Cole, 2007b). Interdisciplinary work gives English teachers the freedom to explore this terrain, and to teach students relevant skills for today's workforce. Vocational project managers believe that English should be aligned to new workplace arrangements and the communication skills necessary to succeed in these environments.

Tireless Bookworms

These English teachers will accept the fact that the world is changing—but simultaneously believe that the basis for secondary English teaching and learning is print literacy. Students should therefore study written text in a direct manner, learning about written effects such as metaphor, verisimilitude and hyperbole. Bookworms will search out reading opportunities for their students and design pedagogies that enhance the reading experience. For example:

> *Teacher E*: Last year I read a book called *Hana's Suitcase* by Karen Devine. I found it so moving that I wanted to share it with my class. Even though I only had one copy, I was determined to use this book and we worked our way through it together and it has turned into one of the best teaching experiences that I have ever had. I believe that the class felt that I had been moved by this book, and they were too.

Bookworms will organize writing exercises that test the skills of their students to work in different genres (Derewianka, 1998). They will look at interdisciplinary work with suspicion, as it may constitute a threat to their understanding of reading and writing print text as primary. Bookworms will use many discursive and oral strategies in their English teaching, but these lesson segments and connectives will not usually be too far removed from a printed text source such as a script or a speech.

Critical Literacy

The issues about the status and use of critical literacy in English get to the heart of the changes that these Discourses explore. The ELs framework has put critical literacy at the centre of *Being literate* and therefore prioritizes its potential. This is perhaps an ironic counterpoint to traditional notions of textual authority and the mandates that emerge from governmental and bureaucratic offices. It could be suggested that most system control centres would not encourage critical exploration of controversies and the questioning of their texts. After close and animated scrutiny, it was found that teachers reacted according to two opposing Discourses to questions about critical literacy.

Textual Revolutionaries

This research found that there are English teachers who are wholly in agreement with the critical literacy approach to English teaching. Not only does it fit in with their beliefs about making a difference in the classroom, but it also gives their lessons a purpose and meaning beyond confined interaction with the students. Such teachers will seek out text that can be used for the purposes of social justice and egalitarianism. They will not shy away from exploring the media, and addressing issues such as racism, misogyny and the environment. Textual revolutionaries will include post-structural thinking in their approaches to text (Mellor & Patterson, 2004).

> *Teacher F*: The problem with English teaching has been for many years that it has not addressed fundamental social problems. Therefore, there was no point to it other than improving the student's level of English and perhaps some polite edification through reading. Now we have a framework to make a difference – I really appreciate that.

The textual revolutionaries will highlight the ways in which those in power have constructed meaning, and they will look for different positions in English teaching to make sense through text, using post-colonial, feminist or environmentalist perspectives for instance. These English teachers will be politically motivated to make a difference in society—and they will use this objective as an animating force in English classrooms. They believe wholeheartedly that it is a teacher's job to educate their students to be able to articulate their own opinions, especially if this means going against the norm (Cole, 2007c) or standing up for fundamental rights.

English "Royales"

Counter-arguments against critical literacy were not found to be as prevalent in the English teachers questioned for this research. Perhaps this was because the teachers in Tasmania were acting through the Discourse of pragmatic neutrality, as they thought it might be imprudent to speak out openly against critical literacy. Those who did, however, spoke about the suffocating and conformist English teaching agenda that critical literacy can produce. They indicated that changing the world through English teaching is unrealistic and idealistic. These English teachers believe that students need sets of values that may be delivered through quality literature. For example:

> *Teacher C*: You should remember that English isn't just about language and literacy skills – it is about ideas. In the absence of philosophy being well taught in schools, English can be a quasi-philosophy at times – it's about coming to terms with issues in life and the textual responses to these issues. It is not about giving students one certain answer or point of view.

The English "royales" are sceptical with respect to politically motivated teaching and suspicious of leading the students to a preconceived position on a text. They are aligned with the defenders of the canon, and select their texts from English literature to give their students a flavour of writing throughout history.

Emotions and Teaching English

The second part of the research presented the greatest challenge for the pre-service students. The aim was to examine the emotional side of English teaching. Once the teachers' ideas with respect to the ELs had been ascertained, the researchers were to pursue the emotions involved with teaching English. Clearly, this could lead the interview in several different directions (Strauss & Corbin, 1998). The pre-service students used open-ended questions to allow the teachers to tell their stories, and to explore how emotion permeates their practice. The teachers were encouraged to speak about their personal emotions, student emotions, emotions in the books that they were studying, or emotions that might be stirred up in the classroom due to the examination of text-related issues. The second part of the research depended upon the quality of the relationship that the student-researcher had managed to strike up with the teacher, and was not designed to be psychoanalytic. It should be noted that the representation of emotional phenomena in English teaching has come about in the context of a trainee teacher interviewing a fully trained teacher. This introduces a certain angle to the data, in that the teachers may well have added pedagogic value to their "emotionality" as they spoke to the trainees.

The analyzes that follow about emotions and English cannot be differentiated as Discourses of interrelated teacher types. This is because the emotional factors that are being represented here are by nature complex in that they are not unambiguous labels or clear categories that separate opinion (Chevellard, 1991). The following headings were arrived at after rigorous discussion between the pre-service students and the main researcher. In a parallel manner to the Discourse types, they are highly interrelated, and represent a qualitatively themed analysis of the data on emotions and secondary English teaching in Tasmania during 2004–2007. The primary research question here was: What are the ways in which emotion works in your English class?

Maturation

Research has shown that teachers construct English teaching differently as they mature into the job. At the beginning of their careers, many of them were trained to use emotions in the text to create lively and interactive learning environments. Perhaps they were responding to reader response or the personal growth theory of English teaching (Sawyer, 2004). Whatever the precise reason for the initial integration of emotional textual stimulation into their practice, they tended to personally value these tactics less as they matured. For example:

> *Teacher G*: My ideas have changed over the years – when I was an early teacher, I did a lot of teaching that I hoped was affecting students in an emotional and empathetic way – now I'm moving away from that model. I'm still looking at literature in the way it has an effect on students, but I don't want my students to be affected by the characters and the work in the same way. I actually want them to be more involved with the writer, the intended audience, the gaps and silences in the text, the purposes within the text.

Teachers at the beginning of their careers found it more difficult to speak about ways of working with text to enhance emotion, both in terms of their own emotions and emotions that come about due to reading texts. For example:

Teacher L: I have just started teaching and I have had a terrible time getting the kids to talk about anything! I remember having great discussions at school about characters in books and important issues. My students just don't want to say anything.

Perhaps because beginner teachers are sometimes under emotional pressure in the classroom context, textual emotions are more difficult to locate, address and articulate (Holland, 1968). The interview transcripts point towards a complex relationship between the use of emotions in English as a textual practice, the understanding of how to use emotions by particular English teachers and the articulation of emotion in their work. This relationship must also consider the ways in which habit and conditioning may make emotions part of the automatic dynamic in the classroom (Varela et al., 1993)—which also points to maturation as being pivotal when it comes to English teaching and emotion. This is reinforced by the ways in which English teaching becomes easier as practitioners mature into the job. At the beginning of their careers, English teachers might find it hard to separate their own emotional involvement with a lesson from the emotions that might be stirred up from reading a text (Doecke, 2006).

Gender

The interviews show that gender has a part to play with respect to emotion in English learning, both in terms of students reacting to texts and gendered emotional relationships in the English classroom. For example, boys sometimes found it difficult to take on role-plays, or to empathize with characters in the text. Girls, however, more frequently have no problem in identifying with characters, understanding the emotions in the text, and completing work that requires them to analyze relationships in the text. Gender therefore plays a role in secondary English in that engagement with literature requires emotional processes that may become gendered: For example:

Teacher H: ...it can be a struggle with boys to get a deep response out of them. It just usually requires you to pull back or alter the task in some way so that they are not obviously traumatized by the experience.

Teacher I: Something I find interesting though is that girls, perhaps because they are conditioned, are more likely to identify with the obvious male characters and feel quite happy talking about that identification, the emotions and the situation than boys do with female characters.

Teachers commented that work around gender stereotypes and relationships between genders can have a positive impact in English classes, in that the emotional proclivities stirred up by gender in the classroom may be resolved and articulated through the third person of the text. Teachers willing and able to use textual emotion positively in the classroom will stimulate differences through these practices (Cole, 2007a); those perhaps preferring a quiet life will yearn for single-sex English classrooms! The results of this research do not point to binary gendered opposites in English teaching, but show how classroom experience may be intensified through understanding the role of gender in English studies.

Power

The third theme that this research and the debriefings picked up was power. Many pre-service students have benefited from this as they may have come into teacher training with misconceptions about teacher power and the use of power in the classroom. They have found out that teachers feel empowered through an emotional connection with their job—they could also feel disempowered if this emotional connection is broken. The power of the English teacher was prevalent when he or she worked with a group with definite objectives and processes. The disempowered teachers were still working through power differentials. For example:

> *Teacher K*: At the end of the year, the grade 11 class wrote a letter about the behavioural problems that we had been experiencing. They said that there had been a personality clash. I don't believe in personality clashes myself. The secret to survival in that class was one boy who took an age to come around. Once he was on board and working with me, the rest of the group complied. They realized that I was the one with the power, and that the student was engaging in a power-stunt.

This teacher shows how power problems in the classroom may resolve themselves through dialogue and emotional alignment. The disempowered teacher is unconnected to the will of the group, and feels a gulf between their expectations and the class reality. Clearly, this emotional aspect of English teaching has a lot to do with behaviour management. Teachers who perceive their job to be a daily battle with teenagers will feel disempowered; those who understand their working lives as a synchronized movement towards enhanced communal literacy are more likely to revel in their existence (McWilliam, 2000).

Affects in English Teaching

The students and the main researcher discussed affects and their relationship with teaching English before doing the fieldwork. Affects were distinguished from emotions by understanding that emotions are connected to the personality of the teachers, whereas affects are connections between people and text and reading that may provoke emotions (Holland, 1968). It was agreed that affects were useful while talking about how English classrooms work on a less personal level than emotions (Keen, 2006). It was hoped that discussing affects would elicit less reactive responses from the English teachers than directly asking them about emotions, whilst still producing useful information on current English practice and identity. Affects can only be differentiated via interrelated themes, which do not define Discourses or identity resources since the conversations that emerged around them are not structured by subjects. The headings below were arrived at after rigorous and open analysis of the interview transcripts between pre-service students and the main researcher. The research questions here were: What affects help to make your classes work? What affects might cause difficulties in your English teaching?

Creativity

Many teachers spoke to the students about how to be creative in the English classroom. This is a personal goal——in terms of not endlessly repeating the same photocopied lessons—as well as being a social objective (Houtz & Krug, 1995). Students need to be skilled and creative in their language usage, as the communication abilities demanded of them in the contemporary workplace are increasingly disparate (Cope & Kalantzis, 1995). Affects are related to these changes in English teaching and identities that the improved creativity demands, as teachers have to continually work on the level of relationships with their students. Affects are also expressions of desire (Semetsky, 2007) that may be differentiated from emotions in that they relate to the atmosphere that the English lessons produce. For example:

> *Teacher H*: So sometimes very deep affective learning can come out of life writing and I have to try and say you are not writing just to be cathartic and for your own personal counselling here, there has to be an awareness of audience as well as learning outcomes and a valid learning experience going on. At this level teenagers sometimes don't know the difference and I feel I've got to be the one that arbitrates.

This teacher pinpoints how affects are connected to creativity, and the ways in which language use may alter when engaging with creative writing. In an increasingly diverse social environment and with the acceptance that this diversity should be used and celebrated (Graham, 2007) in teaching, English teachers should look at new ways to make their lessons appealing. The use of technology shows one possible route and the affects that are produced through multimedia are an important zone for English teachers to explore: for example, media studies, film, advertising and the Internet (Cole, 2005). Furthermore, the increasing prominence of family literacy, personal literacy and English as a second language as part of mainstream English practice (Cardiero-Kaplan, 2004) shows us how English teaching is evolving and affects are part of this evolution. The students found that some teachers were reluctant to talk about these changes in English, as it can involve new skills for them to learn. However, those who did accept changing demographics would engage in discussing the use of affects to get their classes to work creatively through building positive relationships. Examples that were given of using affect for creativity included: scenarios to build vocabulary, working with communicative competence and engagement, and exploring the cultural perceptions and desires that are brought to the English classroom by the students through the media and popular culture.

Rebellion and Dissonance

The last category of affects that this research with English teachers uncovered involves rebellion and dissonance in the classroom. Critical dissonance is a research methodology which encourages teachers to critique and explore the social consequences of their knowledge (Cochran-Smith, 2003). Several English teachers agreed with this approach to the contemporary English curriculum as it enables inquiry-based learning and teaching for understanding:

Teacher J: The way I work through a book is a semi-reflexive process. I gauge the ways in which the class might react before I bring literature into the room. It's a kind of experimentation. I have to set all of these ideas up before we start reading a text or they won't learn.

This way of using affects taps into pervasive discourses of rebellion and dissonance (Cole, 2005, 2007b, 2007c) that may be present in the cohort. Teachers will structure lessons around literature that expresses these ideas, or introduce the topics of rebellion and dissonance through examining current news events. These lessons should not have a negative feel, but use the desires of the participants (affects) to engage with the texts to the advantage of the English teacher. Many of the pre-service students were impressed and surprised at this development in English teaching—as it marks out the ways in which the profession is evolving, as the nature of textual authority changes in society. This point also shows how English teachers now need to work with cultural seduction in language and affects to make their classes work (McWilliam, 2000).

Polarization and Emergence

The teacher identity Discourses that have been put into play by the ELs and brought to light through this research may be represented through polarisation and emergence: Polarization is a useful term in this context as it describes the ways in which the Discourses may be connected to friction and antipathy between groups involved in curriculum reforms (Lyotard, 1991, p. 76). This points to the fact that there is lateral movement between Discourses and that they are not sealed or constituted by privileged spaces. This notion of polarization and emergence could be added to indefinitely show how polarization may also work along different axes, yet this complexity would make it impossible to understand this as a summary of the results of this research project.

Polarization is the most conspicuous aspect of this mapping as the teachers are forced into positions by the introduction of the new knowledge framework. It could be said that many of them had been happily performing their jobs for many years without having to consider their positioning. In many ways, as has already been discussed, the introduction of critical literacy as a headline governmental objective may augment polarization (Hargreaves, 1994). Most governments content themselves with functional and linguistic, rationally defined discrete learning outcomes (Eisner, 1994). These outcomes usually do not produce polarities—in fact they often work to do the opposite and to neutralize debate. I am sure that many English teachers, especially those who endorse critical literacy, have welcomed the *Essential Learnings* for exactly the reason that serious critical examination of text is now on the agenda. Many teachers may have been working to produce critical thinkers for many years, and perhaps for the first time this is in line with explicit governmental outcomes.

The emotional and affective factors that this research has uncovered may be represented as a spiral that oscillates between personal English teaching development and the ability to articulate one's philosophy of English teaching (Arnold, 1991). At the top of the spiral is one's power as an English teacher at any given time during a career—below this, the factors of maturation and gender also heavily influence one's emotional state and the consequent textual emotions that one may be able to induce at any given point through the application of affect. Running through these emotional factors in English teaching are the affects of rebellion, dissonance and creativity. Creativity goes through the whole of this representation, and to a certain extent defines the emergent qualities of the teacher (Tochan & Munby, 1993). These qualities include the ability to work through change, the establishment of shifting yet positive learning relationships and inspirational teaching with elements of spontaneity and surprise. It should also be noted that emergence is non-linear and includes retardation as well as development (Casti, 1989).

Power should not be thought of as the goal of English teaching—though it is always part of any pedagogic and professional role that one might inhabit. This representation of English teachers is an attempt to present the complex nature of emotion in English teaching, and this point was discussed in detail throughout the course of the project by the main researcher and the pre-service students. This discussion had the aim of looking at the nature of complexity in English teacher identity, and what we may learn from this (Purcell-Gates, 2004). The overall impression was that lessons learnt from life, for example, communicating with one's children or taking on roles of responsibility in the community will help with understanding how this representation might help to structure English teaching development.

Conclusion

This research gives pre-service students an insight into English teaching in Tasmania. On one level, it shows how changes due to curriculum reform can polarize English teachers and make them shift with respect to their job positioning—and on another, it gives them an introduction to the emotional and affective parts of the daily work. As Muchmore (2001, p. 28) has explained when investigating the personal pedagogies of an English teacher, there is a "complex and multi-layered system of beliefs" to understand. It is only when the teacher is challenged in some way that the transformation of these beliefs happens (Tann, 1993), and the relationships between these beliefs come into the light and may be articulated. The ELs framework functions on this level as it has shaken up the idea of English in many teachers' minds, and its introduction in Tasmania has produced the questioning of cultural and social assumptions. These are several excerpts from the pre-service students' self-reflective diaries that relate to these points:

Student A: I was actually teaching today when one of the interviews came back to me. The teacher had been speaking about the ELs and how it was attacking the subject fidelity of English. He wanted more Shakespeare in the curriculum! The kids in the room were bored by the literacy project that had been set, and I was wondering if I could ask the colleague teacher if I could use a different text.

Student B: The project has really helped me to think about my emotions and those in the English teaching classroom. Before I just thought it was a

> matter of going in there and getting through the text in a professional manner. Now I realize that I bring a whole lot more of "me" in there.

The knowledge that the students have learnt by taking part in the research is subjective as well as discursive (Masny, 2006). This means that they are assimilating ideas about the construction of English not only as public output, but also as personal experience. On this level, the forces of identity are activated by polarized beliefs (Leach & Moon, 1999), as described above. This aspect of synthesis and analysis of English is concerned with having the will to carry on, and considers the ways in which English may be recast through the unconscious and the imaginary. These long-term goals deal with the possibility that exterior and interior factors in English might not form a dualistic system of division between the inner and the outer in the minds of English teachers. The benefit of this research is to address this possible dualism early on, and to set a course for English teaching careers where the interior and exterior are aligned and reconciled to enhance the power of the future teachers that take part.

References

Arnold, R. (1991). *Writing development: Magic in the brain.* Open University Press.

Cardiero-Kaplan, K. (2004). *The literacy curriculum and bilingual education: A critical examination.* Peter Lang.

Casti, J. L. (1989). *Nonlinear system theory.* Academic Press.

Chevellard, Y. (1991). *Le Transposition Didactique: Du savoir savant au savoir enseigné.* La Pensée Sauvage.

Cochran-Smith, M. (2003). Learning and unlearning: The education of teacher educators. *Teaching and Teacher Education, 19*(1), 5–28. http://dx.doi.org/10.1016/S0742-051X(02)00091-4

Cole, D. R. (2005). Education and the politics of cyberpunk. *Review of Education Pedagogy and Cultural Studies, 27*(2), 159–170. http://dx.doi.org/10.1080/10714410590963839

Cole, D. R. (2007a). Teaching *Frankenstein* and *Wide Sargasso Sea* using affective literacy. *English in Australia, 42*(2), 69–75.

Cole, D. R. (2007b). Techno-shamanism and educational research. *Ashé: Journal of Experimental Spirituality, 6*(1), 6–34. https://citeseerx.ist.psu.edu/viewdoc/download?doi=10.1.1.518.4633&rep=rep1&type=pdf

Cole, D. R. (2007c). Virtual terrorism and the internet e-learning options. *E-Learning, 4*(2), 116–127. http://dx.doi.org/10.2304/elea.2007.4.2.116

Cope, B., & Kalantzis, M. (1995). *Productive diversity: Organisational life in the age of civic pluralism and total globalisation.* HarperCollins.

Derewianka, B. (1998). *A grammar companion for primary teachers.* Primary English Teachers.

Doecke, B. (2006). Teacher quality: Beyond the rhetoric. In B. Doecke, M. Howie & W. Sawyer (Eds.), *Only connect: English teaching, schooling and community* (pp. 195–209). Wakefield Press (AATE).

Doecke, B., Howie, M. & Sawyer, W. (Eds). (2006). *Only connect: English teaching, schooling and community*. Wakefield Press (AATE).

Dowden, T., & Nolan, P. (2006, November 30). *Engaging early adolescent students in their learning via student-centred curriculum integration* [Paper presentation]. Australian Association for Research in Education Conference, Adelaide, Australia. https://www.aare.edu.au/data/publications/2006/dow06285.pdf

Eisner, E. (1994). *Cognition and Curriculum Reconsidered*. Teachers College Press.

Fairclough, N. (1992). *Discourse and Social Change*. Polity Press.

Gee, J. P. (2003). Literacy and social minds. In G. Bull & M. Anstey (Eds.), *The literacy lexicon* (2nd ed., pp. 3–15). Pearson Education Australia.

Graham, L. (2007). Done in by discourse … or the problem/s with labelling. In M. Keefe & S. Carrington (Eds.), *Schools and Diversity* (2nd ed., pp. 46–65). Pearson Education Australia.

Gubrium, J. E. & Holstein, J. A. (Eds.). (2002). *Handbook of interview research: Context and method*. Sage.

Hargreaves, A. (1994). *Changing teachers, changing times: Teachers' work and culture in the post-modern age*. Teachers College Press.

Holland, N. N. (1968). *The dynamics of literary response*. Oxford University Press.

Houtz, J. C., & Kroug, D. (1995). Assessment of creativity: Resolving a mid-life crisis. *Educational Psychology Review, 7*(3), 269–300. http://dx.doi.org/10.1007/BF02213374

Keen, S. (2006). A theory of narrative empathy. *Narrative, 14*(3), 207–240. http://dx.doi.org/10.1353/nar.2006.0015

Kress, G. (2006). Reimagining English: curriculum, identity and productive futures. In B. Doecke, M. Howie & W. Sawyer (Eds.), *Only connect: English teaching, schooling and community* (pp. 31–42). Wakefield Press (AATE).

Leach, J., & Moon, R. (1999). *Learners and pedagogy*. Paul Chapman.

Lyotard, J.-F. (1991). *The inhuman: Reflections on time* (G. Bennington & R. Bowlby, Trans.). Polity Press.

Marshall, B. (2000). *The Unofficial Guide: Researching the philosophies of English teachers*. Routledge.

Martin, G., Hunter, L., & McLaren, P. (2006). Participatory activist research (teams)/action research. In K. G. Tobin & J. L. Kincheloe (Eds.), *Doing educational research* (pp. 157–190). Sense Publishers.

Masny, D. (2006). Learning and creative processes: A poststructural perspective on language and multiple literacies. *International Journal of Learning, 12*(5), 147–155.

McWilliam, E. (2000). Stuck in the missionary position? pedagogy and desire in new times. In C. O'Farrell, D. Meadmore, E. McWilliams & C. Symes (Eds.), *Taught bodies* (pp. 27–39). Peter Lang.

Mellor, B., & Patterson, A. (2004). Poststructuralism in English classrooms: Critical literacy and after. *International Journal of Qualitative Studies in Education, 17*(1), 83–98. http://dx.doi.org/10.1080/0951839032000150248

Mills, K. A. (2005). Multiliteracies: Remnant discourses and pedagogies. In *Pleasure, passion, provocation: Proceedings of the ALEA/AATE National Conference 2005* (pp. 1–15). Aust. Assoc. for Teaching English/Australian Literacy Educator's Association.

Mills, K. A. (2006). Critical framing in pedagogy of multiliteracies. In *Voices, vibes, visions: proceedings of the ALEA/AATE National Conference 2006* (pp. 1–15). Aust. Assoc. for Teaching English/Australian Literacy Educator's Association.

Muchmore, J. A. (2001). The story of "Anna": A life history study of the literacy beliefs and teaching practices of an urban high school English teacher. *Teacher Education Quarterly, 28*(3), 89–110.

Purcell-Gates, V. (2004). Ethnographic research. In N. K. Duke & M. H. Mallette (Eds.), *Literacy research methodologies* (pp. 92–114). Guilford Press.

Sawyer, W. (2004). Seminal books on English teaching. In W. Sawyer & E. Gold (Eds.), *Reviewing English in the 21st century* (pp. 23–36). Phoenix Education.

Semetsky, I. (2007). *Deleuze, education and Becoming.* Sense Publishers.

Shulman, L. S. (1986). Those who understand: Knowledge growth in teaching. *Educational Research Review, 57*(2), 4–14.

Strauss, A., & Corbin, J. (1998). *Basics of qualitative research: Grounded theory procedures and techniques* (2nd ed.). Sage.

Tann, S. (1993). Eliciting student teachers' personal theories. In J. Calderhead & P. Gates (Eds.), *Conceptualising reflection in teacher development* (pp. 53–69). Falmer Press.

Tasmania Department of Education. (2002). *Essential learnings: Learning together.* Tasmania Education Authority.

Tochan, F., & Munby, H. (1993). Novice and expert teachers' time epistemology: A wave function from didactics to pedagogy. *Teacher and Teacher Education, 9*(2), 205–218. http://dx.doi.org/10.1016/0742-051X(93)90055-L

Upton, P. (2005). *Re-positioning the Subject: Trainee English teachers' constructions of grammar and English* [Doctoral dissertation]. University of Nottingham. https://core.ac.uk/download/pdf/33563813.pdf

Varela, F. J., Thompson, E. T., & Rosch, E. (1993). *The Embodied Mind: cognitive science and human experience.* MIT Press.

Watt, M. G. (2005, November 1). *Looking back at curriculum change in Tasmania: Is the essential learnings framework promoting successful curriculum reform?* [Paper presentation]. "Blurring the Boundaries: Sharpening the focus", ACSA Biennial Conference, University of the Sunshine Coast

Globalisation

CHAPTER THIRTEEN

Deleuze and Globish: Imperial Tongues, Faceless Coins, War Machines

This is what is beautiful in global capitalism, what I really love: Even the English language itself is being taken away from the English.

Žižek (2013)

I only have one language, yet it is not mine.

Derrida (1998)

From the idiosyncratic perspective of Deleuze and Guattari's thought, this chapter makes the case that the Globish can be construed as a "war machine" against English. Given the author's own brute facticity of living and working in Japan, we shall test the propensity for Globish in the context of language learning and discuss why Globish and variants have gained much attention in the archipelago. The argument not only focuses on the desire to escape from "native speakerism"—the widespread ideology found in the ELT industry, which conveys the notion that "native-speaker" teachers represent a form of "Western culture" from which spring the ideals of both the English language and English language teaching methodology (Holliday, 2006)—but also hones in on Japan's unique and schizoid love-hate relationship with the world's de facto lingua franca (Sauzier-Uchida, 2008). Contra the image of ownership of language as a desire for otherness, the exotic, second selves, etc. (Takahashi, 2013), what we find is a conception of Globish stripped of the desire for a particular geopolitics of Western, Anglo-Saxon identity. At its heart, the desire for Globish expresses the tension between English viewed, on the one hand, as a neutral, cultureless pragmatic language, which is to say, a de-Anglo-Americanized English which serves Japan's drive to internationalization and globalization, and, on the other hand, as one tied to historical, imperialist practices that threaten local languages and cultural values (Depardon & Nougaret, 2008; Lecercle, 2002).

This chapter will explore the genealogy of the "real global communication tool" of Globish (Nerrière, 2009, p. 14) to highlight the desire for a transnational common tongue, free of origins and home. While the primary focus is on language education and second language acquisition, I shall endeavor to connect Guattari's notion of the "flattening of [capitalistic] subjectivity" (Alliez & Goffey, 2011, p. 41) (*laminage de la subjectivité capital-istique*) with the "flattening of the world" (Friedman, 2009) so as to think in a fresh light the notion of the hybridity of languages and the problem of learner identity.

Using the philosophical concepts of Deleuze and Guattari, and thinking Globish from a poststructuralist point of view, this chapter explains how minor languages both inflect and affect major languages or dominant tongues. I conclude by considering Globish as a war machine, "a battering ram" as Deleuze says of Nietzsche (Allison, 1985), which affects, shapes and moulds the contours and shape of "English" (Kohl, 2009). I shall endeavor to speculate beyond the somewhat tired debates and critiques of both native-speaker English and linguistic imperialism (Phillipson, 2014).

In the first part of the chapter, I set out the context of how Globish quickly gained popularity in Japan and further afield, specifically focussing on the question of desire and affect. In the second part, I explain its historical predecessors before detailing how Deleuze's and Žižek's respective philosophies may help to decode the logic of Globish. In the third part, after interpreting Globish through Deleuze's language theory and Guattari's general semiotics, I move on to think of Globish as a means to expunge the babble of the world, the cacophony of difference as such. I conclude with two thoughts:

1. an affirmation of the thought-provoking nature of Deleuze and Guattari's philosophy of language (for teachers and/or learners in foreign language classrooms); and

2. a rumination on the phenomenological ideas on communication and creativity. This is to disclose the potential for hijacking dominant speech (standard forms of English), for creating vacuoles of noncommunication

or circuit breakers which can "elude control" (Deleuze, 1995, p. 175), for moving from order words to disordering words (graffiti, slogans).

Jean-Paul Nerrière's Tool of Communication

As this chapter designates Jean-Paul Nerrière's (2005; 2009) tool of communication named Globish as a war machine against standard, received forms of English, and by way of Deleuze and Guattari's (1987) distinction between minor/major languages, I consider how one might construct a prototypical non-capitalist, universal subject "*without identity*", that is to say, how the war-machine may subvert models of the imperial subject (White, Anglo-Saxon Protestant (WASP) in the United States or "native speakerism" in Japan). This is precisely and importantly from a position of being *without national language, location or culture*. I examine Žižek's dialectical logic *vis-à-vis* Indian national identity and the question of the English language as a case in point.

Moreover, as I am both mounting a critique of the desire for Globish and construing it as a schizophrenic form of capitalistic dyslexia or illiteracy (Deleuze & Guattari, 1983, p. 241), I shall treat communication as somehow operating between monads who use it without risk of infection of the Other. As Peters puts it (2012):

> Too often, 'communication' misleads us from the task of building worlds together. It invites us into a world of union without politics, understandings without language, and souls without bodies, only to make politics, language and bodies reappear as obstacles rather than blessings. (pp. 30–31)

Expressed phenomenologically, this is undertaken to ask—what does it mean to say that in contamination and contact with alterity, in relations of exposure and abandon, that fundamental communication takes place *beyond language* (Lingis in Mitchell & Kemp Winfree, 2009)? The point to be made is that behind the desire for the Other's language are questions of identity, power and, pivotally, desire. Simply put, if proponents of Globish desire a global subject stripped of identity and culture, which is to say, a desire for a perfect tool of global human resource management, they fail to understand the essential functioning of language. They contribute to the impoverishment of natural language.

Escape from Globish

In preliminary remarks in his 2010 lecture entitled Der Guattari-Effekt at the University of Bochum's Institut Für Medienwissenschaft in Germany, the philosopher Éric Alliez (2010) said the following in the lingua franca of our day: "Thank you very much for giving me the opportunity to read my paper in French. I think it is absolutely great to escape global, Globish". In further comments regarding the outline and protocols for his talk, Alliez went on to say: "You can read it in German and I'll be able to speak French", suggesting there was little need for the global common tongue. He appeared most relieved by this fact, and happy that there was a complex babble of languages, resistant to the glottophagic thrust of a majoritarian English code (Calvet & Petheram, 1998). His comments came at the time when his compatriot Jean-Paul Nerrière, a retired French IBM-businessman, who had spent some time working in Japan, was promoting his own brand of Globish—a portmanteau word signifying the conjunction of global and English. Finding something uncanny occurring in international business meetings with British, Americans, Europeans, Japanese and Korean attendees, Nerrière describes how he coined the term:

> The communication was close to excellent between the British and the Americans. But it was not good between those two and the other people. Then there was a big surprise: the communication between the last three groups, continental Europeans, Japanese, and Koreans, was among the best. There seemed to be one good reason: they were saying things with each other that they would have been afraid to try with the native English speakers—for fear of losing respect. So all of these non-native speakers felt comfortable and safe in what sounded like English, but was far from it. (2009, p. 35)

To the apparent chagrin of those present, Nerrière explains, when the Americans started speaking, "everything changed in one second" (2009, p. 36): "The non-native speakers stopped talking; most were afraid of speaking to the native English speakers. None of them wanted to say a word that was incorrect" (p. 36). Speaking in a hybrid form of English, a kind of English lingua franca (ELF) according to Jenkins (2012), Nerrière noticed that in meetings with colleagues, he and the other non-native English speakers were speaking in distinct communication patterns that were seemingly "incomprehensible" to most native speakers. While "incomprehensible" might appear hyperbolic, we do find an interesting, similar example of Globish in the Taiwanese/Japanese film Yi Yi: A One and a Two (ヤンヤン 夏の思い出) (2000) directed by Edward Yang, in which over an evening meal, Taiwanese businessman N.J. and his Japanese counterpart Ota discuss in Globish the prospects of international collaboration:

N.J (Nien-Jen Wu): Yes, we are very impressed. But you know … we think your pro-posal is very advanced. So, my company need more time to …

Ota (Issey Ogata): You are like me. We can't tell a lie. My company, last year lost big money … Not successful … Because we tried to repeat the old way so, too many same products, too many competition, almost not profit. That is why I suggest to you we try at new way. It's okay. If we don't sign, I understand. Risk is high, when you do any-thing for the first time. No problem. Just let me know when your company makes any decision. Ok? Let's toast. Thanks.

Here we find neither Taiwanese nor Japanese, nor perfect English, but a middle ground, a workable albeit imprecise common tongue.

Desire for Globish

Interpreted through a Deleuzian lens, desire (joy/anxiety) for language operates on a pre-personal level, in terms of impersonal affect. Here the concept of desire can be read through the understanding of the role of affect (Cole, 2011; Cole & Bradley, 2014). There is no transparent desire to learn the language on the level of the first person singular. I do not just desire in vacuo. I am, rather, part of a net-work or agencement (assemblage) of desire. While we discern the desire for a for-eign language as creative, energetic, replete, and subtle and through it a means to achieve certain ends such as learning in and for itself, or more instrumentally, for financial or professional gain, there is also present an existential desire: there is the desire to become-other through foreign language learning, a desire for a second self (Bradley, 2015), which is to say, a desire to say something that can only be said in another language (Dörnyei & Gardner, 2012). We may find a desire for inde-pendence from families or to be a master of a minor language that few speak. We also find sexual desire: an investment in learning for amorous ends; a desire to be called "darling" in a foreign language; a desire to have "a" darling (Oguri, 2010); a desire to be told "I love you" in English (Kim et al., 2006). For example, in the 2003 South Korean comedy film 영어완전정복 [*Please Teach Me English*], we hear the following from Park Moon Su:

When I find a woman to love, I'll confess to her in English. 'I love you' in Korean is so corny. I love you, darling. English feels different, doesn't it?

We also find a desire to be simply desired by the Other (Takahashi, 2013). Furthermore, the desire to learn a foreign language can be linked to the desire to have Asian, African, European, or North American friends: a desire to sing opera, hip-hop or the blues in another tongue. There are also more complex desires which are arguably more manufactured and ideologically fixed, desires to acquire a global identity (in Japan this is called グローバル人材 or global human resources), a desire for global thinking or global perspective, a desire to be less insular. So there is never simply a desire for someone or something (for a white, blue-eyed Western, English-speaking boyfriend for example) as one always desires an aggregate (living the American dream, a big house, baseball games, American fast food).

Deleuze says we never desire something to the exclusion of other elements. Moreover, one never simply desires an aggregate either, as one is always bound up from within an aggregate (compulsory English language learning from primary through secondary, high school, university, graduate school, the workplace, endless evening classes and finally hearing and seeing English announcements during the train commute home). Through all of this we are told and told how we must learn this and that and for this and that exam.

This is shown well in the film *Please Teach Me English*. Riding the bus on her way to register for English class Nah Young-ju sees a schoolgirl rip and swallow indigestible pages from an English dictionary. She bemoans the fact that English is so desired: "Everybody's obsessed with English. What's wrong with being born in Korea and just knowing Korean?" (Kim et al., 2006). Deleuze will say that desire always flows within an assemblage. To affirm the joy of learning language then one must in some sense flow within an assemblage (less testing, less rote learning, more communication, escape from the teacher and classroom, the joy of contact with others from overseas, a joy in saying something in your own name in a language of your choosing, free of the conventions, rules, formalities, strictures of Japanese honorifics for example, the selling of your own cultural belongings to cross distant seas for other exotic climes). Deleuze adds that to desire is to construct an assemblage. This means one imagines a self other than those manufactured by educational institutions. A becoming other of oneself. A becoming-speaker of other languages. A new comportment to the world. There is then an aggregate of a dictionary, a textbook, your first passport, of being totally lost in an exotic land, smells of foreign food, different climates, new alphabets, different writing styles, a different comportment of the body, an assemblage of foreign friends (parties, clubs, names), your first kiss, of breakdowns and breakthroughs, and then not knowing who you are. You are constructing an assemblage of language learning, even while enjoying a romantic sunset and future dreams, with thoughts of international marriage or just being different, of getting away, breaking away from social mores and obligations, and finally saying "who the hell am I?" This is what desire is, Deleuze tells us—constructing an assemblage, constructing, assembling. Desire for foreign language learning is both creative and destructive; it is a constructivism (Boutang et al., 2012).

Machine Parts of Globish

Globish, which can be distinguished from global English, from global or international English and its variants, uses 1500 common English words mostly drawn from a corpus derived from the *Voice of America*. As a kind of Twitter-regimented code, it mostly uses the active voice and short sentences (26 words or less). Globish pronunciation has fewer necessary sounds than traditional English and avoids idioms and jokes. It is as such a simple, pragmatic form of English. With the erasure of the presence of the "native speaker", Globish proponents claim it is essentially devoid of *culture*. Even though a scant examination of the etymology of the corpus would challenge this assertion, this is not the main concern of this chapter and so we shall leave it to others to test such a view. Rather this chapter is concerned with the *desire* for a form of language devoid of culture.

Mistakes are tolerated more in Globish than in English because what matters is the communicative act or performance as such. Moreover, this simpler form of English also assists computer machine translation. The defenders of Globish claim that English simply has too many words for non-native speakers (NNS) to remember and use effectively. This is deemed unfair as NNS, who outnumber native speakers by three to one in the world, are more likely to converse with someone from a non-English speaking country than someone from a culture of the English-speaking world. It is estimated that one quarter of the world's population—over 1.5 billion—speak some form of English, and learners of English will reach two billion by 2020. In *Don't Speak English, Parlez Globish*, Nerrière (2006) insists that Globish users must speak slowly and in short sentences and avoid humor and metaphor to ensure optimal understanding. Globish, based on the Special English of the *Voice of America* and Business English Lingua Franca (BELF), a "neutral professional language" (though not without its own problems) is used as a "neutral" code by business practitioners. In brief, it is not specifically designed to emulate "native-speaker discourse" but simply to get the job done.

Ressentiment, Globish, Desire and Japan

In the *portmanteau* coinage Globish, do we not find a visceral *ressentiment* against the English language, against soft power as such, akin to the psychosomatic reactions of Louis Wolfson (2009), the schizophrenic who literally suffered from

English, his mother's tongue? This is the man who translated English into other tongues and codes to escape the somatic pain of its utterances. In *Essays Critical and Clinical* (1997), Deleuze describes Wolfson's labors to translate all dominating signifiers back into a scrambled code as a babbling code to escape everyday chatter and communication. In this reading, the production of Globish is itself a kind of expression of schizophrenia. It is a scrambling and deterritorializing of the dominant linguistic code. In what sense then can it be said that Globish is a war machine (*machine de guerre*)? It is my contention that Globish, while valiantly seeking to extricate itself from the politics of minor languages, only becomes ever deeper embroiled. It itself succumbs to the desire to be a major, dominant, and imperial language.

Indeed, after newspapers featured Globish in 2010, it soon gained great attention. The following year the Japanese translation of *Globish: The World Over* (2009) became a bestselling language-related book (Nerrière & Hon, 2011). There is a discernible desire or delirium for Globish, which is in part derived from forms of social anxiety, from being "left behind" in the global society. Similar to this view, outside of Japan, Warschauer, Black, and Chou (Kirkpatrick, 2012, p. 491) find a "growing movement around the world to teach a denationalized version of English based on local and regional standards of pronunciation, syntax and usage, rather than US or British English".

The desire for another means of communication, to escape English, has a long history. In Japan, Globish has several precedents with scholars setting out their visions for foreign language education over the years. Englic is one such alternative model (Tanaka & Tanaka, 1995). Englic's *raison d'être* object was to distinguish the actual use of English from the cultural and linguistic hegemony of "inner circle" countries. The proponents of Englic claim that it can be justifiably influenced by native languages and personality and as such can be used with "confidence" (Tanaka & Tanaka, 1995, p. 127). Other writers such as Takao Suzuki (see Kachru, 2010, pp. 77–78) have called for a form of English disconnected from "dominant" Anglo-English speaking countries. Indeed, some writers argue that to teach English in Japan is misguided given the country's cultural and geographical uniqueness. Indeed, Kubota (1999, p. 302) reinforces this view by claiming that the rationale behind Englic models is one which allows the Japanese to communicate with other English speakers "without sacrificing their own cultural identity" (1998, p. 295). More recently, the renowned Japanese linguist Kazuo Misono, in assessing whether Globish can be a tool to bring people together asks the question, "Can Globish become a world language to save us all?" (Misono, 2011)

Historical Precedents

In the 20th century, other hybrid variants of English vied for linguistic hegemony. These include Esperanto, Basic English (Ogden, 1934), and many others like Interlingua, Kosmos, Volapuk, Nuclear English, BGE to name but a few. Indeed, in the 1920s, the critic I.A. Richards formulated Basic English, an 850-word version of English, initially for use in China. Richards's initiative was followed in 1930 by the Swedish philologist Robert Eugen Zachrisson who proposed another international language, Anglic. Clearly, Globish draws much inspiration from this legacy and its more recent predecessors which include many similar sounding variants including David Crystal's World Standard Spoken English, global English, Globalish, Toolan's "Global" or "the public international English used by globetrotting professionals" (Toolan, 1999, p. 3). Acutely aware of the problems a simplified, common denominator form of English may inspire, Toolan writes (1999):

> 'Pure Global English', as a vehicle of verbal art, like a diet purely of Pepsi's and McDonald burgers, an audiovisual experience comprising only MTV and SkySports, and so on and so forth, would be a grim version of Bakhtinian monologism, a doped, desensitized, automotized, worldspeak: a language detached from the pains and joys of identity.

The last sentence clearly echoes the above arguments regarding the desire to escape the forced adaptation of other identities.

Nerrière's compatriot, Michel Serres, critiques the dominance of English in France. He suggests hyperbolically that the invasion of English in France threatens the national language more than the Nazis did during the Second World War. His words echo those of the ALF or Avenir de la Langue Française (Future of the French language) and other groups. Writing in Le Monde and l'Humanité, Serres (Samuel, 2010) bemoans the fact that French is being "methodically ousted" in favor of simplified English that "zealously promotes the international business oligarchy". Deploring the impoverished state of the French language, Serres decries the apparent omnipresence of global English and describes French as "the language of the poor". Those people in power, he argues, "no longer speak my language".

For Nerrière, the antidote to the linguistic imperialism of English is precisely Globish. He insists that given the widespread use of English in non-Anglocentric countries, as Anglophones no longer own English, Globish can limit the influence of the English language "dramatically". As he says (2005):

> I am helping the rescue of French, and of all the languages that are threatened by English today but which will not be at all endangered by Globish.

While there is some credence to the idea that English as a form of soft power effectively sustains Anglo-Saxon hegemony through social and economic inequality across the world, the link is not unidirectional as there is clearly a desire for a global language which transcends national borders. Indeed, artist Jennifer Allen (2011) adopts both a pro-Globish position and invokes a Deleuzian motif when she describes Globish as a "language liberated from all the old structures that we associate with the nation state, with a fixed territory". As she says, Globish is a "nomadic, moving language". Explaining further that Globish is more oral and corporeal, she argues:

> Globish is much more oral; it's a spoken language. It is closer to the body, and has a lot to do with gestures. So whether I speak Globish or I write Globish, this language has a strong physical presence, a strong now.

Deleuze and Globish and Translation

Globish does not exist *in vacuo* as it inflects and is inflected by a major language. It affects that language with the goal of rendering it minor. It makes minor usage of the major. Globish as a constant and homogeneous system sets English in continuous *variation*. Globish is thus a becoming, a becoming-minor of the majority code. Deleuze explains: "For the more a language acquires the characteristics of a major language, the more it tends to be affected by internal variations that transpose it into a 'minor' language" (Deleuze, 1997, p. xvii).

A different perspective can be taken *vis-à-vis* the notion of computer code and the grammaticality of language by Janell Watson (2011). Computer code for Watson is "cryptic and agrammatical, because it leaves out most of the redundancy which is essential to human languages" (2011, p. 85). Redundancy is the identity of the other, in particular, the complex identity and language of those from cultures of the English-speaking world. For Moles (Watson, 2011, p. 85) redundancy occurs in human speech, when regular patterns provided by redundancy ensure that a message will be understood in spite of "noise" (mispronunciations or unfamiliar words), strange pronunciation, or exterior sound. The idea of Globish operates in a relationship to information science and the notion of redundancy, a quantitative concept, which can be defined as a measure of the efficiency with which a message transmits information. This point is echoed in the linguistic theory of philosopher

Alphonso Lingis (1994), whose phenomenology explores the limits of the sayable in words and thoughts. In thinking the outside of language, the unsayable, the non-rational and unrepresentable and transgressive, Lingis interprets Serres' communication theory as the search for a cleansed linguistic *utopos*, an ideal city of communication, a nonplace *purged of noise*.

In probing the talk and the idle chatter of *the they*– the talk which passes for communication, Lingis interprets the will to eliminate noise as a plot to eliminate the power of the Other, a xenophobic move to eviscerate the Other. As he says, communication is an effort to silence not only the Other, the interlocutor, but the outsider: the barbarian. In a discussion on the role of computers in "The Murmur of the World" in *A Community of Those Who Have Nothing in Common* (1994), Lingis suggests an intimate relationship between communication, computing and language:

> Computer technology driven by the pilot industries of the military industrial complex, places top priority on transmitting the message as effectively, efficiently and effortlessly as possible. It is computer technology that shapes and forms contemporary communication theory. (p. 104)

In a similar vein, Boris Groys (2011) argues that Google works to produces asyntactic word clouds—words beyond grammar—which do not "say" anything as such. Rather, words are liberated from their grammatical chains. There is an equality of words, operative in a particular word cloud. The house of language is transformed into a word cloud. Man becomes linguistically homeless, extra-linguistically aloof with no fixed abode, and ceases to speak as words merely appear or disappear in different contexts "in a completely silent, purely operational, extra- or meta-linguistic mode of practice" (2011, p. 11). Groys picks up the comments by Marinetti in the Italian Futurist's text of 1912, in which he comments on the destruction of the "syntax" and explicitly calls for the liberation of the words from syntactic chains. Around the same time, Marinetti proposes an early version of Groys' word cloud thesis which he named *parole in libertà* or words in liberty. In Deleuzian terms we can say again that this is a kind of schizophrenia, the expression of the absolute decodification of flows.

On this view, Nerrière's dream is the déjà vu of Serres' idea, a phantasmogoria of harmonious dialogic modems in the ideal city of communication, purged of noise. What the IBM-employee desires is to extract the message from its background noise and the noise internal to the message. Negating interference and confusion, deleting the cacophony of irrelevant and ambiguous signals—the regional accents, mispronunciations, stammering coughs, forms of irony and sarcasm, jokes, redundant words, ungrammatical formulations—we arrive at the sonority of immediate communication, stripped of linguistic imperialism, domination, violence, power, army. In sum, this is a desire for a tool of communication designed for the transmission of information, "without depth or past" (Lecercle, 2009, p. 4). One of the best interpreters of Deleuze's philosophy of language, Lecercle writes on this point:

> But to attack the history-culture nexus, the cultural past that is inscribed in the English language, out of which the English language is made, presupposes a conception of language as tool and lingua franca, a simple instrument for the transmission of information and knowledge, without depth or past. (2009, pp. 3–4)

For other critics, the goal of Globish as undistorted immediate exchange is but another expression of human hubris, in the sense that optimum communication signifies *more not less* discord; maximal communication means less not more transparency. In other words, the problem of communication continues to escalate despite efforts to eliminate the noise of the Other. According to Pinchevski (2005, p. 5), the problems of communication continue to expand in correlation to the expansion of communication technologies in everyday life. Pinchevski explains that the beginning of ethics in Emmanuel Levinas's philosophy is a state in which we are literally at a loss for words. This denudes the speaker of cliché and official ordinance or in Deleuze and Guattari's parlance *order words* and opens the speaker and his interlocutor to a dialogue without parameter or *telos*. Here a conversation without pretext carries a fecund moment when one may speak in one's own name, which is to say, to speak candidly, resolutely, openly. This is the ethical basis for the fearless speech act, or act of *Parrhesia* (Foucault & Pearson, 2001).

So on this view, Nerrière aims to erase the babble, the cacophony of the world of work and reason and if we put it in Emmanuel Levinas's terms, Globish is a more recent incarnation of "the said", that is to say, the complete reduction of language to the circulation of information: a language addressed to everybody in general and no one in particular. Indeed, in the essay *Des Tours de Babel*, Derrida (1991) contrasts the violence of universal language—a violence inherent in calls for a universal tongue to the exclusion of the babble of multiple languages. In the confusion of languages, there is "the irreducible multiplicity of idioms", and the challenge of translation—a challenge at once necessary and impossible. Taken in this way, the transparency of communication is thus a reduction of difference, a debarring of empathetic contact; it signifies the erasure of alterity. Yet, the rupturing of an imposed rational transparency contests the imperial violence of the master signifier. So, the interruption of universal code condemns speakers to translation. To convey meaning it is necessary to transform meaning from one language to another which is to confront alterity as such. This is one of the arguments in Barbara Cassin's recent work for example (Apter et al., 2014). Her work has focussed on "untranslatables", words that one cannot simply render into another language. This for her signifies difference, "symptoms of the difference of languages" (Cassin, 2017). Moreover, it is in the interruption of universal code that Maurice Blanchot finds permission to exchange (Blanchot & Hanson, 1993). In interrupting we come to understand, and we understand "in order to speak" (1993, p. 76). The interruption of communication signifies the beginning of the ethical. The task of the translator then is one of finding traces of otherness in the other's language. Translation then is a question of exposing and expressing the fundamental relation of one language with the other. On this level, language is always more than a tool of communication as it expresses expressibility itself. On this line of reasoning, Globish would be anathema to the phenomenologists of otherness.

Faceless Coins

One is tempted to say that Globish itself is glottophagic, in the sense of the devouring of other languages (Calvet & Petheram, 1998): it is ravenous of other dialects, patois, and creoles. The desire for Globish is one of desiring a universal means of linguistic exchange, a non-national currency in a global marketplace of abstract exchange, competing for and coveting planetary exchange value.

There is thus no means of exchange bearing national emblems or images—no forms of British or Canadian English but only Globish as such. It would seem that advocates of Globish like Nerrière wish to put such a newly-minted linguistic unit into mass global circulation with coins denuded of national imagery and of exact value: to swap one equivalent means of abstract exchange for another, making the code interchangeable. What is desired is a currency swap of nationless denomination, with coins of abstract equivalence, coins devoid of cultural import, of national symbol and determination; a simple exchange of imperial code for a depoliticised other. It is to transform the world through a singular code. As such, it is yet a minor imperium cajoling its molar rival. In this way, and from a Deleuzian standpoint, it is perhaps more thought-provoking to view Globish as acting *within* the master tongue as a war machine forcing it into disequilibrium, compelling it to "stutter" or "stammer" languages of myriad forms and compositions—new englishes, Englics, Anglics, ELFs, Globishes etc. Deleuze (1997, p. 112) would call this "a grammar of disequilibrium". On this Deleuzian reading, language is a heterogeneous system in perpetual disequilibrium, in possession of "style" and different syntax. Globish is a worthy object of study from a Deleuzian point of view.

Žižek and Malcolm X

At this juncture, it is worth exploring Žižek's argument on the use of English as it has an interesting contrary position *vis-à-vis* the argument above concerning the universality of Globish. Exploring the ambiguities and paradoxes of the dialectic of linguistic and cultural colonization, and challenging the notion that to win power one must imitate and adopt the code of the colonizers, Žižek contends that a space of liberation is precisely cleaved open from the social disintegration which ensues from the colonization process. Against the complaint that resistance to colonization is formulated detrimentally in the language of the colonizer, Žižek writes that the glottophagy of "English" does not so much imperil local and cultural identities but rather offers a tool of resistance. Speaking with reference to India's experience of colonization at the hands of the British Empire, Žižek insists that in the very use of an imposed alien tongue there inheres the spectre and possibility of a new universalist, democratic state, a new radical possibility in contradistinction to a precolonial, mythic past. In other words, there is a kind of futural utopia of language at work. This possibility is created through colonization itself as the adopted new language symbolizes the absence of a primordial, autochthonic identity. In the long search for origin, there is no more mythical "India" or mythical "England" to be found. The universalist language means there are no roots, places, originary pure, virgin identities or territories—no belonging or origin or nationhood. Against critics who question the *a priori* alienation which manifests in the use of the language of the colonizers, and other forms of cultural colonization, Žižek outlines what he designates as the Malcolm X factor, or the Hegelian "absolute recoil" (2015)—in the very loss of something one creates a lost dimension. This is not taken in the sense of a pure, unadulterated, reclaimed pristine past, a nostalgia for the good old days, for roots, but rather the possibility of something new to come.

With precolonial India "irredeemably lost", "without any genuine tradition to rely on", Žižek argues that in this condition there inheres a desire for a new identity, for "a unique opportunity of freedom" (2015, p. 150). Colonization is not so much the obstacle to freedom, but "the condition of possibility is radically and simultaneously the condition of impossibility: the very obstacle to the full assertion of our identity opens up the space for it" (Žižek, 2015, p. 148). X signifies the unknown root. For Žižek (2014), the X of Malcolm X is the marker of a history in which slaves have been torn out of their African ancestral homes. Yet, as there is no return to roots, the X is a possibility of forging or inventing new forms of freedom, new universalist credos and new subjectivities, precisely from this torn asunder state. His retort is that the very X of a rootless origin opens up the question of both the heterogeneous territory of multilanguages and identities in India as well as the meaning of an "authentic dream of a new universalist democratic India" (2014, p. 17).

As a universal language, English is "stolen from British people themselves" (Žižek, 2013) whose own claims to universality are exposed as particular interests of the ruling imperialist class. As he says (2013):

> [C]olonialism is not overcome when the intrusion of the English language as a medium is abolished, but when the colonizers are, as it were, beaten at their own game – when the new Indian identity is effortlessly formulated in English, i.e., when English language is 'denaturalized', when it loses its privileged link to 'native' Anglo-Saxon English-speakers.

What has this got to do with the desire for Globish? If X signifies the refusal to dream of a return to origins, the point is not to limit oneself to valorising the "vulgar, western mechanical, materialist, non-holistic civilization" (Žižek, 2013) but to exceed it, to become more universal than the West, to beat the West at its own game, to surpass and undermine such universalist pretensions.

In *Imaginary Homelands* (1991, p. 17), Rushdie writes that the desire to stutter English would be on the basis of particular, counter-hegemonic purposes, which is precisely consistent with both Žižek's argument and the principles of Globish; if the drive is to be more universal or global than the West. Rushdie writes:

> Many have referred to the argument about the appropriateness of this language to Indian themes. And I hope all of us share the view that we can't simply use the language in the way the British did; that it needs remaking for our own purposes. Those of us who do use English do so in spite of our ambiguity towards it or perhaps because of that, perhaps because we can find in that linguistic struggle a reflection of other struggles taking place in the real world, struggles between the cultures within ourselves and the influences at work upon our societies. To conquer English may be to complete the process of making ourselves free. (1991, p. 17)

And so, regarding the desire for Globish, new identities are formulated when English is denaturalized, or in Žižek's language, decaffeinated, when it is itself torn away from a motherland, when it loses its Anglo-Saxon focus and privilege. On this reading, global English, the *de facto* lingua franca of business, popular culture, and higher education across the globe, no longer emanates from a small, insular island cut off from the European continent but rather manifests through its constant deterritorialization or globalization. Global forms of English signify that the universal lingua franca is liberated from Anglo-Saxon roots. This too discloses the *desire* of Globish. Anglo-Saxon identity is itself displaced, forced to linguistically migrate, which is to say to compete on a more democratic market of linguistic exchange.

Within the confusion and erosion of identity, there is an opportunity to create an authentic universality contra a Western-inflected particularity. The imposition of a foreign language creates the very conditions for a universal tongue. English, then, is a code spoken transnationally and transversally, by people across all continents, from Indian merchants in Bombay, to bankers in Singapore, and entrepreneurs in Gambia. It is the tool or code which one utilizes as one passes through the nonplaces of the world (Augé, 1995), or the gleaming commercial archipelago of urban technopoles of work and reason as Lingis puts it (Sheppard & Sparks, 2004). The desire for Globish is consistent with the desire to pass through the nonplaces of the world (airports and hotels) smoothly and efficiently. It is the desire to communicate without fear of the Other. This is the desire for Globish as a planetary means of exchange. It is the "limited English" tool travelers use at airports across the world. It is the patois a Peruvian businesswoman and Mongolian businessman might converse in if they met at Dubai airport. Globish has no single metropolitan base or homeland. It is an "exemplary product of postmodernity" (Toolan, 1999) as it is always in exile. On this account, Globish is the *sine qua non* of deterritorialization, which is to say, its simplified code functions to scramble linguistic code further and quicker.

If Globish aims to reveal the truth of English, to restore true communication between interlocutors, it in effect acts as a war machine against English. In doing so, it sets in variation new forms of modulation, new forms of becoming. As Deleuze and Guattari insist, master or major languages like English are perpetually haunted by such minorities, by a multitude of minor dialects, registers and styles. To clarify the point, Globish can be considered akin to a war machine because of the way translation machines create a substitutable, simplified code (smartphone apps for use abroad for example) from natural languages such as English. This is part of a wider program to make all languages interchangeable. Think about the way we are now increasingly dependent on Google to translate and make sense of the multiliteracies that we come across constantly on our screens. Think of the way we use such mobile devices as translating machines when we travel to other countries. Simply take a photo of a menu or train timetable and let the translation app do the rest. Downloadable apps offer instant translations from one language into another so long as what you want to say has already been codified (Kohl, 2009)—get me a taxi, where is such and such hotel? How much is that? We will buy 500—these can be thought of as Globish order words, or asyntactic word clouds (Groys, 2011). Here it is not so much an argument over the dominance of the *de facto* language of world communication but a question of the way the use of computers is transforming English itself through instant translation software and the streamlining of Globish English for computer programmers.

Vernacular and Vehicular War Machines

Nerrière's compatriots Deleuze and Guattari have much to say of the becoming-minor of dominant tongues. The minor use of language results in both the deterritorialization and reterritorialization of English as the major language. It is futile, they argue, to criticize the worldwide spread of English—linguistic imperialism—by denouncing the unholy birth of Franglais or the corruptions introduced into other languages (as Serres does). In *A Thousand Plateaus*, in the plateau "Postulates of Linguistics", Deleuze and Guattari (1987, p. 102) argue that even though English is one of the major common world languages, it is worked upon by all the minorities of the world, "using very diverse procedures of variation" (1987, p. 102). In a strict sense then, it may be argued that "English" as such is a fabrication and ruse and strictly speaking does not exist. It is always already reducible to a variation of dialects, levels of language, and registers (De Landa, 2011). It is vernacular and vehicular through and through.

"Standard English" is an artificial construct, imposed by ideological state appa-ratuses for the purposes of domination and conquest. English Received Pronunciation (RP) is one example of this. The unity of language is constantly haunted by death, by the war machine. One political power fades, and with it its centralizing code, so the rise of the vernacular. This is exemplified well in the creation of standard forms of English pronunciation in India during the height of the Raj for native inhabitants of the British Isles who needed a common form of pronunciation to make sense not only of local Indians but, and because of their strong, regional accents, between themselves.

A war machine works against and is internal to English rather than always situated outside. We can say then that the problem is not the distinction between major and minor language as such but one of becoming, of the in-between or the interstitial. It is a question not of reterritorializing oneself on a dialect or a patois but of deterritorializing the major language further. Look at Black English as an example, Deleuze and Guattari observe. Black Americans do not oppose Afro-Caribbean codes to English as such but transform American English, "their own language", through and into Black English. Those people who speak Black English are bilingual or plurilingual in their own language as they work to "conquer the major language in order to delineate in it as yet unknown minor languages" (Deleuze & Guattari, 1987, p. 105).

Acting as a microcosm of linguistic change and transformation, a megalopolis like New York becomes virtually a city without a language as there is no language that has single dominance. There is no language that does not have "intralinguistic, endogenous, internal minorities" (1987, p. 103) as Deleuze and Guattari insist. And again, as English is the de facto lingua franca, Deleuze argues (1997, p. xvii), it is "constantly being worked on from within by the minorities of the world, who nibble away at that hegemony and create the possibility of new mythic functions, new cultural references, new vernacular languages with their own uses". In throwing down the gauntlet to Noam Chomsky, Deleuze and Guattari charge him with failing to countenance the material movement and transformation of language, and to understand that English is under assault from the small lettered englishes. We might add: why does Nerrière pretend not to understand this?

Globish as Means of Protest

Contrary to my argument above, McCrum (2010) finds in cultures that have imported English a conspicuous erosion of the autonomy of the native language and culture. American-English and English are considered the principal agents in the destruction of natural linguistic diversity. Yet, while the dissemination of English as the language of neoliberal globalization may weaken native languages, on the other side the inflow of other cultures has augmented the vitality of English and enriched its vocabulary. In *Globish: How the English Language Became the World's Language* (2017), McCrum's analysis is interesting in the way it suggests that Globish can be used as a war machine against global hegemonic political power. From McCrum's perspective, Globish has become a language of protest, of slogans. He detects the presence of Globish in popular protest, for example, when South Koreans protest against the north about nuclear weapons testing, in the hope of addressing a wider global audience through the media, they display placards written in English that demand "Stop the nukes". Similarly, in the Middle East, Globish is used in Iran to convey political grievances to a worldwide audience. McCrum explains that at the time of writing his book in 2010, during elections in the Middle East state, "cell-phone images of crude slogans like GET AWAY ENGLAND and FREE, FAIR VOTING NOW, and innumerable tweets from Westernized Iranians communicated the strength of the emergency to the West" (2010, p. 7). Yet, the use of Globish through global media has earlier precedents. We find an upsurge in Globish usage in 2005, when the Danish newspaper Jyllands

Posten published a dozen satirical cartoons depicting the Prophet Muhammad. As a consequence, and largely despite ignorance of the Danish language, parts of the Muslim world mobilized, with riots across Afghanistan, Nigeria, Libya, and Pakistan. McCrum estimates that 139 people died in the ensuing chaos. With excellent use of irony, something perhaps entirely lost in translation into Globish, he notes a bizarre incident of the "fundamentalist" Muslims outside the Danish Embassy in London, chanting in English and carrying placards with English slogans such as FREEDOM OF EXPRESSION GO TO HELL and DOWN WITH FREE SPEECH (2010, p. 7).

Conclusion

In some ways, Globish is a form of speech without response, pure *animus*, a Ya-Boo form of political communication based on the immediacy of sentiment. So, on two fronts, Globish is a war machine: It is used both in international business meetings and in protests against the abuse of political power across the planet. The war machine of Globish strives for a single, artificial, and universal code; a tool, a weapon, a deterritorialized patois, a vagabond, vehicular and vernacular code. Such a code acts as a weapon to oust English, the predominant and contemporary language of power. As such Globish is entirely suited to the language of slogans, to the modes of expression found on Twitter or other forms of social networking. It is the code for business meetings, for conference talk and for protest: a tool to use to seal a business contract before the lawyers get to the fine print. It is both the tool used to send messages to unmanned planes flying over suspected terrorist sites across the planet and to protest against the abuse of power. Globish symbolizes the tearing of language away from land, culture, and station: it is a linguistic *curettage* machine. It is the language of the non-place—based on a register of instant emotive feedback without reflection and thought. It is the language of instantaneous exit polls and surveys, of immediate visceral reaction. Accompanying the "flattening of the world" (Friedman, 2009), there is an even more deadly "flattening of subjectivity" (Alliez & Goffey, 2011, p. 45). As a tool of communication, a universal tool demanded by capitalism, Globish becomes machinic, practical, *ad hoc*. In this respect, in *Anti-Oedipus* (1983), Deleuze and Guattari are entirely correct when they describe capitalism as "profoundly *illiterate*". It has little need for writing. It is the code that matters, binary strings of zeroes and ones. Deleuze and Guattari explain (1983, p. 262): "Electric language does not go by way of the voice or writing: data processing does without them both". In this context of the ongoing data and information processing revolution, Globish seems an entirely suitable vehicle to deliver *information* as such. Already young people are adapting to this Globish trend. For Mark Fisher (2009, p. 25), teenagers process "image-dense data" effectively without the need to read, in the sense, as he says, slogan-recognition is sufficient to navigate the "informational plane".

On the Japanese archipelago, there is thus a form of schizophrenia at work in the learning of English. It is a tool to serve "internationalization" and globalization strategies for Japanese multinationals on the one hand, and, for some, a natural, authentic language which threatens the de-Japanization of the national language on the other (for example, as fears among teachers that more English classes in primary school will detrimentally affect the acquisition of Japanese). Perhaps the desire for Globish stems from the "de-Westernization" of the Western world, which emerges not only from East Asia (Japan, Korea) but, in terms of geopolitical changes, from the emergence of BRICS (Brazil, Russia, India, China, South Africa), and the growth of China, the world's second largest economy. The world is no longer paranoid bipolar (West versus the non-West) but multipolar, filled with multiple competing identities jostling for linguistic position.

References

Allen, J. (2011). Speak easy. The ramifications of "Globish"—Global English. *Frieze, 137*. Retrieved July, 18, 2019, from https://frieze.com/article/speak-easy

Alliez, E. (2010, January 11). *Lecture entitled Der Guattari-Effekt*. Institut für Medienwissenschaft, University of Bochum, Germany. Retrieved July 18, 2019, from https://ifmlog.blogs.ruhr-uni-bochum.de/1101-eric-alliez-im-bkm/

Alliez, E., & Goffey, A. (2011). *The Guattari effect*. London: Continuum.

Allison, D. B. (1985). *The new Nietzsche: Contemporary styles of interpretation*. Cambridge, MA: The MIT Press.

Apter, E., Cassin, B., Lezra, J., & Wood, M. (2014). *Dictionary of untranslatables: A philosophical lexicon*. De Gruyter. https://doi.org/10.1515/9781400849918

Augé, M. (1995). *Non-places: Introduction to an anthropology of supermodernity*. London: Verso.

Blanchot, M., & Hanson, S. (1993). *The infinite conversation*. Minneapolis, MN: University of Minnesota Press.

Boutang, P. A., Deleuze, G., & Parnet, C. (2012). *L'abécédaire de Gilles Deleuze: avec Claire Parnet*. Los Angeles, CA: Semiotext(e).

Bradley, J. P. N. (2015). Becoming-literature: Deleuze and the Craquelure. *Lit Matters—The Liberlit Journal of Teaching Literature, 1*(2), 79–11.

Calvet, L.-J., & Petheram, M. (1998). *Language wars and linguistic politics*. Oxford: Oxford University Press.

Cassin, B. (2017, March). More than one language. *Eflux, 80*. Retrieved July 18, 2019, from http://www.e-flux.com/journal/80/100018/more-than-one-language/

Cole, D. R. (2011). *The actions of affect in Deleuze: Others using language and the language that we make*. Oxford: Wiley-Blackwell. Retrieved July 18, 2019, from http://handle.uws.edu.au:8081/1959.7/512960

Cole, D. R., & Bradley, J. P. N. (2014). Japanese English learners on the edge of chaosmos: Félix Guattari and "becoming-otaku". *Linguistic and Philosophical Investigations, 13*(1), 83–95.

De Landa, M. (2011). *A thousand years of nonlinear history*. New York, NY: Zone Books.

Deleuze, G. (1995). *Negotiations, 1972-1990*. Columbia University Press.

Deleuze, G. (1997). *Essays critical and clinical*. Minneapolis, MN: University of Minnesota Press.

Deleuze, G., & Guattari, F. (1983). *Anti-oedipus: Capitalism and schizophrenia*. Minneapolis, MN: University of Minnesota Press.

Deleuze, G., & Guattari, F. (1987). *A thousand plateaus: Capitalism and schizophrenia*. Minneapolis, MN: University of Minnesota Press.

Depardon, R., & Nougaret, C. (2008). *Donner la parole = Hear them speak*. Göttingen, Germany: Steidl.

Derrida, J. (1991). *A Derrida reader: Between the blinds*. London: Harvester Wheatsheaf.

Derrida, J., & Mensah, P. (1998). *Monolingualism of the other; or, the prothesis of origin*. Stanford, CA: Stanford University Press.

Dörnyei, Z., &. Gardner, R. C. (2012). *Motivation and second language acquisition*. Honolulu, HI: University of Hawaii Press.

Fisher, M. (2009). *Capitalist realism: Is there no alternative?* Winchester: Zero Books.

Foucault, M., & Pearson, J. (2001). *Fearless speech*. Los Angeles, CA: Semiotext(e).

Friedman, T. L. (2009). *The world is flat: A brief history of the twenty-first century*. Bridgewater, NJ: Paw Prints/Baker & Taylor.

Groys, B. (2011). *Google: Words beyond grammar* [Google: Worte jenseits der Gramma- tik]. Ostfildern, Germany: Hatje Cantz.

Holliday, A. (2006). Native-speakerism. *ELT Journal, 60*(4), 385–387.

Jenkins, J. (2012). *English as a lingua franca: Attitude and identity*. Oxford: Oxford University Press.

Kachru, B. B. (2010). *Asian Englishes: Beyond the canon*. Hong Kong: Hong Kong University Press. Retrieved July 18, 2019, from http://www.myilibrary.com?id=301661

Kim, S.-S., Lee, N.-Y., Jang, H., & Kelly, A. (2006). *Please teach me English*. San Francisco, CA: Tai Seng Entertainment.

Kirkpatrick, A. (2012). *The Routledge handbook of world Englishes* (pp. 490–505). Oxon: Routledge.

Kohl, J. R. (2009). *The global English style guide: Writing clear, translatable documentation for a global market*. Cary, NC: SAS Institute.

Kubota, R. (1999). Ideologies of English in Japan. *World Englishes, 17*(3), 295–306.

Lecercle, J.-J. (2002). *Deleuze and language*. Basingstoke: Palgrave Macmillan.

Lecercle, J.-J. (2009). *A Marxist philosophy of language*. Chicago, IL: Haymarket Books.

Lingis, A. (1994). *The community of those who have nothing in common*. Indiana University Press.

McCrum, R. (2010). *Globish: How the English language became the world's language.* Toronto: Anchor Canada.

Misono, K. (2011). Globish: Can it save world languages? *Bulletin of Faculty of Letters, Kanto Gakuin University/Humanities and Science Research Center of Kanto Gakuin University, 124,* 135–173.

Mitchell, A. J., & Kemp Winfree, J. (Eds.). (2009). *The obsessions of Georges Bataille: Community and communication.* Albany, NY: SUNY Press.

Nerrière, J.-P. (2005). Globish—The communication of the future. *Epoha.*

Nerrière, J.-P. (2006). *Parlez Globish! Don't speak English.* Paris, France: Eyrolles.

Nerrière, J.-P., & Hon, D. (2009). *Globish the world over a book written IN Globish.* Lexington, KY: International Globish Institute.

Nerrière, J.-P., & Hon, D. (2011). *Sekai no gurōbisshu: sengohyakugo de tsūjiru kyōi no eigojutsu.* Tōkyō, Japan: Tōyō Keizai Shinpōsha.

Oguri, S. (2010). *Dārin wa gaikokujin in English = My darling is a foreigner.* Tokyo, Japan: Mediafakutorīe.

Peters, J. D. (2012). *Speaking into the air: A history of the idea of communication.* Chicago, IL: University of Chicago Press.

Phillipson, R. (2014). *Linguistic imperialism.* Oxford: Oxford University Press.

Pinchevski, A. (2005). *By way of interruption: Levinas and the ethics of communication.* Pittsburgh, PA: Duquesne University Press.

Samuel, H. (2010, January). English invasion "threatens French language more than Nazis did'. *The Telegraph.* Retrieved July 18, 2019, from https://www.telegraph.co.uk/news/worldn ews/europe/france/6952462/English-invasion-threatens-French-language-more-than-Nazis-did.html

Sauzier-Uchida, E. (2008). Japanese learners' choice to overcome Babel: Standard English, Globish or Japlish? *Departmental Bulletin Paper, Waseda University, Faculty of Political Science and Economics Studies, Research on Liberal Arts Studies, 124,* 55–68.

Sheppard, D., & Sparks, S. (2004). *On Jean-Luc Nancy: The sense of philosophy.* London: Routledge.

Takahashi, K. (2013). *Language learning, gender and desire: Japanese women on the move.* Bristol: Multilingual Matters.

Tanaka, S. O., & Tanaka, H. (1995). A survey of Japanese sources on the use of English in Japan. *World Englishes, 14*(1), 117–36.

Toolan, M. (1999). *Nation languages, local literatures, and international readers: A new indigenization in native English writers?* Retrieved July 18, 2019, from http://artsweb.bham.ac.uk/MToolan/nationlanguage.html

Watson, J. (2011). *Guattari's diagrammatic thought: Writing between Lacan and Deleuze.* London: Bloomsbury Publishing.

Wolfson, L., & Deleuze, G. (2009). *Le schizo et les langues.* Paris, France: Gallimard.

Žižek, S. (2013). Love as a political category. *Subversive Festival, 6.* Zagreb, Croatia. Retrieved July 18, 2019, from http://www.youtube.com/watch?v=b44IhiCuNw4

Žižek, S. (2014). The impasses of today's radical politics. *Crisis and Critique, 1*, 9–44. Retrieved July 18, 2019, from http://crisiscritique.org/wp-content/uploads/2014/01/Zizek_Polit ics.pdf

Žižek, S. (2015). *Absolute recoil: Towards a new foundation of dialectical materialism.* London: Verso.

CHAPTER FOURTEEN

Reading in the Future: Literacy and the Time of the Internet

In fractal mapping—like the famous Mandelbrot Set, that supreme fashion hieroglyph of the 1980s—the basic pattern keeps repeating itself, ad infinitum apparently—the deeper & more enfolded you go, the more it repeats—till you get tired of running the program. After a certain amount of time, you might say, the fractal appearance has been theorized satisfactorily. No matter how much more exploitation of conceptual space occurs, the structure of the space is now *defined* for all practical purposes. Hasn't something similar happened with the Internet? (Bey 1997, p. 152).

The initial technological hype of the internet is subsiding as the ennui of informational overload begins to become apparent. It could be said that the internet signifies more than just the dream of educational technologists in terms of an unlimited realm of resource; it is also the pretext for a brand of western nihilism containing a sense of relativism, collapse of meaning and cultural schizo cynicism. As an exemplar of a perspective that deals with the educational consequences of this nihilism, Patti Lather has described the dénouement of the Enlightenment, positivism, and secular humanism, in the postmodern scene (Lather, 1991, pp. 86–101). Following Lather, it could be said that human reason as it has been rigorously defined in the west through science, and the will that this has engendered, has undergone a series of involuntary changes; scientific male phallocentric thought has begun to explore its foundations for the puissance to encounter yet untheorized categories and institutions. Through her research and writings, Lather has attempted a reconciliation of the grounds for education (though not male rationality) through deconstruction of the assumptions for research, and the treatment of scientific method as fiction and text (Lather, 1991, p. 91). Lateral thought of this type is useful in that the authority of scientific education may be transferred away from the linear transmission of knowledge and taken into contextual moments of critical inquiry. Yet, in a similar and parallel manner to the ways in which the deconstruction of Derrida may lead to the continuous lateral questioning of textual reference to discover the self-sameness of logos; in the case of Lather, educational authority may loop back and become embroiled in the text through the conjunction of simultaneous fictions that explain the functioning of postmodern educational power. In other words, the recursive action of fictional analysis reconstructs and reconfigures the power of the word through learning about text. This chapter does not tend towards such a movement because the collapse of textual meaning is not the object of analysis. To state the point directly, this chapter shall explore the literacy of the internet through an understanding of the time-based qualities that the internet offers to the learner when they are reading.

The Advantages and Disadvantages of Hypertext

However, it is propitious at this point to question the authority of the text of the internet in terms of the literacy that it might produce. This process of questioning involves the unveiling of the power relations that the electronic medium has negotiated. George P. Landon has figured this problem in terms of the convergence of hypertext and critical theory, and the replacement of conceptual systems founded upon ideas of center, margin, hierarchy, and linearity with ones of multi-linearity, nodes, links, and networks (Landow, 1992, p. 2). Using the work of Derrida, Theodor Nelson, Roland Barthes and Andries van Dam, Landow suggests that the convergence tendency of the electronic medium is an introduction to new modes of thought which shall become as important as the reading of narrative became through the technology of the printing presses. These modes of thought define a restructuring of time, and prepare us for a complex, non-linear time, where the acceleration in literacy learning on the internet is one of a gamut of survival techniques present in the vernacular of global postmodern capitalism. Landow and his associates have researched into this field, and report that students at the university level develop lines of "asynchronous communication" during their courses conducted through hypertext (Landow, 1992, p. 132). This communication preserves the structure of the courses whilst dispensing with the pressure of deadlines, or preset scheduling procedures. Students learn in an atmosphere of continuous discussion and project linkage, with hypertext documents serving to make the study of text a non-linear process of cross-referencing and the exploration of a plethora of connected material. These hypertext courses took on a different aspect to the presentment of isolated and studious competitors attempting to take out limited numbers of books from the library on any one subject at the same time. The real-time (and stored time as artifact) linking of the students meant that ideas could be shared during their development, and projects could be left or restarted depending upon answers to questions, or the settlement of discussion (Shields, Bader, McQuillan, & Beeman, 1988).

The implications for higher education are clear if such pilot projects were to be extended. Students would learn about internet literacy more broadly and they would produce work in a more communal atmosphere on the net. Positions of difference could be rigorously maintained through discussion, topics could be brought into line with the desires and interests of the students, instead of being dominated by the wishes of the academic designing the course. Evaluation in this context clearly cannot be a summative but involves the immersion of the student in a process of collaboration. The roles of the students, teachers and any other participants who might become involved in the literacy-learning unit, result in an energy center for the transmission and reception of code. Internet learning micro-cultures are beginning to be understood (Plant, 1996), though the translation to recognizable cultural formations is blurred by the potential for camouflage and piracy, which the electronic medium affords. Non-linearity begins to take on real force when it is not merely consigned to the scrambling of the code of the text, but it is also a part of the life choices of the participants in the process. Contrary to Landow, who begins to sound like a salesman for all things non-linear, and tries to position himself as the instigator of complex hypertextuality, (and there is undoubtedly immense potential here), we must not allow the time of literacy on the internet to subsume or dominate other learning paradigms, or, put another way, we cannot move to enforce a grand narrative of non-linear literacy learning at the expense of the actual life choices of the players caught in the systems of internet literacy.

Ted Friedman, for example, notes that hypertext is a transitional genre particularly appealing to literary academia because it dresses up traditional literary study with postmodern multimedia flash (Friedman, 1995, p. 74). Dull literary courses may be given the appearance of relevance and current style through the presentation of ideas in hypertext. The authority of the linear narrative is questioned by this procedure; however, the production units of hypertextual critique are also ideal places for students to be carried through the system without interacting with the text in question. The agents in these courses may become discouraged due to the intensity of communal scholasticism. Reading immense amounts of cross-referenced and interconnected publications, as Landow suggests, extends the linearity of the narrative form of literacy through non-linear acts. On the contrary, the internet offers much more than protracted reading projects, in that it introduces the student to a maze of contemporary artifacts. The interactivity of hypertext learning is linear since it produces and reinforces a narrative structure of reading and writing. The non-linear learning structure of the internet incorporates heterogeneous elements such as video, music, VR environments, graphics, as well as screens of text. The non-linearity of learning is dependent upon the feedback system that is produced between the student and the material. The complexity of the feedback on the net does not result in simple extensions of linear methodology (i.e., reading and writing exercises), but introduces the students to other worlds of complex non-linear literacy.

The *Machina Mundi*

The cutting edge of the internet are the other worlds; they represent the science fiction of the digitized medium, the sites where the future collides with the chaotic present. The communications systems connected to the internet present perhaps the most powerful technology that has ever been invented. In a sense that has never been understood, the internet reverses the relationship that humans have with technology. It could be said that it is no longer a question of humans inventing technology, but of technology reinventing the human. Reinvention involves the way in which humans communicate and the communicative resources that humans have, to define themselves (Ansell-Pearson, 1997, p. 152). Reinvention may be understood through the many escape routes from the constraints of sedentary society that the internet affords. The space for literacy learning on the internet opens a complex, non-linear time that does not totalize or accumulate experience, but places it through the maelstrom of accelerated dimensions. This is the chaotic material space where chronological time breaks down. The chaotic material space cannot be eternalized into a Platonic heaven or reproduced as perfunctory knowledge (the internet is not a library); on the contrary, the space of the internet coheres the glutinous remnants of intellect and desires driven by excess (proto-materialist libido). In other words, the cybernetic machine that the internet is a vital segment of is an immense system of constraint, turned into a hierarchy by economics and shaped by flows of communication and capital (polarization). To challenge this machine in terms of the literacy learning parameters of the net is to move the pragmatic and theoretical emphasis away from its automatic binding elements (capitalist control), and to enter a fluid relationship with the spaces left by repetition and by control (virtual terrorism).

It could be argued that the literacy of the internet is by analogy the end game of western theology. Nicholas de Cusa conceived of the notion of the *Machina Mundi* in terms of the Great Chain of the World (1440), with a God that was not separated from nature, but was an intrinsic part of it as steersman (Greek, *kubernets*) or governor (Latin, *gubenator*). This *Machina Mundi* has a center that is everywhere and a circumference that is nowhere, for God is its center and circumference and God is everywhere and nowhere (Cusa, 1997). The Great Chain of medieval theology that de Cusa theorized, operated as a hierarchy of constraints, governing various subsystems, including human society, within an organically organized whole. The ultimate constraint on all communication in the system (production, reproduction, exchange, maintenance, interaction) is embodied in the mysterious principle called God. Anthony Wilden has argued that God in this system is a metaphor, and taken seriously as a metaphor, it symbolizes the ultimate constraint on all past, present, and future behaviour on the planet; this constraint we now call entropy (Wilden, 1997, p. 225). Wilden contends that entropy is qualitative as well as quantitative, depending on "the qualitative signification of a chosen relation between order and disorder" (Wilden, 1997, p. 226). Entropy is a characteristic of arrangement, the arrangement of God being the maximum concordance of differences, (*De concordantica catholica*, 1433); total entropy is also achieved when a system is described as having all differences equalized. Wilden contrasts the hierarchically constrained universe (a simple ecosystem), from the linear or efficient causality that is assumed to operate in the isolated, mechanical, equilibrium systems of a Newtonian universe.

Using the notion of the *machina mundi* to analyze the literacy of the internet, we may perceive how the theology of the whole, that requires an unmoved mover, is a metaphor for the stasis of the system, and this allows us to access an overview of the form of constraint that the organization defines. Global, late, or post-modern capitalism, that is accelerated and defined through its communication systems, provides the pretext for understanding the post-modern shifts in control, down to semiology, literacy, and social relations. However, this analysis does not provide meta-statements as Wilden hoped. This is because the gap or space between the representation of capitalism and capitalism *qua* capitalism is unrepresentable as capitalism circumvents linear development. What we are left with are the coding techniques of global capitalism on which we may perform a destructuralization in terms of the forms of constraint that have been set in place to control the literacy learning process. The digital medium of the internet, where signs are reversible, dispersed and in many ways viral, substantiates the claim that the cybernetic equation of the global communication system acts in such a way as to simultaneously provide almost total control of any communicative interaction (tracking) and release from intentional face-to-face interactivity (digital camouflage). It is also the space in which the unconscious surges, and where agents may learn about digital literacy, also termed "selective exposure" (Foster, 1997).

Computer Mediated Community

The mapping of the coding techniques of post-modern capitalism, and the constraints that this imposes upon literacy learning on the internet, presents a complex arrangement of signs and relations in time and space (local interactions leading to universal interruptions). The time of the internet incorporates a form of communication that resembles an immense digital marketplace, selling everything from people to software, from holiday homes to maps of the moon. This gigantic commercial enterprise never rests, it depends entirely on the interest generated from the identity and the design of the web pages and has a quick turnover of sites and innovation as companies go to the wall or servers are not maintained. Agents learning on the net encounter multiple inducements to part with the details of their credit cards and can satisfy their desire for products not readily available in their local neighborhood. Marshall McLuhan (1964) would have considered this aspect of the internet as being hot media. The commerciality of many parts of the net initiates a type of dumbing down of the agent, and a passive acceptance of uncritical desires. The lack of imagination that this type of media may induce does not bode well for creative education (in terms of produced artifacts). However, the motivation to learn about literacy is galvanized by using the internet, as specific desires are distilled and brought to the surface of the learning activity using a digital medium to discover information. The quality of striving in learning, known as conation, is strengthened using the internet as the access to information is increased. Kathryn Atman has argued that conation is one of the principal factors that determine success in distance learners (Atman, 1987, p. 14), and learning literacy on the net may be placed into the category of multi-directional distance learning.

The *machina mundi* of the internet constrains the learner in terms of being driven by postmodern illusion (capitalist entropy), but rather than this signifying an ultra-modernism or the extension of the senses that McLuhan has theorized, this constraint defines a space for difference in terms of cultural artifact. The increasing ease of the production of websites means that agents will be able to actively transfer their desires into individual or collective electronic creativity. Steven G. Jones has looked at this development in terms of a socially constructed space and the post-modern geography that it entails (Jones, 1995, pp. 10–35). Jones has located the need for new notions of community as the old ones break down, and points to the fact that we are now able to create community technologically. As society moves in this direction, education benefits from what has been termed as the "rhetoric of the electrical sublime" (Carey, 1989, p. 23), whereby the investment in electronic hardware is touted as the solution to social problems. Setting schools up with computers, in these terms, is a simple political fix to broader social problems, since it could be claimed that the social space that is created on the net does not equalize the differences in societal wealth. The social space that is constructed on the net is highly illusionary and virtual, and it does not address issues of the permanent underclass. Jones questions the authentic nature of the cyber society created through computer mediated community (CMC), as it is basically a *use* of space and time, rather than being an abstraction in space and time, which was the case in society constructed before technology allowed for extensive mediation (Mumford, 1934). The CMCs are characterized by a fluidity and mobility (and not place), in that the constructed social space does not remain fixed in narrative terms or in terms of the status of the participants in its fold (the literacy of digital nomadism).

Jones, paraphrasing Carey, puts many of the claims about the new cyber society down to the "mythos of the electronic revolution" (Carey, 1993, p. 171), where the fidelity of cyber-spatial social relations is kept as an analogue to physical social relations, and a false homology is made between the two (Jones, 1995, p. 19). This could also be applied to many of the claims about new literacies or multiliteracies (Cope & Kalantzis, 2000) that are developing due to the explosion in electronic communication. Jones argues that this action misunderstands the notion of community by replicating the rhetoric of the fascists, who built a deeply divided and oppressive society through technology and social production and called it community *(Volk)*. On the net, in conceptual terms, the technology is not so much a space for community, as a passage point or medium for the ritual sharing of information (Stone, 1991, pp. 81–118). Social scientists have found it extremely difficult to define community precisely, falling prey to the commonly known errors of instrumentalism, and the replication of subjective belief (about community) in objective study (on community). At best, communities may be understood as complexes of variable social relationships and ideas, yet they escape identification of vital character or structure (from the outside). Jones identifies the need for the conceptualization of space and the social, and the inquiry into connections between social relations, spatial practices, values, and beliefs. The ability to create, maintain and control space, whether it is virtual, non-place or net-world, links us to notions of power and necessarily to issues of authority, dominance, submission, rebellion and co-option, which Etzioni (1991) has established as primary criteria for community and is immanent in the production and maintenance of internet literacy.

Power on the Net

The identification of communal power relations on the net, however, does not bring us nearer to the unconscious learning and particular literacy that will proceed there. It is not clear how the struggles of history and the formation of tumultuous communities, are going to be uploaded into cyberspace on the large scale. Whilst the interactivity and power relationships of the new media cannot be denied, the question remains as to whether they will lead to communities vying for power in ways which reflect this media, or whether processes which have already shaped history shall be repeated on the web. Currently the commercial wars among servers, O/S mediums, software designers, PC manufacturers and dot com companies, are primarily a technical sparring to fill out the needs of the market for cheap and reliable access to the internet and an adequate choice of useful and interesting services. The alleged feedback for real communities is a leap into the science fiction of the social. It should be noted that the emergent culture of the net inscribes a pre-written space in contrast to literary culture, and that digital literacy-learning will take place in this space to accelerate the processes of inscription. This pre-written space, however, has not led to idealized tribal village communication as Howard Rheingold has suggested (the electronic village), but points more obliquely and disparately to the hunters and gatherers in the electronic media (Meyrowitz 1986).

Notions of the electronic village or community of computer mediation derive in part from the understanding that the internet is the end game of western theology. By tending towards the whole, it is possible to conceptualize the equalizing of difference in a fully entropic global communication system. Yet the tendency towards the whole is also an escape route from it. The political forces that have placed the internet into the classroom as an educational tool cannot predict the literacy and outcome of this placement, as the students learning on the internet will not conform to the same forces as their placement (it is a complex non-linear arrangement). Allan E. Goodman (1993, p. 56) predicted that the computerization of the classroom will lead to its deconstruction as a formal structure. The variously formulated virtual classrooms have taken similar lines into the future in that they have extended ideals of choice and have made literacy learning a lifelong occupation to be married with work or play. In this case, agents placed in these technological settings of the future benefit from a universally wired and interactive society. However, beneath this ideal structure, lie the power centers where real people exist and desire, even if more of their daily experience is mediated through computers. Deleuze and Guattari have provided an analysis that engages with these micro powers:

> Each power center is also molecular and exercises its power on a micrological fabric in which it exists only as diffuse, dispersed, geared down, miniaturized, perpetually displaced, acting by fine segmentation, working in detail and in the detail of details. Foucault's analysis of disciplines or micro powers (school, army, factory, hospital, etc.) testifies to these focuses of instability where groupings and accumulations confront each other, but also confront breakaways and escapes, and where inversions occur. What we have is no longer The Schoolmaster but the monitor, the best student, the class dunce, the janitor, etc .. .. . We would not say that the proper name loses its power
>
> when it enters these zones of indiscernibility, but that it takes on a new kind of power ... . And every power center has this micro texture. The micro textures—not masochism—are what explain how the oppressed can take an active role in oppression: the workers of the rich nations actively participate in the exploitation of the Third World, the arming of dictatorships, and the pollution of the atmosphere (Deleuze & Guattari, 1992, pp. 224–5).

It is on this level of micro-organization that the changes triggered by the time of the internet are happening. There is not a conscious non-linearity occurring as direct positive feedback in response to the electronic circuitry (except perhaps in populations deprived of the technology); the non-linear process is more concretely, an unconscious restructuring of the micro texture of the power centers within it. In contrast to the dualism of the public and the private or the political and the personal; the time of the internet presents a non-diachronic investment in heterogeneity. It could also be said that the machinic phylum of the internet is a focused instability, which implicates communication and intelligence with a bizarre range of new powers that have direct implications about our notion of literacy. The ability to access immense amounts of information, to perceive extremely idiosyncratic desires and to examine the cultural artifacts of the electronic herd—all point to new forms of internet literacy. Jerome Bruner has expertly presented the difference being drawn out here, when he said that, "the ways of the mind are enabled, indeed often brought into being, by learning to master what has been described as a culture's toolkit of symbolic systems and speech registers. There is thinking and meaning making for intimate situations different in kind from what one uses in the impersonal setting of a shop or office" (Bruner, 1996, p. 25). This is precisely what the internet does not provide. The symbolic systems and speech registers are obviated or at least rearranged, and they are replaced and overlaid by non-situational complexities of undirected inscription. The unconscious literacy learning of the internet, therefore, does not provide a training ground for the mores of sedentary society. The proper name (the personal project and consequent symbolic register), towards which the student of Bruner would strive, is dissolved beneath a host of micro-textual and avataristic internet identities and power.

The Distinction Between Form and Expression

Gilles Deleuze (1992, pp. 280–294) has complained about the incessant chatter of undirected speech that arises from mediocre cultural production, such as the French literary TV program *Apostrophes*, or the omnipotence of boring couples, or formulaic novels written by journalists. He claims that if literature is going to die it will be by assassination, as the conformity of production for the market will subsume creative forces, and no one will notice singular creation (that is not represented in the market). Audio-visual production does not replace literary pro-duction in these terms but suffers from the same reduction in creative possibilities that bowing to a mass market engenders. The internet particularizes a similar move-ment towards hyper-commercialism, which is precisely why strategies that unfold the time of the internet in terms of singular educational pursuits and an identifi-cation of internet literacy, are a creative necessity for computerized learners. The prizing apart of thinking and meaning-making as, for example, Bruner proffers, does not take place on the internet in terms of a situational or contextual analysis, which enables systematic and specific skill-learning. Instead, the literacy-learning structure meshes with and spreads instantaneously through the virtual and the non-directed. The micro-textures present in the power structures of the internet process this procedure, and allow its dispersal in terms of information, and in-formation about the information, *ad infinitum*. In these micro-textures there are unprecedented opportunities for zones of indiscernibility, where identities circu-late, and information loses its meaning (as to who benefits from it and its inten-tionality). Concurrently, the results of the analyzes of modernist power structures in the manner of Foucault lose their rhetorical placement as postmodern or the capacity to be detectable as such; they are merely layers that we may increasingly put on top of one another when we are talking about literacy on the internet.

However, it is futile to define the time of the internet with post-(x), as if the mediated future disavows the past. Douglas Englebart's (1962) vision of human intellect being augmented through technology depends upon the system of power that the technology defines. For example, Alvin Toffler (1970, pp. 360–386), investigated the future and saw global capitalism determining a new genre of education that would replace the factory skills of the past with the flexibility necessary for jobs in high technology (information and control). His predictions regarding super-industrialism combined with councils of the future to speculate about curricula and teaching methodology, assume that the extension of control shall permeate in the social direction of hyper-industrialism; and he subsequently frames worrying possibilities such as the educational use of smart drugs to enhance IQ. Some industrialists would undoubtedly concur with several of these predictions, and the merging of education and industry, especially in higher education, has transpired along some of the lines that Toffler predicted, leading to a stark division between those advocating an art-based approach to education and those siding with industry. Studies such as *The Information Society* by William J. Martin (1988), confirm the movement of control throughout society, by pinpointing the flows of information at each conjunction. With information packaged and processed into any shape that it could ever take (through digital convergence); systematic regulation of any communication and therefore literacy becomes possible. This is because a form is discernible that connects the most innocently naive utterance to intelligence secrets at the heart of governments (communicative continuity). Information theorists work under the assumption that universal units of information (bits) flow like electricity to animate the circuits that they visit. Yet the quantification of information is not directly analogous to the quantification of energy; whilst both mechanisms serve objectified ends, the means of production (an energy plant, and a state system) are clearly divergent.

Governments do wish to capture, regulate, and control the literacy and the flow of information present on the internet, but the raw material of the net is cultural production (the bit is a tool); which can extinguish or expand the distinction between expression and content. At the furthest extent of rigorous (Newtonian mechanical) scientific discourse, the distinction between expression and content is at its strongest, and the bits of information are clearly definable and able to be used in formal situations (literacy=verifiable truth). In the confused communicative arena of the net, where power approaches a micro-texture, and the focus of instability designates a zone of indiscernibility; content and expression are merged, and they are translatable onto a smooth plane of digital interaction (literacy= flux). The distinction between expression and content is not only merged, but also complexified. The duality that exists between formal expression and folk psychology dissolves, beneath a bewildering array of communicative possibilities (digital synthesis). The linguist Louis Hjelmslev untied the duality between expression and content by "weaving a net out of the notions of matter, content and expression, form and substance" (Deleuze & Guattari, 1992, p. 43). The unmetaphorical net of postmodern communication technology does not only have implications for language, but permeates society and literacy, or the strata of society as Deleuze and Guattari term them with reference to geology. It is clear from the work on emergent communities on the net, that the complex movements associated with the new media are sufficiently differentiated to be stratified, yet this stratification also forms intricate crossover points, through which there exists the possibility of an undifferentiated plane. Hjelmslev termed this plane as matter, Deleuze and Guattari use the expression body without organs, and digitalization creates its own singular plane of interactivity through which we may encounter the literacy of the internet.

The Literacy of Quantum Materialism

Hjelmslev's net leaves no ground for dualism between expression and content, as he utilized all the resources of real distinction, reciprocal presupposition, and general relativism, to define each in their mutual solidarity as opposed (relative) functives of one and the same function (Hjelmslev, 1969, p. 60). In so doing, the space is produced for theories to matter in a quantum universe and as the medium of the internet for literacy. Echoing the quantum mechanics of Niels Bohr, the relativisation and implication of any procedure (in others) concerning the plane of matter—is the "unformed, unorganized, non-stratified or de-stratified body and all its flows, for example, subatomic and sub molecular particles, pure intensities, pre-vital and pre-physical free singularities" (Deleuze & Guattari, 1992, p. 43)—and this makes it possible to de-structuralize the work of procedure. Niels Bohr was concerned with the distinction between the scientific observer and the phenomena under scrutiny, and the fact that any *interaction* between measuring devices and that which is measured, defines a quantum relationship. Bohr speaks of the impossibility of any "sharp separation between the behaviour of atomic objects and the interaction with the measuring instruments which serve to define the conditions under which the phenomena appear" (Bohr, 1987, pp. 39–40). This irreducible interaction does not form a unity between observation and phenomena governed by a classical economy of synthesis, but it defines a complex and shifting *complementarity* (Plotnitsky, 1994, p. 103).

The complex complementarity from Plotnitsky and Bohr, where the procedures and methods of investigation are rigorously implicated in the matter under investigation (and any escape routes from it), define an educational stance for understanding the literacy of the internet. It is a relative stance, and in no way does it define a non-theoretical or "mystical" space which defeats the interruptions of investigation, but, as Bohr elaborates with relation to physics, "the notion of complementarity points to the logical conditions for description and comprehension"

(Bohr, 1978, p. 91). The conditions under which investigation into the literacy of the internet is possible require that non-directed, unorganized, subconscious particles of learning are "mapped" on a field that does not attempt to solidify this fluidity into structured methods of comprehension. Similar in kind to the discoveries about behaviour at the subatomic level, where particles exhibit complex non-linear behaviour in time and space, the literacy of the net does not need abstract models for its comprehension, but rather channels of complementary theory that turn in swathes with the transitory and ubiquitous formations of internet-students. The procedure of investigation into the literacy of the internet cannot be seen to impart stratified notions that are not implicated in the undifferentiated mass of the net. This is because closed systems of theoretical placement would be subsumed by the complexity of the communication involved, and the irreducible gap between the notion of net understanding, and the processes of the net themselves.

To this extent, the quantum materialism of the net opposes metaphysics. As a dynamic field of investigation, the internet is a real formation of power centers, material transaction and literacy learning about the future. In his study of emergent net culture, Manuel Castells (1996) integrated the informational mode of development with the modes of production in their historically determined heterogeneity of institutional arrangements. The most distinctive result of this investigation is the theorization of what Castells called "the space of flows" through integrated global networks. The space of flows is described as having at least three layers that are: (1) Technical: the circuit of electronic impulses (the microelectronics, telecommunication, hardware in general) that form the technological infrastructure of the network. (2) Geographical: the topology of the space formed by its nodes and hubs. The networks define hubs that link them to specific places under definite social and cultural conditions. Nodes are the "location(s) of strategically important functions that build a series of locality-based activities and organizations around the key functions of the network" (Castells, 1996, p. 413). And (3) Social: the spatial organization of the managerial elite using the network.

Castells uses the ideas of timeless time and placeless time to describe the sequence of the space of flows. Timeless time occurs when the characteristics of a given context, namely, the informational paradigm and the network society, induce systematic perturbation in the sequential order of phenomena performed in that context. Placeless time refers to the dissolving of geographical distance in the space of the flows—as organizational logic is placeless; it is fundamentally dependent upon understanding the space of flows that characterizes information networks and resultant literacy.

The Epoch of Schizo Literacy

However, we may legitimately ask the question, do we want our identities and consequent literacy to be washed away by this timeless space of flows? It could be said that the time of the internet defines a set of entanglement strategies for post-modern literacy education. This means that it gives the agents in the system the chance to scramble the codes that would wash away their identities. Castells (1997), however, addresses this question through an analysis of the self in the network society, and the sites of resistance to the omnipotence of global network capitalism (and its corporation models). He identifies the "condition of structural schizophrenia" as characterizing the work of the space of the flows, as it impinges upon the self. He differentiates between three different types of identity when approaching the structure of schizophrenia.

1. Legitimizing identity: this is introduced by the dominant institutions of society to extend and rationalize their domination over social actors. Legitimizing identities generate civil societies in the sense of the original Gramscian concept of a set of apparatuses that were mirrored by Althusser's State Ideological Apparata (SIA). These reproduce what Max Weber called *rationale Herrschaft* (rational power).
2. Resistance identity: this is produced by those actors who are in a position/condition of being excluded by the logic of domination. Identity for resistance leads to the formation of communes and communities as a way of coping with otherwise unbearable conditions of oppression.
3. Project identity: these are proactive movements which aim at transforming society, rather than merely establishing the conditions for their own survival in opposition to the dominant actors. Feminism and environmentalism fall into this category (Castells, 1997. p. 254). Castells theorized the weakening of the influence of traditional legitimizing identities such as the nation state as they are under attack from the space of flows. Global monetary markets from the late 80s onwards have connected, and now form a structure that defies central organization from any one nation state (this is the undifferentiated plane of postmodern capitalism into which digital envelopment feeds). Castells put his hope in the rise of resistance identities and their links with the project activists, to fill the social hole left as civil society loses its legitimacy, and the structure of schizophrenia in the space of the flows threatens to knock stable identity out of the water. This chapter places the communicative transformation and literacy of the net in this

space, which doesn't preclude this type of Castellan linkage and creates room for undirected subconscious literacy learning.

Yet even these formulations seem to be tainted with schizophrenia. Perhaps it is better not to try to demarcate stable identities in the time of the internet at all, but to follow the aim of Deleuze and Guattari, and to draw escape routes from the prisons of the self through schizoanalysis. However, we ask the question as to whether we wish our identities, literacy, and values to be washed away in the flood of electronic circuitry, do any answers to this question hold any truth or singularity, given that the act of legitimization depends upon a reflexivity not possible in the channels of the flows? Students learning literacy on the internet will encounter and be able to take on various social, sexual, political, spiritual, and intellectual identities; these are certainly not stable, but they are intricate, real, and impossible to contain within a limited rendering of the human or the self. On a larger scale, the groupings that will arise out of this mediated exploration of internet literacy and identity depend strongly upon the cultural artifacts that they produce, and the material conditions that allow agents to get up from behind their monitors and socialize. The internet social formations include Star Trek societies, sexually liberated group meetings, self-help psychology, ecological anti-capitalist anarchists, UFO and New Age religious units, ravers and right-wing militias. The process of formation and literacy that is taking place within the space and time of the flows, is often located within the logic of corporate organization even though they are literally anathema to it. This is the wholesale movement of culture and the entanglement processes that internet literacy seems to encourage; it is the mixing up of the codes on which society is based to reveal other possibilities. The linearity of the virtual majority defines the intentionality of the most homogenous organizations (for example the Bush administration), whilst the time of the internet allows heterogeneity to emerge within the tenets of postmodern literacy-learning about culture and consequently lifestyle choices—this is the epoch of schizo literacy.

References

Ansell-Pearson, K. (1997). *Viroid life: Perspectives on Nietzsche and the transhuman condition.* Routledge.

Atman, K. S. (1987). The role of conation (striving) in the distance education enterprise. *The American Journal of Distance Education, 1*(1) 14–24.

Bey, H. (1997). Notes for C theory. In A. Kroker & M. (Eds.), *Digital delirium* (pp. 123–165). New World Perspective.

Bohr, N. (1987). *The philosophical writings of Niels Bohr*, (3 Volumes). Ox Bow Press.

Bruner, J. (1996). *The culture of education*. Harvard University Press.

Carey, J. (1989). *Communication as culture*. Unwin-Hyman.

Carey, J. (1993). Everything that rises must diverge: Notes on communications, technology and the symbolic construction of the social. In P. Gaunt (Ed.), *Beyond agendas* (pp. 171–184). Greenwood.

Castells, M. (1996). *The rise of the network society: The information age: Economy, society and culture, Volume 1*. Blackwell Publishers.

Castells, M. (1997). *The power of identity, the information age: Economy, society and culture, Volume 2*. Blackwell Publisher.

Cope, B., & Kalantzis, M. (2000). *Multiliteracies: Literacy learning and the design of social futures*. Macmillan Press.

Cusa, N. de. (1997). On learned ignorance. In *Selected spiritual writings* (pp. 90–115). Paulist Press.

Deleuze, G. (1992). Mediators. In J. Crary & S. Kwinter (Eds.), *Incorporations*. Zone Books.

Deleuze, G., & Guattari, F. (1992). 1933: Micro politics and segmentarity. In *A thousand plateaus: Capitalism & schizophrenia II* (pp. 208–231). Athlone Press.

Englebart, D. (1962). *Augmenting human intellect: A conceptual framework*. Stanford Research Institute. https://apps.dtic.mil/sti/pdfs/AD0289565.pdf.

Etzioni, A. (1991). *The responsive society*. Jossey-Bass.

Foster, D. (1997). Community and identity in the electronic village. In D. Porter (Ed.), *Internet Culture* (pp. 23–38). Routledge.

Friedman, T. (1995). Making sense of software: Computer games and interactive textuality. In S. G. Jones (Ed.), *Cyber society: Computer-mediated communication and community* (pp. 73–89). Sage Publications.

Goodman, A. E. (1993). *A brief history of the future*. Westview Press.

Hjelmslev, L. (1969). *Prolegomena to a theory of language*. University of Wisconsin Press.

Jones, S. G. (1995). Understanding community in the information age. In S. G. Jones (Ed.), *Cyber society: Computer-mediated communication and community* (pp. 10–35). Sage Publications.

Landow, G. P. (1992). *Hypertext: The convergence of contemporary critical theory and technology*. John Hopkins University Press.

Lather, P. (1991). *Getting smart: Feminist research and pedagogy with/in the post-modern*. Routledge.

Martin, W. J. (1988). *The information society*. Association for Information Management, London.

McLuhan, M. (1964). *Understanding media: The extensions of man*. Random House.

Meyrowitz, J. (1986). *No sense of place: The impact of electronic media on social behavior*. Oxford University Press.

Mumford, L. (1934). *Technics and civilization*. Harcourt, Brace & World.

Plant, S. (1996). On the matrix: Cyber feminist simulations. In R. Shields (Ed.), *Cultures of internet: Virtual spaces, real histories, living bodies* (pp. 170–183). Sage Publications.

Plotnitsky, A. (1994). *Complementarity: Anti-epistemology after Bohr and Derrida*. Duke University Press.

Shields, M., Bader, G., McQuillan, P., & Beeman W. O. (1988). *Intermedia: A case study of innovation in higher education.* Office of program analysis/Institute for research in information and scholarship, Providence, RI, United States.

Stone, A. R. (1991). Will the real body please stand up? Boundary stories about virtual cultures. In M. Benedikt (Ed.), *Cyberspace* (pp. 81–118). MIT Press.

Toffler, A. (1972). *Future shock.* Pan Books.

Wilden, A. (1979) Changing frames of order: Cybernetics and the *machina mundi*. In K. Krippendorff (Ed.), *Communication and control in society* (pp. 9–29). Gordon and Breach.

CHAPTER FIFTEEN

Deleuze and Narrative Investigation: The Multiple Literacies of Sudanese Families in Australia

Introduction

This chapter introduces the reader to concepts from the philosopher Gilles Deleuze and asks how we might put those concepts to work in thinking about education. It introduces a new way of conceptualizing knowledge and asks how that new way of thinking might be used for teaching and learning purposes. Deleuzian philosophy asks us to put to one side many of our everyday concepts based on humanism and moralism, since those everyday concepts tend to undermine the critical narrative of investigation that we are trying to explore (see Denzin, 2003). The primary point of this paper is to enhance empirical study through Deleuzian concepts in such a way that we can open a new understanding of the narratives of the Sudanese refugee families, and to grasp the implication of that new understanding for the teaching of literacies. From a Deleuzian perspective, "the Sudanese" should not be understood in terms of fixed or stable categories. Rather they can be thought of in terms of their stories, and the elements that go to make up those stories. These are what Deleuze might call the "narrative real". Beginning with those stories, we can rethink educational practice (see Davies & Gannon, 2009) as teaching through multiple literacies.

As such, this chapter seeks to go beyond humanist impositions on the lives of the Sudanese Australians. I have located the notion of the "narrative real" from Deleuze as relevant to this process since dormant forces often lie within the Deleuzian "field of the real". As Jeffery Bell (2011) has argued: "For Deleuze, the real is to be associated with processes that constitute the givenness of objects rather than with the constituted, identifiable objects and categories themselves" (p. 4). In other words, there are elements within what is happening—and has happened—to the Sudanese refugee families that act as "markers" in the "narrative real" of the Sudanese Australians, and these markers may be reformulated as evidence for claims about how to offer more effective education through multiple literacies. One might cogently argue that it is not adequate to state the empirical facts of the dislocation of the Sudanese according to the humanitarian programme in Australia. The truth of what is happening to these families lies in their thought processes and in a complex, of "becoming Sudanese Australian". The field of inquiry is henceforth open and includes the contingent, anomalous or extraordinary. This study signals a Deleuze-inspired take on ethnography, in the sense that the Sudanese-Australian families are not considered as "ethnographic others", or representative of a qualitative study of Sudanese family life in Australia. Rather, the givenness of their lives is opened and explored through this work, with the aim of discovering an unknown point, whereupon the Sudanese-Australian "narrative real" is emergent and incipient learning of this real is understood.

Deleuze and the "narrative real"

What was real for Deleuze, and why is it important? Recent critiques of Deleuze and Deleuzian philosophy have targeted the notion of the real in Deleuze as being a weak point in his philosophy (e.g., Žižek, 2004). The argument is that Deleuze's promulgation of the "narrative real", which is at heart a dissection of Lacan's emergence of the real due to a symbolic lack, sets the unconscious up as being consummately productive. Deleuze (1990) in the *Logic of Sense* is searching for the real through a psychoanalytic "curtain" that had been drawn by Freud, Lacan and Melanie Klein. The Freudian analyst engages the patient in a narrative monologue whereby the real emerges from the entanglement of adult and child oedipalized sexualities and fantasy, until the therapeutically healed "ego" can emerge, free from the initial psychic impingement and impact of oedipal desire. Yet how do we know when this has happened? What if the psychoanalyst becomes superimposed as the parent, and thereby co-opts oedipal desire through analysis? Lacan set about refining and focusing the Freudian story about the real, in that he made the real a player in his structural analysis of the psyche. In fact, Lacan (1966) called the link between one's reality of desire and any articulation of this reality "the real"—to emphasize its importance and provide a symbolic marker in the "order of things". For Lacan, Oedipus is not a real impingement on psychic development, but a symbolic artefact of living and desiring, whereby the mind has produced a piece of dramatic attachment, embedding the real as a lack in life.

Deleuze and Guattari (1984) work on desire in a parallel manner to Lacan and Žižek (1989) in *Anti-Oedipus* though they arguably go further than both in that the "narrative real" of desiring machines and "schizo-analysis" inverts and re-channels capitalist desire through synthesis, to deal with capitalism's othering effects. Capitalism according to the "narrative real" in *Anti-Oedipus*, does not fundamentally incur a symbolic or linguistic lack in desiring, which could be located between the things one wants and the things that one is able to get, but is part of a disjunctive synthesis through which one may understand becoming in the world. The apartness and confusion that capitalism incurs may be traced back to the power structures in primitive societies according to Deleuze and Guattari (1984). Therefore, the "narrative real" of capitalism was already present in human society (Deleuze & Guattari, 1984) and is lodged in our collective unconscious through the flows and material practices of history and the drives that successive power structures have created (e.g., agrarian, industrial, technical, etc.). Deleuze and Guattari (1984) worked to unlock the "narrative real" from such successive historical markers that can produce madness.

Importantly, the nonconformist, "anti-herd" real of *Anti-Oedipus* comes about after examining the play of forces in the "death drive". In contrast, the "narrative real" of the *Logic of Sense* is a paradoxical series of events that presents an accumulation of experience and is a means to understanding how sense emerges under the influence of synthesis. Yet key to this understanding is the "death drive" and how it ultimately overrides Oedipus as an external influence (Freud), a symbolic other (Lacan) or a capitalist dictate (Žižek). The death drive has a formative part to play in Deleuze's formulation of the "narrative real" as it is fundamentally connected to one's notion of life and the in-between play of forces that life entails (see Deleuze, 2005). Deleuze is here referencing Nietzsche, to construct a philosophy of the future that outmanoeuvres Oedipus, and to present a positive rendition of the functioning of the drives. Deleuze presents thinking around this philosophy of the future as the "virtual"; not as a reflection or copy of reality or reconstruction of the actual, but to creatively invent the world through the unconscious, by following the lines of power and language (see Cole, 2011a, 2011b). The "virtual" does not merely transcribe life, as it includes contingency, personal memories, the imaginary, chaos and the dramatic. This philosophy of life critically includes reference to Spinoza and Bergson, as the subject is redesignated through pre-personal affect and biological vitalism by thinking in the "virtual". In other words, one begins a search for anomaly when one engages fully with Deleuze. The consequence of the "virtual", explained here as the "narrative real" of this paper lies at the edges of consciousness, as one articulates the influences of desire on perception, or begins to understand how actions have been conditioned and controlled for many years before one's body has experienced affects. In corollary, Deleuze's "narrative real" helps to understand the narratives of the Sudanese in Australia and their deeply felt experience of displacement by using the "virtual" as a form of tiered, analytical and synthetic thought process.

Deleuze and Investigations of the "virtual'

What are the consequences of Deleuze's "virtual" for empirical studies? In *Difference & Repetition* (1994), Deleuze characterized his philosophy as transcendental empiricism. This means that the object of thinking, in the virtual or "narrative real", is out there in the world, outside of human consciousness, and yet is simultaneously subject to the contortions and distortions that human thinking can produce. This is because the "virtual" includes aspects of contingency, chance, the memory, the imaginary, affection and the creative unconscious playing with time and space (cf. Deleuze, 1994). For example, if one is examining bacteria and their place in the world, one can deploy the "virtual" to extend empirical observations to explain the unpredictable ways in which bacteria can reproduce and relate to their outside. As such, Deleuze's philosophy opens scientific thinking and produces resonance between precise observation and documentation, and modes of writing executed by, for example, Marcel Proust or James Joyce. In contrast to the description of Deleuze's thought as being based on simple affirmation (see Massumi, 2002) or the efficaciousness of human desire; the "virtual" is when one is confronted face-on by a reality that is impossible to fully embrace or is "leaky". To a certain extent, this entails a type of manoeuvring in reality—as a researcher and writer—to make sure one comes to the "narrative real" as an outsider, so that one does not reproduce normative assumptions or familiar perceptions of reality that are relayed through the "average consciousness" or "everyday banality". One could say that the use of the "virtual" is a means of disentangling the influences of science in terms of phenomenology or the assumptions in psychology that have come to dominate investigations of the real, especially in the humanities and education (cf. Woolfolk & Margetts, 2007). Putting oneself outside psychological and phenomenological paradigms to investigate the "narrative real" by using Deleuze's "virtual" is a risky move, yet one that could prove to be invaluable to understanding the Sudanese Australians and their multiple literacies in education.

Such understanding of the Sudanese Australians comes about because the "virtual" is a means to examining forces and relationships that bisect, define and run through the "narrative real". One could say this is a type of slow investigation of the real, allowing for and encouraging a thoughtful sedimentation of the ways in which the "narrative real" is immanent and pantheistic for the Sudanese in Australia—in that their stories include evidence from all aspects of their lives and may give rise to many gods. In other words, in this study, we are searching for the multiple, geo-plastic forces embedded in the narratives of the Sudanese Australians. The meaning that one might take from these forces can be particularly bent and misshapen, and not respond to any form of equilibrium or constancy within the real. These geo-plastic forces are part of the slow revelations of the "narrative real" from a Deleuzian philosophical position (see Cole, 2010, 2012). The layers of the real must be peeled away by deploying the "virtual" to get to the "narrative real", before any core concerns and drives can be understood; in the case of this paper, this process involves examining the narratives of the Sudanese Australians.

Sudanese-Australian Immigrant Families: Two Narrative Case Studies[1]

The two Sudanese families (A and B) in this study came to Australia during the last 10 years. The two families travelled from the far south of Sudan (A), and the central highlands (B) respectively, and yet have settled approximately 30 km apart in the western Sydney districts of Penrith and Prospect. The project involved filmed observations in English adult classrooms, interviews with the adult Sudanese-Australian English learners, interviews in the houses with the family members and giving the participants "flip cameras" so that they can make short films about their everyday lives in Australia. The project lasted 8 months, with the families working with the researchers[2] to enable insights into their lives in Australia and particularly into their experiences with education. In the first family (A), the male (Nallowa) joined his wife and seven children two years ago; he is an Arabic and Dinka speaker and is learning English at the local adult centre for Technical and Further Education (TAFE). In family (B) the couple, Ema (male) and Serena (female), came to Australia together three years ago, and are both learning English at the local TAFE centre. Family (B) has nine children, with the eldest still in Egypt. Family (A) was much more forthcoming and ready to help with the research, which was mostly since Nallowa encouraged interaction between the researchers and the family, as he saw advantage in taking part. Nallowa wore suits to the adult English classrooms when we were filming and told the family members what to do in the house when we visited. To understand the "virtual" from his perspective, I would like to take a phrase from the interview transcripts and dwell on it so that the synthetic connections may become apparent in the construction of a Sudanese-Australian "narrative real".

Nallowa said in the second interview: "Now I ah ah, because I'm like to say in in ah, Africa you don't have ah, a country now, Africa you have two river" (interview transcript). Nallowa discussed the issues of drought in the interview and how the populations must live close to water to survive; but beyond this survivalist point is the deeper relationship that the Sudanese have with the land and how they conceptualize space. Something that was especially noticeable while working with the Sudanese Australians was how they meet and congregate at the intersections of streets and buildings. For example, Sudanese-Australian youth gather in groups in Blacktown at night in the small squares between commercial buildings and around the railway station exits. Nallowa was usually late for appointments, yet when he did turn up, his arrival was always unexpected and a surprise. The "virtual" for Nallowa and the Sudanese-Australian youth did not include timetabled schedules and designated queuing spots, but rather followed flows and points of confluence, whereby the map of the place or time was altered to fit in with the "virtual". The connections and relationships that the Sudanese Australians are developing, as part of their "narrative real", depend on their mapping processes of the terrain, and how the Sudanese Australians are forming new ways of working in "the real". This aspect of the research has less to do with consciousness, as it has to do with the inward journeys that the Sudanese migrants have embarked upon and are still living through in terms of their realities in Australia.

The "narrative real" of the Sudanese-Australian boys in the study contributed to the impression of "mute disparity" and an inward journey. The boys' habits consist of playing sport, attending school, dressing up and going out with their friends and dealing with their masculinity via media images of teenage male heroes framed and produced in the United States. Beyond this reality lies the deeper and more dangerous memory and concern of being a young Sudanese male in the war, where child soldiers are common (see AHRC, 2010). The gendered "virtual" of this study is due in part to the fact that the boys were questioning the reality that confronted them in Australia and were often finding it unexciting and banal. The allure of consumerism, educational success and the "petit bourgeoisie" may be diminished if one has the embedded memory or thought of war, however much that memory may be mediated by displacement or supported by family life (cf. Brown et al., 2006). The 18-year-old, eldest teenage male in Australia in family B was especially susceptible to such thoughts, and barely took part or expressed any opinions in the research project interviews. He would not talk about such events, as he was unwilling or unable to divulge such information, yet the atmosphere of a child soldier hung around him like the unnatural framing of some supernatural, unearthly force.

The Sudanese-Australian boys are strong-willed, attracted to American gangster rap, designer clothes and gold-plated jewellery. Outside school, and beyond the articulation of the research interviews involved with this project, the boys are lively and fun, forming close-knit groups who like to go out and inhabit the streets with their own sense of space as has been noted above. In contrast, the girls would willingly express random desires to the researchers such as wanting to become sportswomen, actresses or pop stars. The girls were able to easily converse about their developing Sudanese-Australian identity, what they thought of school and Australian life. The gender divide in the empirical field of investigation of this study is principally a question of desire, and this may be profitably approached through the Deleuzian-inspired "narrative real". This real offers through-lines and potentially new ways of looking at the development of Sudanese-Australian identity. The "virtual" is not a set cognitive ability or patterning of thought (see Cole, 2011); rather, the "virtual" signals the ways in which the Sudanese Australians are able to express themselves, currently outside institutional situations. These habits and abilities are henceforth folded into understandings about Sudanese-Australian learning and adaptive potentials through multiple literacies in the next section.

The observations and videotaping in the English language classes revealed the clear fact that the Sudanese-Australian adults were in the main struggling to learn English. Nallowa (family A) is a fluent Arabic and Dinka speaker, who has previously studied English in Kenya. In family (B), Ema and Serena were both learning English at TAFE. Serena especially needed special attention with her English exercises, and her teacher usually stayed behind to help her catch up. Nallowa considered his involvement in the project and his relationship with me very hopefully, and to bettering his position and his family's. He showed the researchers traditional embroidered materials that the women had prepared, perhaps with the hope that we might buy them. Both families (A and B) go to church and were involved with church community-ties. The Sudanese Australians have extensive support networks, and their houses are meeting places and crossroads for relatives and friends. In one of the flip-cam videos, a wake was filmed, where family members and relatives congregated in the house for several days.

The Sudanese-Australian "virtual" consists of a highly sociable bricolage (Harris, 2011). Neither loneliness nor isolation figures in their world. Equally, the place of study and reflection does not have an obvious position in the Sudanese-Australian "virtual". Sudanese-Australian homes contain large sofas and padded chairs, TVs, religious imagery on the walls and flashy stereo systems, and do not have the ordered demarcation of separate areas for discrete functionality. There are no books on display or within easy reach of the children. Rather, the "virtual" of the Sudanese Australians reinstitutes tribal and village spaces in their homes, without the mapping of petit bourgeoisie capitalism or reification of the home amongst the oedipalized English middle classes (cf. Vickers & McCarthy, 2010). However, the atmosphere of such places is not an unhappy one, with the constant movement of young children threading with the chatter of African conversation, TV sounds and low music. The "virtual" of the Sudanese Australians and the consequent "narrative real" depends greatly on the ways in which the children emerge from these family homes with a distinct African flavour. The children want to get jobs, earn money, buy cars and have attractive clothes. The indications are that they will achieve such goals, as they leave their parents behind in terms of their linguistic abilities in English, understanding mainstream Australian mores and their resultant chances of securing employment. How much they will recreate their African heritage in their subsequent homes is a matter for speculation. The Sudanese-Australian children will retain strong Sudanese-African connections because the diaspora from Africa has created powerful and supportive social networks through dedicated communality. These forces will play out in the "virtual", as the seductions of commerciality, ownership, capitalism and sedimentation within Australian society jostle with embedded Sudanese-African identities.

Multiple Literacies as Narrative

How do these case studies and the resulting "narrative real" help practitioners in education? The Deleuzian "virtual" in this paper takes the case studies of the Sudanese in Australia, with the aim of extending such an emergent reality, to bend and shape pockets of Australian society and any consequent narratives. This study and its consequences are not types of social constructivism, phenomenology or educational psychology, as has been discussed above; rather, this study aims to take the current functioning of the Australian education system, and alter its track given the "virtual" from the Sudanese-Australian case studies and create a new form of storytelling or "narrative real". Such an intervention implies that pragmatic measures could be adopted that consider the "virtual"; this pragmatism has been described as a form of "shimmering web" with respect to the Deleuzian notion of affect and how it applies to the humanities, arts and science as political science (see Gregg & Seigworth, 2010). This web could be figured as a material lens through which new possibilities in education are viable, and that take away the normative blueprints for development as they currently exist (see Cole, 2010, 2011a, 2012). This point has been previously taken up by qualitative researchers in education, who have used Deleuzian theory to break up the "everyday banality" of doing video research in the classroom:

> *"The need for new thought seems especially urgent in research concerning children, buried as they are under the weight of psychological and educational narratives that frame them into generality and string them out along the predictable plot of 'normal' development. Children who offer resistance, whether intentionally or not, to the disciplinary embrace of this employment risk becoming invisible or deviant. Research frequently fails to interfere with this everyday banality of the normal child and thus unwittingly colludes with the production of exclusion, dis-advantage and a stunted set of possible futures for children"* (MacLure et al., 2010, p. 544).

The new thought that can be used with respect to this study is multiple literacies theory or MLT (Masny and Cole, 2009). MLT is an example of a Deleuze-inspired literacy theory, which acts parallel to the "virtual" and the construction of the "narrative real" of the Sudanese Australians. MLT is a form of unhinging and reworking that releases multiple and minor literacies from their iron castings inside of, for example, English language development or a predefined "refugee African self". MLT is not a form of straightforward reflective practice, but suggests diffractive practices (see Cole, 2011a). MLT joins the specific socio-cultural needs of the Sudanese in Australia with the ways in which their stories may be read and reread as perturbation with respect to the dominant affective processes produced by their resettlement in Australia. Literacy is here not only a result of being able to speak and listen, read and write, but it is any form of communication in life. The Sudanese Australians, perhaps except for the oral abilities of the young girls, were clearly struggling with respect to most aspects of standard English literacy. This section henceforth describes the pragmatic, minor and multiple literacies that would help to extend the Sudanese-Australian "virtual" into the mainstream of education practice, and act as a new "narrative real" for teaching and learning with the Sudanese in Australia. The multiple literacies elaborated below are a result of considering the evidence of the case studies, and applying the processes of the Sudanese-Australian "virtual" in education:

1. Peer and youth literacies
    The Sudanese Australians respond well to kinship and group bonds being preserved. In mainstream educational practice, children are traditionally assessed, streamed and divided into year, subject and class groupings. The Sudanese Australians thrive in social arenas where they can listen to peers

and older members of their community speak about educative or social matters. For example, a Year 7 Sudanese-Australian student would respond well to being taught Mathematics by a Year 10 Sudanese-Australian student, or at least to having them available for peer support, and for cultural knowledge and context.

2. The literacy of synthetic time

The clockwork mosaic of discrete knowledge areas to be studied one at a time and after each other, and the often-confusing multitude of subjects in the secondary context, is a hindrance to the development of the Sudanese-Australian "virtual" and their consequent "narrative real". Rather, the Sudanese students could be taught for extended periods of unequal length and duration to encourage the synthesis of time, whereby their knowledge-acquiring apparatuses are switched on and they are attuned to learning. The introduction of the literacy of synthetic time requires a new timetable for the Sudanese Australians to be used for their schooling, with different subject and study periods (see Cole, 2011).

3. War literacies

The reality of war must not be watered down, sublimated or diluted in the context of schooling the Sudanese Australians because it is strongly present in their "narrative real". Rather, the "virtual" of the Sudanese would be stimulated and engaged by understanding what war means and in being able to articulate and discuss ideas connected to war, and not only be confined to how they have impinged upon Australian life and its people. This type of literacy cannot be taught discreetly or designated as being only relevant to the academic subject of Australian history.

4. Oral literacies

Spoken language takes precedence for the Sudanese Australians and their "narrative real". The imposition of non-oral literacy too quickly and too universally, that is, the deployment of educational practice involving reading and writing with the Sudanese Australians, will take the study focus away from their oral abilities and the sense of community that orality has embedded within it. Oral literacies coincide with the need for code switching in the classroom (see Milroy and Muysken, 1995)—in this case between Dinka, Nubian, Arabic and English—so that their knowledge, cultural understanding and conceptual development may be supported.

5. Tribal literacies

The tribalism of the Sudanese Australians cannot be overlooked but should be used effectively as part of their learning practices. This set of literacies would benefit the "virtual" of the Sudanese Australians and their narrative construction—because of the modes of socialization that tribalism includes, it requires educators and students to re-introduce a pre-modern space into the teaching and learning arena, whereby neither capitalist nor industrialized education is incumbent on the forms of sociality that are apparent.

6. Physical literacies

The use of sustained abstract knowledge in the classroom will hinder the progress of the Sudanese-Australian students in the mainstream. Physical literacy is important because the ways in which their "narrative real" is constructed through the "virtual" necessitates the physical reality of what is being discussed or studied to be paramount in the minds of the students. Education should be a physical experience for the engagement and development of the Sudanese-Australian "virtual" and the production of their narratives.

Conclusion

It would be hard to imagine that Deleuze could have envisaged the use of his conception of "the virtual" to help Sudanese-Australian students and their learning adaptation(s). However, the fit between philosophical conception and its application for the Sudanese Australians in education is compelling. Such a relationship has been mapped in this paper through the "virtual", "narrative real", case studies and finally in multiple literacies. This mapping is robust because Deleuze (1990) was concerned with questions of empirical realism, and how psychoanalysis can be taken away from the confines of a self-serving practice. Rather, we may take from Deleuze an ontology of becoming that works on a pragmatic, political and scientific level, in this case through multiple literacies and education (see Cole, 2010, 2011a). In this study, the careful observation and research work with the Sudanese Australians has not led to verifiable categories of qualitative data, or to sets of analysable phenomena, but to a conception of the Sudanese-Australian "virtual" that points to necessary changes in the educational system along narrative and multiple literacy lines. These changes need to be made if the Sudanese Australians are to succeed in Australia, and not be consigned to a peripheral sphere in the mainstream and subsequent welfare dependence. Recent studies on African communities in Australia have indicated that young Sudanese (under 25) are especially prone to becoming involved with crime and the infringement of Australian law (see AHRC, 2010). The introduction of the six types of multiple literacies as mentioned above into mainstream secondary and primary education as a practice could be a starting point to address the tendency towards failure that some Sudanese Australians are currently demonstrating in mainstream education. This is because the deployment of these literacies would help the Sudanese to construct a substantive educative "narrative real" in Australia of their own. Such a change in the fortunes of the Sudanese Australians would benefit the whole of Australian society and make real the possibility of a true multiculturalism as "multiple culturalisms" and as a new "virtual" of Australian educative life—which is often still dominated by a white, colonial past.

Notes

1 This study was funded by the SSHRC (Canada) International Opportunity Grant—*Immigrant Families and Multiple Literacies: Policy, Classroom and Community Connections Across Australia and Canada*. Full ethics permissions were obtained for this study and all names have been de-identified.
2 This study was carried out by Professor Diana Masny (University of Ottawa), Associate Professor David R. Cole (University of Western Sydney) and a research assistant.

References

AHRC (Australian Human Rights Commission). (2010). *In our own words: African Australians: A review of human rights and social inclusion issues*. Australian Human Rights Commission.

Bell, J. (2011). Between realism and anti-realism: Deleuze and the Spinozist tradition in philosophy. *Deleuze Studies, 5*(1), 1–17.

Brown, J., Miller, J., & Mitchell, J. (2006). Interrupted schooling and the acquisition of literacy: Experiences of Sudanese refugees in Victorian secondary schools. *Australian Journal of Language and Literacy, 29*(2), 50–62.

Cole, D. R. (2010). The reproduction of philosophical bodies in education with language. *Educational Philosophy and Theory, 42*(8), 816–829.

Cole, D. R. (2011a). *Educational life-forms: Deleuzian teaching and learning practice*. Sense Publishers.

Cole, D. R. (2011b). The actions of affect in Deleuze—others using language and the language that we make . . . *Educational Philosophy and Theory, 43*(6), 549–561.

Cole, D. R. (2012). Matter in motion: The educational materialism of Gilles Deleuze. *Educational Philosophy and Theory, 44*(S1), 3–17.

Davies, B., & Gannon, S. (2009). *Pedagogical encounters*. Peter Lang.

Deleuze, G. (1990). *The logic of sense* (M. Lester & C. Stivale, Trans.). Columbia University Press.

Deleuze, G. (1994). *Difference & repetition* (P. Patton, Trans.). Athlone Press.

Deleuze, G. (2005). *Pure immanence: Essays on a life* (A. Boyman, Trans.). Zone Books.

Deleuze, G., & Guattari, F. (1984). *Anti-Oedipus: Capitalism and schizophrenia* (R. Hurley, M. Steem & H. R. Lane, Trans.). Athlone Press.

Denzin, N. K. (2003). *Performance ethnography: Critical pedagogy and the politics of Culture.* Sage.

Gregg, M. & Seigworth, G. J. (Eds.). (2010). *The affect theory reader.* Duke University Press.

Harris, A. (2011). Singing into language: Sudanese Australian young women create public pedagogy. *Discourse: Studies in the Cultural Politics of Education, 32*(5), 729–743.

Lacan, J. (1966). *Ecrits.* Seuil.

Maclure, M., Holmes, R., Macrae, C., & Jones, L. (2010). Animating classroom ethnography: overcoming video-fear. *International Journal of Qualitative Studies in Education, 23*(5), 543–556.

Masny, D., & Cole, D. R. (Eds.). (2009). *Multiple literacy theory: A Deleuzian perspective.* Sense Publishers.

Massumi, B. (2002). *Parables for the virtual: Movement, affect, sensation.* Duke University Press.

Milroy, L., & Muysken, P. (Eds.) (1995). *One speaker, two languages: Cross-disciplinary perspectives on code-switching.* Cambridge University Press.

Vickers, M. H., & Mccarthy, F. E. (2010). Repositioning refugee students from the margins to the centre of teachers' work. *The International Journal of Diversity in Organizations, Communities & Nations, 10*(2), 199–210.

Woolfolk, A., & Margetts, K. (2007). *Educational psychology.* Pearson Education Australia.

Žižek, S. (1989). *The sublime object of ideology.* Verso.

Žižek, S. (2004). *Organs without bodies: Deleuze and consequences.* Routledge.

Index